THE
HULL
ZEPPELIN
RAIDS
1915–1918

THE HULL ZEPPELIN RAIDS 1915-1918

ARTHUR G. CREDLAND

FONTHILL

Learn more about Fonthill Media. Join our mailing list to
find out about our latest titles and special offers at:
www.fonthillmedia.com

Fonthill Media Limited
www.fonthillmedia.com
office@fonthillmedia.com

First published in the United Kingdom 2014

British Library Cataloguing in Publication Data:
A catalogue record for this book is available from the British Library

Copyright © Arthur G. Credland 2014

ISBN 978-1-78155-252-0

The right of Athur G. Credland to be identified as the author of this
work has been asserted by him in accordance with the Copyright,
Designs and Patents Act 1988.

All rights reserved. No part of this publication may be reproduced,
stored in a retrieval system or transmitted in any form or by any means,
electronic, mechanical, photocopying, recording or otherwise, without
prior permission in writing from Fonthill Media Limited

Typeset in 10pt on 13pt Sabon
Printed and bound by CPI Group (UK) Ltd, Croydon, CR0 4YY

Contents

1	Prelude to War	7
2	Terror from the Skies	10
3	No Defence	15
4	Warnings: The 'Buzzers'	17
5	The First Hull Raid, 6 June 1915	23
6	The First Women Police and Self Help by the Citizenry	32
7	Counting the Losses, and those Seeking Advantage from the Raid	36
8	Public Reaction to the Bombing	39
9	Attacks on the German community	43
10	An Organised Defence	52
11	Raids in 1916	57
12	Success in the South	75
13	Further Raids in 1917 and a Royal Visit	78
14	1918: The Last Raids	83
15	Measures and Countermeasures	85
16	Götterdämmerung	88
17	Reactions to the Raids	91
18	Aftermath	96
19	A Consideration	99
20	Anti-War Propaganda and the Bolshevik Scare	105
21	Lessons Learned	106
22	Summary of the Hull Raids 1915–1918 and Lists of Casualties	108
	Acknowledgements	113
	Appendix I List of Zeppelin Raids across Britain	114
	Appendix IIa The Reports, Correspondence and Photographs of T. C. Turner	117
	Appendix IIb T. C. Turner's Report, from the *Hull Times*	119
	Appendix III More Photographs of the Hull Raids	126
	Appendix IV Fryer's Maps	127
	Appendix V Memories of an 'Old Town' Special; and another Town 'Special'	128
	Appendix VI Dressing stations	134
	Appendix VII Buzzer Nights	135
	Appendix VIII Artefacts in Hull Museums	136
	Appendix IX Winifred Holtby; Shelling of Scarborough	140
	Appendix X Aerial Bombardment	143
	Endnotes	145

Where is the man that can fail to see that no city would be proof against surprise when the ship could at any time be steered over squares, or even the courtyards of dwelling houses, and brought to earth for the landing of its crew? Iron weights could be hurled to wreck ships at sea, or they could be set on fire by fire-balls and bombs, nor ships alone, but houses, fortresses and cities could thus be destroyed with the certainty that the aerial ship could come to no harm, as they could be hurled from a vast height.

    Francesco Lana de Terzi, *Prodroma overo saggio di alcune invenzione etc.*, Brescia, 1670

...every year the instruments of war were vaster and more powerful, and that armies and explosives outgrow all other growing things...

    H. G. Wells, *War in the Air*, 1908

The catastrophe was the logical outcome of the situation, created by the application of science to warfare. It was unavoidable that great cities would be destroyed.

    Wells, 1908, Ch. VI, section 5, pp 206-7

CHAPTER 1

Prelude to War

The day after the announcement of the assassination of Archduke Ferdinand, 28 June 1914, Gustav Steinhauer was on his way to Britain to check on his agents in the east coast ports.[1] In 1901 he had been appointed head of the British section of German naval intelligence, the Nachrichten-Abteilung, and his main purpose was to establish the state of preparedness of the Royal Navy and the reactions of the British to the events in central Europe. One of his informants was Otto Weigels, a fruit trader in Hull who was in a good position to know what was going on in the shipping world. Steinhauer warned Weigels of impending war but the latter's reaction was:

'You are mad,' he said tapping his head. 'These people in the Kriegsministerium have got war on the brain. At any rate, there is no chance of war with England. The people go about their business as usual, and only rudely tell me that our Kaiser is riding the high horse again.'[2]

It is noteworthy to find this response from a German resident in England, and in Britain as a whole, and indeed throughout the Empire, this was probably the general opinion, though a few were very vocal in their attempts to convince the majority of the dangers presented by Germany. They pointed to the intensely nationalistic spirit engendered by the Kaiser, the huge and well-equipped standing army, and the growth in the Imperial navy, all of which they considered a threat to the British Empire and indicative of a desire to expand Germany's colonial territories at our expense.

The more general view, right up to the July 1914, was that which Basil Thomson, appointed Assistant Commissioner of the Metropolitan Police in 1913, gives us in an autobiographical volume, quoting from his daughter's diary:

No one except a few 'alarmists' foresaw that the murder of an Austrian Archduke and his wife was to cost the lives of many hundred thousand men, the flower of both races, who were destined never to see another Christmas. We were dancing on the steps that led up to Armageddon.

Some of these controversial individuals, notably William Le Queux, a journalist and novelist, exposed their fears in newsprint and in sensationalist books.[3] Le Queux certainly had a wide range of contacts, was multilingual, and according to Steinhauer 'had more than a nodding acquaintance with most of the spies in Europe.'[4] A particularly influential product of his pen, which became a bestseller, was an imagined invasion of Britain by Germany, published in 1906 and entitled *The Invasion of 1910, With a Full Account of the Siege of London*.[5]

It came with a preface which included a facsimile of a letter of support[6] from Field Marshal Lord Roberts who complained about the reduction in military expenditure despite the expansion of the Empire and the increase in our responsibilities.[7] He had been trying to convince the government for many years that our small professional army was not enough to withstand a determined assault on Britain and its dominions and there was a necessity for an armed reserve. The navy, dominant on the oceans of the world, was regarded as the main defence and the army was largely intended to deal with sudden uprisings in the Empire. In 1905, Roberts had resigned from the Imperial Defence Committee after less than a year, when his proposals for compulsory military training were rejected.

A salutary lesson had been provided by the Boers, farmers hastily turned soldiers, who in the South African War had demonstrated their effectiveness against regular troops, and great skill as sharp-shooters in irregular 'commando' formations. Roberts actively promoted the setting up of rifle clubs throughout the country to improve the general standard of shooting and thus help provide a body of men which would provide useful recruits for any future hostilities.

After leaving the defence committee Roberts headed the National Service League, a body founded in 1902 which actively campaigned for compulsory training. Le Queux was a prominent member of the NSL and also active in the League of Frontiersmen formed in 1905 by Roger Pocock, a Boer War veteran and former constable in the NW Mounted Police. He, like Le Queux, perceived the threat of German expansionism and from its headquarters in London branches of the organisation soon spread throughout the Empire, and remarkably it survives to this day, though in a much reduced condition.[8]

In Le Queux's book, which dealt with events projected for only four years into the future, the Humber and Ouse rivers were rightly seen as the major route of an invading army into the heart of the industrial North and Midlands. The people of Hull wake up one morning to witness a flotilla of barges on the river proceeding towards Goole filled with German soldiers:

> I mounted my bicycle and ran along the Beverley road through Prospect street to the dock office, where around the Wilberforce monument[9] the excited crowd now already collected was impossible, and I was compelled to dismount.

Soon afterwards German naval vessels arrived off Victoria pier[10] and started disembarking troops into launches. The upshot of this was the determination to hastily improvise barriers on the bridges and the roads around the docks using timber and iron, furniture, trams, buses and paving stones dug from the streets:

> At the first moment of alarm the East Yorkshire Volunteers hurried on their uniforms, and assembled at their regimental headquarters for orders. There were of course no regular troops in the town, but the Volunteers soon obtained their arms and ammunition, and after being formed, marched down Heddon [sic][11] road to the Alexandra dock.

Needless to say they were quickly overwhelmed by the enemy forces and from the impact of a high explosive shell from one of the cruisers in the Humber 'one of the black cupolas of the dock offices was carried away'.[12]

The capital was seized though in the meantime the main German naval force had been destroyed by the Royal Navy. The invading forces in London eventually proved inadequate against an insurrection by the citizenry who dubbed themselves the 'The League of Defenders'. This popular uprising by the citizens included, sharp-shooters, rifle club members, and Frontiersmen[13] who, with a scratch collection of firearms and artillery, eventually overcame the German forces albeit with great loss of life.

The impact of this book was considerable, and the message was clear, that a civilian reserve was a necessity for the protection of Britain and the Empire. Probably most people still thought that a war with Germany was neither inevitable nor even likely, but the demand for the establishment of a citizen army received growing support. In 1907 the Territorial and Reserve Forces Act was passed under the guidance of the Secretary of State for War, Richard Haldane. This enabled the amalgamation, in 1908, of the Volunteer Force, a body administered by civilians, together with the Militia, and the Yeomanry, to form the Territorial Army. This was a trained reserve of civilians, available for call up whenever needed, a body which was to form such a vital part of our forces in the Great War and subsequent conflicts.

Le Queux played a not insignificant role in the lobbying which preceded these army reforms, and also in the formation of a British secret service. His *Spies of the Kaiser*, published in 1909, postulated a huge network of German agents working throughout the British Isles laying the foundations for invasion and conquest. The book made a tremendous public impact and helped to convince the committee of imperial defence to sanction the formation of the Secret Service Bureau in that same year.

Six years after *The Invasion* appeared in print war was declared, not in 1910 but in 1914. To quote Sherlock Holmes pronouncement immediately after the arrest of Von Bork, the fictional German master spy:

> There's an east wind coming all the same, such a wind as never blew on England yet. It will be cold and bitter, Watson, and a good many of us may wither before its blast.[14]

CHAPTER 2

Terror from the Skies

There has been an increasing interest in the aerial bombardment of Hull in 1939–45, its intensity and extent, and impact on the civilian population[1]. What has been largely forgotten is that Hull was also the target of German bombers in the Great War. The attacks on Hull and other towns were of course not remotely on the scale of those in the Second World War but those on the receiving end were the first ever British civilians to suffer the effects of aerial bombing and the resulting injury, death and destruction. The psychological impact of seeing the Zeppelin airships drifting across the sky, huge gas-filled balloons and apparently unstoppable, followed by the impact of incendiary and high explosive bombs can only be imagined. It was certainly something totally outside the experience and the imagination of the ordinary citizen if not of visionaries such as H. G. Wells and the Jesuit priest Francesco Lana, mathematician and one of the pioneers of the science of aeronautics.[2]

Hot air and gas balloons appeared in the late eighteenth century but were largely an object of spectacle and amusement, though the military possibilities, at least for observation on the battle field, were developed using small balloons filled with hydrogen gas.[3] The massive rigid airship designed by Graf Ferdinand von Zeppelin[4] was completed in 1899 and made its first flight in July the following year at Friedrichshafen on Lake Constance (Bodensee).[5] A canvas cover enveloped an aluminium metal framework enclosing several bags filled with the hydrogen which gave it buoyancy. The cotton fabric bags were covered in several layers of gold beaters skin (the outer membrane of calf's intestine) to make them gas tight. In its civilian role the airship was capable of carrying passengers,[6] they and the crew being housed in a gondolas slung below, the controls in the forward gondola and the power units shared between them.[7] The total crew was typically twenty-two but might be reduced according to the weight of bombs, fuel, and water ballast it was decided to carry:

> The crew consists of a commander, a first officer, two warrant officers, including the navigator and the senior engineer, and nineteen non-commissioned officers. These include four petty officers for the rudders and elevators, twelve engine room

artificers for the motors, two wireless operators, and one sailmaker for the outer cover and gas bags. It is obvious that on an airship the crew must be absolutely reliable, and this explains why the crew consists entirely of petty officers. In the ordinary run of events, the crew is disposed in two-hour watches, but this is not possible when making an attack on England, because every possible kilogram of weight must be economised. It is therefore necessary to leave two to five of the crew behind, and it has often happened that the engineers have had to stand by their motors during the whole journey. The navigating personnel did have a change, as they spend two hours at the wheel and then two hours on observation duties on the platform.[8]

Food meant unnecessary weight, and certainly in the later Zeppelins, the 'Height climbers', when every ounce counted, very few provisions could be taken. At great heights it froze and could not be eaten. Small cakes and chocolate were considered the best nourishment.

Several engines drove propellers which impelled the airship in the desired direction, and for military use the weight of passengers could be replaced by bombs.[9] The latter were suspended vertically by cables from hook-shaped tumblers on racks, on either side of the keel in the amidships area. A horizontal shutter ('bomb door') on rollers was slid open when an attack was imminent.

Judging by the memoirs of the former airship pilot Buttlar-Brandenfels, the arrangements in the early Zeppelins were extremely primitive. As he describes it there were initially only three high explosive bombs, each suspended by a length of twine; the 'bomb aimer' sighted with his thumb and cut the cord with his penknife![10] As mechanisms developed the bomb doors could be opened electrically by pressing a button and the explosives were similarly released. At the beginning these were 10 lb (4.5 kg) incendiaries, and explosive bombs of 1 cwt (50 kg), 2 cwt (100 kg) and eventually 6 cwt (300 kg). The first 1,000 kg bomb was dropped on London, on the 16/17 February 1918, by one of the 'Giant' aeroplanes, four engine biplanes with a wingspan of 138 feet. As numbers increased of airships destroyed and the effectiveness of each raid was diminished by improving defences Buttlar-Brandenfels, an experienced Zeppelin pilot, speaking in a lecture in January 1918 still justified their use because:

> an airship carries as much weight of bombs as twenty aeroplanes, and can, therefore, do more work when over the object of our attack, besides, the airship carries bombs of much heavier calibre than it is possible to take on an aeroplane. In the second place, the whole of England is within range of an airship, while the radius of action of an aeroplane is still very limited.[11]

Up till the 1914–18 war Britain had not suffered war casualties on its native shore since the Jacobite rebellions of the eighteenth century, and on any great scale since the Civil War in the seventeenth century. More recently, in the nineteenth century, the only civilian casualties from explosions were victims of bombs planted in the Fenian outrages, attacks largely restricted to the capital.[12]

The bombardment by German battle cruisers of Hartlepool, Scarborough, and Whitby, on 16 December 1914, shocked the British public. It seemed that non-combatants could now be regarded as legitimate targets by the enemy, or at least that significant numbers of civilian deaths were acceptable as a 'by product' of military action. More than 100 people, mostly civilians, were killed and over 500 injured, the greatest number in Hartlepool which suffered a sustained attack, receiving more than a thousand shells from the *Blucher*, *Seydlitz* and *Moltke* resulting in eighty-six deaths and 424 casualties. Hartlepool was the only significant military target and 'Remember Scarborough' became a national rallying call and a potent recruiting slogan.[13] These shocking events were soon to be followed by a mode of attack as yet unknown to the people of Britain.

There had been considerable agitation within Germany to embark on aerial bombing but still awaiting Imperial consent to attack the capital the first raids were not on London. The campaign commenced in earnest on 19 January 1915, with a raid on Great Yarmouth, after a raid planned for the 13 January involving four Zeppelins was aborted due to bad weather. In a secret order of 12 February 1915, Kaiser Wilhelm sanctioned attacks on docks and military establishments in the lower Thames and on the English coast. London, west of the Tower, was not to be bombed, and it was forbidden to attack royal palaces (it should be remembered that the British and German royal families were closely linked[14]) and historic buildings. To avoid civilian casualties only coastal defences and docks were to be bombed but because the dock areas were densely populated and precision bombing was impossible this was a futile injunction.[15] London was hit for the first time on 31 May 1915 when 3,000 lbs of bombs were dropped by a single raider, and despite the ban on attacking residential areas, houses were destroyed, seven persons killed and thirty-five injured. His Imperial Majesty and Supreme War Lord eventually lifted his caveats, and London received its first unrestricted raid in the summer of 1915. Hull saw the first of eight raids on 6 June 1915 There had always been an intention by the German army to bomb industrial targets in England. If the aims of the Schlieffen plan had been achieved and they had occupied Calais, then this or a neighbouring port would have been the base for aerial attacks with heavier-than-air planes. Instead battle lines were drawn through western Europe in an ever-growing system of trenches from the Channel to Switzerland. Britain therefore remained out of range of aeroplanes and instead airships took the initiative, both army and navy craft but mainly Zeppelins of the Imperial Navy.

A book published in 1907 was both indicative of the strong nationalist currents within Germany and a clear proclamation of superiority in the air. The title could hardly be more explicit *Berlin-Bagdad: Das Deutsche Weltreich im Zeitalter der Luftschiffahrt* ('Berlin- Baghdad: the German World Empire in the Age of Airship Travel').[16] H. G. Wells' apocalyptic novel, *War in the Air*, which appeared the following year, seems to be a direct riposte.[17] It has a graphic account of the destruction of New York by a battle fleet of German airships followed by world war and the collapse of civilisation. Implicit within this story is that aerial bombardment can result in catastrophic destruction but cannot by itself win a war.[18] In the same year in a non-fiction volume, *First and Last Things*, he prophesied:

> Great towns red with destruction while giant airships darken the sky—for the first time in the history of warfare—the rear of the fighting line becomes insecure, assailable by flying machines and subjected to unprecedented and unimaginable panics. No man can tell what savagery of desperation these new conditions might release in the soul of man.[19]

The first ever 'bombs' dropped on their unsuspecting victims below were large hand grenades thrown from the cockpit of an aeroplane, on 1 November 1911. The targets were tribesmen in two oases outside Tripoli during the colonisation by the Italians of Cyrenaica and Tripolitania, that part of North Africa which became known as Libya.[20] Though the possibilities of aerial bombardment had become apparent the large formations despatched from Germany starting in 1915 were not used en masse to attack one particular target. Instead they were split up, either deliberately or as a result of weather and wind conditions, and attacked a variety of destinations, whether those planned or targets of opportunity. Any particular target was usually hit by one or maybe two airships detached from the large group which had been assembled on the other side of the North Sea. Over London up to five airships might appear in one night.

It was the use of heavier-than-air bombers[21] in large formations which, within his own lifetime, made a reality of Wells' imaginings, with the 300–plus bomber formations of the Luftwaffe over London in 1940.[22] Of course, already in 1917 and 1918 the 'Gotha' bomber, a twin engine biplane with large wing span, had attacked London and the Southeast, sometimes in formations of more than twenty aircraft. The ultimate development of mass bombing came with the '1,000-bomber' raids by the RAF over Germany during the Second World War.

The island people of Britain were now in the front line of attack from a continental enemy and the arrival of aerial bombardment was truly terrifying, made even more so because it was neither expected by the general populace nor were its victims prepared for it in any way. At the outbreak of the 1939–45 war not only were there many people who remembered the Zeppelin and Gotha[23] raids but the population at large had read news reports and seen newsreels at the cinema revealing the effects of bombing on towns such as Guernica (26 April 1937) during the Spanish Civil War.

After the war people were only too eager to forget the raids and in Hull, astonishingly, the first systematic attempt to gather eyewitness accounts did not take place until the 1980s,[24] well after the 1939–45 war, let alone the Great War, when the diminishing numbers of survivors were well advanced in age. More recording was undertaken of the last of the survivors in the 1990s by Steven Suddaby, who used the results as the basis of an overview of the raids, but now of course, in 2012, all the eyewitnesses and participants are dead.[25]

CHAPTER 3

No Defence

Within the city and its immediate environs there was initially no means of defence against the Zeppelins, which cruised around at will, and no system of shelters to provide a haven during a raid. At first the only response was 'passive defence', a total blackout and absolute silence. Church and clock bells were, especially in coastal areas, to be put out of action between the hours of sunset and sunrise.

Buttlar-Brandenfels refers to the effectiveness of the black-out on his run in towards London, when, from Winterton, on the Norfolk coast, he 'did not see a single light over the English countryside, although it was very clear, until London hove in sight.' As he points out in areas frequented by airships this would have meant shutting down rail traffic as 'no train can proceed without signals and lights in the stations.'

There was an acute lack of anti-aircraft guns or fighter planes to attack the Zeppelins and in the early raids the airships were often visible over Britain for a matter of hours, manoeuvring until the weather and cloud conditions enabled the selection of an appropriate target.

Railways and docks were the intended focus of attack, but residential properties, transport systems and shipping facilities were closely enmeshed. In addition the Zeiss bomb-sight needed a great deal of practice to use effectively so it is unsurprising that civilians were killed and injured and their homes damaged or destroyed. The strategists behind the raids realised this would be the case and hoped it would diminish the population's will to fight and help speed a German victory. In Britain, the effects on civilians were regarded as yet another expression of 'Hun Frightfulness'. Regarding proposals for Zeppelin raids on London, Konteadmiral Paul Behncke wrote, 20 August 1914:

> Maybe expected whether they involve London or the neighbourhood of London, to cause panic in the population which may possibly render it doubtful that the war could be continued.[1]

Admiral von Tirpitz stressed that London should be the main target not only because of the serious damage that might be caused but also 'for the significant effect it will have in diminishing the enemy's determination to prosecute the war.'

Despite various outbreaks of panic the result was quite the opposite, as also happened in the 1939–45 war when intensive bombing resulted in the 'blitz spirit', the determination to carry on regardless, and a determination to hit back at the 'Hun'. To quote the *Hull and Lincolnshire Times*, in 1919, after the war had ended[2]:

> Instead of stampeding the British people into an early clamour for peace (as they had fondly hoped) they stiffened our backs, and created a whirlwind of enthusiasm for recruiting and the production of munitions which no other means could have achieved. That alone was well worth the price paid for the advent of the nocturnal visitors, because recruiting was the very breath of our existence in the early stages of the war. Had we not been able to rush men into France, the German hordes would have triumphed, and the whole history of the world would have been reconstructed by the downfall of civilisation. It is no exaggeration to say that each night a Zeppelin hovered over English territory thousands of men voluntarily donned khaki in order to give forcible expression to their indignation over the inhuman attacks upon defenceless towns and the slaying of women and children. Count Zeppelin was an unwitting but successful recruiting agent for Great Britain, and was one of the most potent factors in speeding up a colossal production of mighty munitions of war.

The raiders were quickly dubbed the 'baby killers' as the horrors of civilian deaths struck home, the victims often burnt to death by incendiary bombs.[3] Aerial attack was terrifying enough, but with such results it seemed barbarous and more like a form of terrorism than a legitimate act of war. The initial raids were freely described in the press but after the first raid on London, on 31 May 1915, strict censorship was imposed both to prevent the enemy discovering the effectiveness, or otherwise, of the bombing and to prevent alarm and panic across the nation.[4] The result was that the bland government announcements and reports of casualties came to be regarded with scorn and only encouraged rumour-mongering.

Despite the odious effects of the bombing there was certainly no attempt to specifically target civilians with anti-personnel weapons such as the flechettes ('flying darts' or fliegerpfeile) that were used by both sides on the Western Front. These were steel darts, a few inches long, with vanes to direct flight, released from aircraft over trenches and troop concentrations. Dropped from altitude they killed or maimed their victims by entering the body at high speed under the force of gravity.[5]

CHAPTER 4

Warnings: The 'Buzzers'

A system of audible warnings was introduced, which as in the last war were referred to as 'buzzers', the familiar name which workers already gave to the sirens which marked the beginning and end of the working day in a factory (See Appendix VII). There were other nick- names, such as 'Lizzie', and one of the 'specials', recruited to patrol the old town area when a raid was imminent, referred to the warning sound as 'Mournful Mary'.

The first 'successful' raid on Britain was on 19/20 January 1915, involving three airships, *L3*, *L4* and *L6*. One aiming for London suffered engine failure[1] and returned to base while two others flew toward the Humber. Caught by the wind they were carried south and unloaded their bombs on Great Yarmouth, Kings Lynn and Sandringham. The first house in Great Britain to be damaged in a Zeppelin raid still stands at 25 St Peter's Plain (also known as Merlin Villa), Great Yarmouth, commemorated by a blue plaque over the door. Less than twenty feet away on the same night, 19 January, an elderly spinster, Martha Taylor and Sam Smith a shoemaker, became the first two victims of aerial attack on British soil, killed near Drakes Buildings. The first bomb dropped on British soil landed at Sheringham on the Norfolk coast, at Whitehall yard, 8.30 p.m., 19 January.[2] It was dropped from *L4*, commanded by Count Magnus von Platen-Hallermund but failed to detonate. A second bomb did explode but caused no damage. The airship proceeded to Kings Lynn where Percy Goate, a teenager of fourteen, and Alice Gazely, twenty-six, whose husband had recently been lost in France, were both killed.

The *Hull and Lincolnshire Times*,[3] 25 January 1915, in a piece entitled 'Arousing the public':

> In the event of certain happenings for which the Germans will be responsible, the public of Hull are to be warned by the shrill blasts of steam whistles. The steam organ valve whistles are being supplied by Messrs George Clarke and Son, Waterhouse Lane. The type to be used in Hull are 6 in. in diameter.

They were installed at various locations by the Hull Corporation. A typewritten description, dated 24 January 1919, of the 'buzzer' installed at the Blundell and

Spence paint works on the corner of Beverley road and Spring Bank tells us that it was five feet high and nine-and-a-half inches in diameter, activated by steam at a pressure of 80 psi through a 3-inch iron pipe, and placed 100 feet above ground.[4] Erected by Clarkes, on 28 May 1915, it was dismantled by the same company 23 January 1919 and was presented to the Hull Municipal Museums. The buzzer seems to have been particularly loud and from its situation not far from the town centre was clearly heard both across the heart of Hull, and outwards and north along Beverley road as well as west along Spring Bank with all their populous side streets. Unexpectedly this cylindrical brass whistle was to see service yet again; it was taken from the museum in 1939 and erected at the Hull Power Station, sounding the last 'all clear' 8 May 1945.[5]

Other installations had evidently predated it because in the diary of 'buzzer days' the first alert was 12 April 1915, and there were four more alarms before 6 June when the first actual raid took place.

An order was received from the police to sound Blundell's alarm at 12 midnight on 5 June 1915, but there was not sufficient pressure and initially it was unable to respond; the all clear sounded at 2.15 a.m.[6] It failed again on the 6 June but the alarm was blown at 9.30 p.m. by three other buzzers; the first bomb dropped about 11.45. The same typewritten source tells us that it was sounded for the last time on 11 November 1918 (Armistice Day), at 3.30 p.m. by E. J. Nicholson. We might have expected it to have been at 11 a.m. and according to the memories put down on paper by 'Freda' (surname unknown): the air raid alarms sounded for the last time to announce the Armistice at 11 a.m. on 11 November 1918.[7]

A formal vote of thanks was made, 9 December 1918, to those companies or municipal departments which had maintained an air-raid alarm throughout the war, namely: Blundell and Spence & Co., Earle's Shipbuilding and Engineering Co., Reckitt & Sons, Hull Oil Manufacturing Co., the North Eastern Railway Co., and the Water and Gas Committee of the Hull Corporation.[8]

At first the alarm was given as soon as a Zeppelin was sighted on its path over the coast and flying in over the surrounding countryside. In all the alarm was sounded fifty-three times throughout hostilities and the public waited a total of 206 hours for the 'all clear'. This latter phrase familiar from the 1939–45 war was used in the Zeppelin special issue of 1919,[9] but the special constables and the wartime press announcements refer to the 'dismiss buzzer' (see below) or the 'release buzzers'. We also find reference to the 'signal of safety' and the 'all well', which suggest the now more familiar expression only became established towards the very end of the war.[10] 1915 and 1916 were the peak of the raids, with twenty-two and twenty-three 'buzzer days', diminishing to four in 1917 and five in 1918. Between 31 March and 3 April 1916, the buzzer blew five times. A press announcement in April 1916 stated that if the 'release syren [sic]' (all-clear) sounded before 10 p.m. the school register would be taken as usual, but if after 10 p.m. the school would close the following morning. After an active raid schools would close the whole of the following day.[11]

The logbook for Selby Street primary school records ten closures after alarms or raids in 1915 and the introduction of reduced opening hours before Christmas and into February to save on artificial lighting during the dark winter months.[12] To take full advantage of natural light the Summertime Act was introduced in 1916, when the clocks were advanced on 21 May and put back 1 October. On two occasions the school premises were required for billeting troops, January to March 1916 and 26 October 1916 to June 1917, and pupils and staff in the meantime had to share the accommodation at Westbourne Street School.

One of the regiments billeted in Hull was the Lancashire Fusiliers. Shortly after the declaration of war the 3rd Battalion were moved from Bury (Lancashire) to Hull where they remained until transferring, in November 1916, to the east coast at Withernsea, though still as part of the Humber Garrison. A photograph in an album recording events in the mayoralty of J. H. Hargreaves shows some of the troops sat outside their billet, the Presbyterian Lecture Hall and School, with their washing strung on lines across the width of Baker Street, very close to the city centre and emphasising the large military presence in the city.[13]

The City of Hull's *Special Constables' Gazette*, June 1917, indicates the plan for daylight:

> In case of Daylight Alarms the buzzer will continue for 5 minutes (instead of 3 minutes as at night), and the dismiss buzzer will also sound for 5 minutes. Special constables on hearing the signal, proceed at once to the concentration posts to which they are posted for duty when called upon at night.[14]

The gazette was published weekly and was regarded as a confidential document intended for specials and 'officials' only.[15] It contained reports of significant events and in this issue is a thank you from Francis Askew,[16] the Lord Mayor, to all those involved in the arrangements for the visit of the King and Queen on 18 June. Meetings are announced, promotions and resignations, sunset and sunrise times, flag days as well as amendments to the Defence of the Realm Act. There is a note regarding allotments and the impact on their potential for food production as a result of damage by trespassers.

On a war footing the city was divided into six districts each under a Special Constable Commander who was chairman of his local Emergency Committee, of which six subordinates, the Group Leaders, were also members. The latter were allocated two to each of three sub-committees, along with additional members who were designated Sub-Group Leaders.[17] Each sub-group consisted of any number of sections, depending on the total work load and manpower required to undertake particular tasks, each in charge of a Section Leader. All constables were furnished with a warrant, a cloth armlet (brassard) and a badge. SCCs and Group Leaders were provided with blue enamel badges the Sub-Group Leader with a white enamel badge, while Section Leaders had an arm band which they wore on their right arm.[18] The badges were probably enamel plates mounted directly on the arm band.

A badge which has been offered for sale, in the form of a five pointed star, a little over one inch from point to point, is apparently a long service award made to Specials who had attested in 1914. Made of base metal there is an interlaced 'S C' monogram in the centre, surrounded by a roundel with the raised letters and date, *City of Hull 1914*.

A round badge is also found, the centre brass with three crowns in a shield, arms of the city of Hull, surrounded by *Kingston-upon-Hull*, the letters and heraldry in relief. The whole is within an enamel border, red, white or blue, with the plain brass letters *Special Constable 1914*. It has two rings brazed on the reverse through which a cotter pin would pass, and is usually marked J. R. Gaunt, London. These may be what are known as 'mufti' badges worn when off duty.

There was a Central Organising Committee made up of SCCs and other officials under the leadership of Chief Special Constable Commander, James Downs JP.[19] In overall charge was the city's Chief Constable George Morley, who was appointed in 1910 and remained in office for the next twelve years.[20]

First aid posts, usually referred to as 'dressing stations' were set up, headed by a medical officer (a doctor, not just an orderly) who was in complete charge, and manned by personnel of the St John Ambulance association.[21] (See Appendix VI.) Boy Scouts and Special Constables acted as telephone attendants and messengers for the stations. Scouts also acted as guides for old people in the darkened streets. One or two motor vehicles were allocated to each station to enable the injured to be rushed to hospital or transfer medical staff if needed urgently elsewhere.[22]

A detachment of Specials was employed as Cyclist Despatch Riders.[23] Special badges were issued to riders under nineteen years old to be worn as an alternative to the ordinary Special Constable's badge.[24] After an air raid warning and lights out order, barricades were set up on the main roads, Anlaby Road, Beverley Road, Cottingham Road, Hessle Road and Holderness Road. At each of these motor halts, there was a hut with telephone communication, and all vehicles were stopped except those occupied by known individuals.[25] Licences were examined and anybody at all suspicious was subject to questioning. All vehicles were to carry a red light, one hour after sunset to one hour before sunrise and constables were to check that each was carrying no more light than was necessary to warn of its approach and illuminate its identification plate. In addition a check was made inside to see if there was any apparatus capable of signalling.[26] No vehicle was to leave the city without a pass or proper form to be collected at the halt and no alien was to enter or leave without a permit. Resistance by any occupant would result in arrest.[27] The specials were authorised to stop all vehicles, including bicycles, found on the streets a half an hour after the alarm had been given. If not being used for any essential purpose they could be seized and detained.[28]

Later, an organisation entitled the East Yorks Motor Volunteer Corps was established, the members apparently making their own vehicles available for official purposes. It is presumably this body which assisted in moving casualties, as well as medical, military and police personnel, and maintaining general communications so as to enable an effective response whenever danger threatened.[29]

Specials were recruited in large numbers both to fill the gaps left in the regular force by call-up and enlarge the numbers of men available for new duties necessary in wartime. Many specials themselves became eligible for service at the front and it became increasingly difficult to fill the posts. (See Appendix V for memories of a Special.) Overall some 5,000 men[30] served in this volunteer force throughout the war and in 1919 there were an estimated 2,800 on the roll.[31] Uniform was not provided except when Specials did beat duty, when they could collect a coat and cap from Hull Central police station.[32] Each of these men was on duty once or twice a week for three hours at a time covering twelve beats for nine hours a day.[33] In a port town like Hull, foreign seamen and ships' passengers needed to be recorded and their movements checked, so Specials regularly acted as clerks in the alien registration office.

The larger companies organised their own air-raid precautions. For example Wm. Gilyott & Co., warehouse owners, arranged for some eight of their foremen to be sworn in as Specials, designated as Section Leaders. Every time an alarm sounded, five leaders and fourteen men came on duty and had at their disposal fire extinguishers, hand grenades,[34] sand, and water (in buckets). The deputy Sub Group Leader was William Gilyott himself.[35]

People wandering the streets were given shelter in the cellars of some of these warehouses and later in spaces deliberately left between the stored merchandise. Others found temporary refuge in the basements of some of the banks.

Though initially lacking the means to actively defend against the airships, the British at least had a good idea of their movements. The British authorities knew the German naval codes, allowing them to read the busy wireless traffic which accompanied the preparation and execution of an attack. The information derived from the radio messages, as well as position fixes with cross-bearings made from our intercept stations, and sometimes visual sightings from lightships in the North Sea would all be despatched to the appropriate battery commanders.[36]

There was an abundance of radio chatter which enabled the numbers of craft to be estimated with accuracy and their movements to be plotted to and from the target:

> During the whole flight the airship remains in wireless communication with Headquarters in the Heligoland Bight. The first message after carrying out an attack is to send a short report as to where one is at the time, and what object has been attacked. About midnight, then, the various airships send their messages one after the other somewhat as follows:– '1 a.m. North Hinter Lightship, London—

signed, L.30'. It is obvious we look forward anxiously to these messages to ascertain if all ships have reached their objective, what places have been attacked, and above all, whether all ships are safely on their return journey.[37]

Early in 1916 the HVB (Handelsverkehrsbuch) codes were replaced by the AFB or Allgemeinefunkspruchbuch codes. Considerable success was achieved in elucidating this but by great good fortune a copy of the new code book was recovered from the wreck of *L32* which was brought down 24 September 1916, at Great Burstead, with the death of all twenty-two crew.[38]

Though at the beginning of the raids the city itself had no anti-aircraft guns there were batteries down river, on the north bank at Paull,[39] Sunk Island, Kilnsea, and Spurn Point and, and on the Lincolnshire side of the Humber at Stallingborough, Killingholme and Immingham. It is uncertain which, but either Sunk Island or Stallingborough answered the first attack with Maxim guns while quick-firing one-pounder guns (pom-pom) opened fire at the other sites. They could project a shell no more than 3,000 feet and there was little hope of hitting the target, but gunfire, even if the target was unlikely to be hit, always had a disruptive effect on an aerial attack.[40]

CHAPTER 5

The First Hull Raid, 6 June 1915

After the attack on London in January 1915 many remained convinced, until the events of early June, that Hull would remain safe though as we have seen the local authority took the precaution of establishing a system of buzzers to warn of an impending raid. Some at least of the more aware citizens had also considered the possibility of Zeppelin attack when at the beginning of the war there were protests at holding the customary Hull Fair, one of the largest in the country, in October 1914:

> The Corporation had decided to hold Hull Fair as usual and this decision has produced a crop of correspondence in the newspapers mostly in protest, not on account of the unseemliness of such an orgy in face of the stupendous events taking place on the continent, but in fear that the glow of the illuminations at night will attract the unwelcome attentions of the German Zeppelins culminating in a discharge of bombs on the merry makers.
>
> The fear is not quite unreasonable seeing that some of our aviators have made a flight from Ostend to Dusseldorf in Germany a distance both ways of 332 miles without a descent. A Zeppelin starting from Wilhelmshaven would have to cover twice that distance to arrive at Hull and get back again, a feat not impossible but extremely improbable.[1]

An improbability that was to be emphatically disproved, and had been foreshadowed by the airship attack on Antwerp in late August 1914 which had resulted in a number of civilian casualties. On 2 August 1914, a German aeroplane had bombed Lunéville and the French responded with a raid on a Zeppelin hangar near Metz. The German military had made advanced plans to bomb England and the English service chiefs, aware of the potential dangers of the Zeppelin, made a number of 'pre-emptive strikes' before a single enemy airship had been seen over Britain. A poverty of home defences made offence the best form of defence. An attack was made Düsseldorf, 8 October 1914, destroying a Zeppelin in its hangar and the next month, 21 November, the Zeppelin factory itself, at Friedrichshafen was bombed by Avro 504 biplanes. A total of six Zeppelins were destroyed in the first year of the war by carrying the fight to the enemy.[2]

In the collections of the Hull Museum is a series of photographs, some loose and others mounted, which record the effects of bombing, the result of the raid on 6 June 1915. They bear the name of Turner and Drinkwaters, for many years Hull's foremost photographic portrait studio. In fact T. C. Turner, of Regent House, Anlaby Road,[3] played an active role in bringing the attention of the government and the military to the desperate need for air defences. He sent a detailed report of the raid on 6 June 1915 to the Intelligence Department of the War Office, the text of which was reproduced in the *Hull Times* after the war was over.[4] It was written from personal observation from a central position in Hull outside his premises, Regent House, and sometimes from its balcony, with additional material from friends. To protect his 'observation post' Turner had strengthened his house against the effects of bombing and had built what he describes as a basement 'funk-hole', which had brick walls with 10-inch girders and plates over it, and a foot of sand. This may have been the only truly purpose-built shelter for public use, of any substance, constructed in Hull during the Great War. Suddaby tells us that up to a hundred people might seek refuge there during a raid.[5]

The *Hull Times* stated that:

Before the war Mr. Turner had some conversation with a young German girl who had made several trips in Zeppelins in her own country. During her stay in Hull she told Mr. Turner to watch for them, as she knew they were chiefly intended for mischief on England.

This encounter had probably encouraged his efforts to find a way of dealing with aerial attacks.

The text of Turner's report supplied to the authorities was accompanied by copies of his photographs and the position where each bomb had landed marked on Ordnance Survey maps. When no improvement had been made in the city's defences by February the following year he made visits to the Admiralty and General Headquarters, Whitehall, pressing his case for action.

There are, in the Hull Maritime Museum, several copies of typewritten summaries (and some of the handwritten notes from which they were compiled) of damage and casualties accompanying the photographs.[6] Evidenced by the address on the envelope, the pictures, and presumably the notes too, had originally been sent after the hostilities were over, 25 September 1919, to John Wright Mason,[7] Medical Officer of Health, at Hull during the Great War. Mason's annual reports on the state of the city's public health continued to be issued during the period 1914–18, but it is remarkable, and indicative of tight censorship, that there is absolutely no mention of the war in these, neither of its direct casualties, nor even of the impact that must have been made on the organisation and provision of services generally.[8]

The first attack took place on a clear, starlit night, 6 June 1915 by *L9* under the command of Kapitänleutnant Heinrich Mathy,[9] one of the most daring and able of the airship commanders. This was a naval Zeppelin which first flew on 9 September 1915 and was eventually lost on 30 January 1916. A massive 163 m (535 feet) with a range of 4,300 miles, she was powered by four 240 hp Maybach engines. She had departed from Nordholz,[10] near Cuxhaven, a somewhat bleak and isolated location which another airship commander, Buttlar-Brandenfels, described as 'the most God-forsaken, one might almost say man-forsaken, hole on earth.'[11] This was the headquarters of the German Naval Airship Service and was furnished with a revolving double shed for the airships which could be rotated to any point of the compass, depending on which way the wind was blowing. Nordholz also had a direction finding station, part of a system to provide navigational fixes for the airships, and also to plot movements of allied shipping in the North Sea.

Mathy's primary objective was London but he made landfall at Cromer and strong headwinds from the south caused him to fly northward to Bridlington, from where Mathy navigated his craft to Hull, his alternative target. The buzzer had already sounded five times previously but, without any sign of raiders, the latest warning was treated with a lack of concern, and on a fine summer's evening it only encouraged more people to come out onto the streets.

Warning of two airships over the North Sea was received at 7.25 p.m. and two hours later at 9.30. Major General Ferrier, Commander Humber Defences, ordered all lights to be extinguished in Hull.[12] The airship was seen at Flamborough Head (the distinctive white cliffs, providing an unmistakable landmark for the navigator) at 10.20 p.m., at Hornsea 10.30, and then off Withernsea 10.40. At 11 o'clock, the Zeppelin was over Westella and now moving eastwards towards the city, following the railway lines as far as Dairycoates, then veered over the Humber. Two parachute flares were dropped which fell into the water.[13] The initial approach was at an altitude of 8–10,000 feet but becoming aware that there was no anti-aircraft fire the airship dropped down to about 5,000 feet. A little before Marfleet the airship moved inland again and the raid commenced over King George V dock, two or three bombs falling into the water. Then she moved over Earle's shipyard, receiving the only response of the evening from the 4-inch guns of HMS *Adventure* under repair on the slipway. An explosive bomb fell near the ship, then an incendiary, before the craft moved towards the timber yards and sawmills at Drypool on the east side of the River Hull, north of the Victoria dock. The airship then turned towards Holy Trinity before heading in the direction of Rank's mill. A bomb was discovered several months later in Scott's warehouse.

Moving westward towards the goods sheds and sidings of the North Eastern Railway no significant damage was done and no great conflagration occurred because the incendiaries had not landed adjacent to where the explosive bombs fell where they would have magnified the effect of their impact.

At 12.15 a.m. the airship moved east over the Humber dock, where a lighter suffered damage,[14] and followed the Holderness road, then over the village of

Wyton (where an incendiary was later found) and headed towards Grimsby, releasing five incendiaries at about 12.30 or 12.40 a.m. before departing.

Hull was virtually under military control and the commander of the Humber Garrison was General Ferrier. His staff officer in the headquarters building, evidently based in a hotel at the heart of Hull:[15]

> went outside the Hotel and saw a Zeppelin overhead, very distinct against a clear sky, at a height estimated by him as 3,000 feet. He saw three bombs dropped. As each one left the Zeppelin the airship was clearly lit up. He then reported to me, and I saw five explosions, and I saw from my window that two fires had started.[16]

Ferrier's report continues:

> At 12.30 p.m. Brig. General Dixon reported several fires, one serious, which threatened Holy Trinity church, several casualties, but all details working very well. Paull [17] reports that Zeppelin had passed over at 12.15 a.m. going S.E.[18]— counted 32 bombs dropped in Hull city.
>
> All arrangements for collecting wounded and extinguishing fires worked very well. Great credit is due to the troops and fire brigade for saving Holy Trinity Church, which was only 27' away from Messrs. Davis large establishment, which was burnt to the ground.[19]

Edwin Davis' store and Hewetson's sawmill and timber yard, on Dansom Lane, were soon ablaze.[20] The well-known drapers was situated in the heart of the old town alongside Holy Trinity church where some of the stained glass windows were damaged and two youths and a man were killed in the street. They were all residents of Blanket Row where, at number 39, Mullin's grocer's shop, a bomb set fire to the room in which three boys were sleeping. Norman, aged ten, was killed; George, aged fifteen, was dragged out and ran all the way to Monument Bridge before collapsing. Passers-by carried him to the infirmary where he died. A third son, Horace, was also taken to the infirmary, and the father extinguished the fire. Edwin Davis's store burned for more than a day and was totally demolished. Florence Dee (née Mawer) describes visiting the remains of Edwin Davis' store and reminisces on how it used to be. Born in 1906, she would have been only eight or nine years old and her 'memories' are probably as much those from her mother telling her about the time of the Great War as her own recollection of the events:

> Against Holy Trinity Church, where the Labour Exchange is now, that used to be Edwin Davis's. It was a lovely shop, with a broad staircase to go up and floor-walkers brought you a chair as soon as ever you came in. It wasn't a case of

picking and choosing for yourself. Everything was stored behind beautiful long counters and you didn't just pick what it was you wanted from a peg: you had clothes made. [...] I used to love going into Edwin Davis's with the floorwalkers coming up to meet you, 'Good morning, madam, which department did you want? Upstairs? Ah yes,' and he'd call one of the girls, 'See madam upstairs'.

But the shop was bombed and I remember going there with my sister and brother. There were rolls of cloth, all smoking, and rolls of ribbon. There was a policeman on duty and we asked if we could have some ribbon. He said yes and he'd reach it down for us. We got ever so much ribbon. It was all debris, really, and the policeman just let us take some.[21]

It was suspected, but because of the comprehensive destruction never satisfactorily established, that an explosive bomb as well as incendiaries had destroyed the store and the Fleece Inn adjoining. Ten days after the fire a woman's body was found under the debris but she was not identified nor did anyone claim her, or report a missing person. During the fire the heat within the church, only across a narrow road, was terrific and the lead of some of the stained glass melted. Fortunately the wind continued to blow from the northwest, saving the church and the large, four storey, premises of Kings the ironmongers. Demetrius Franks, known as 'Dimmy', the licensee of the Fleece, and his family were sheltering in the beer cellar when the bomb struck, but afterwards came out uninjured.[22] Turner wrote that when on the church roof at 10 o'clock the next morning, photographing the still blazing ruins, the wind began to gently veer round to the opposite direction, the smoke coming up at the camera. A 'fire seven or eight hours later [than the actual time of the raid] would have probably consumed this large and historic building.'[23]

The roof of a garage in Constable Street caught fire[24] and several 'duds' which failed to go off landed in Coltman Street, but a house at 2 St Thomas's Terrace, Campbell Street, was totally demolished. Alice Walker, aged 30, was blown over the terrace walk on to the aisle roof of the church, a distance of some 30 feet, and fell with the mattress to the street. Her sister, Millicent Walker, seventeen, was blown into a yard at the rear, both feet dismembered. Their father, sixty, was killed and a third sister, May Walker, was seriously injured. The upper parts of numbers 1 and 3 were destroyed, the surrounding houses and the roof and windows of St Thomas' church damaged. A Mr Hatfield of the North Eastern Railway police escaped from number 3, with his wife and four children.

Porter Street was a mass of bricks and mortar and an incendiary went through the roof of South Parade, Porter Street, on to the bed where three children were burnt to death. Sarah's Terrace, adjoining, was also damaged, and here Emma Pickering, an infirm 68-year-old unable to get out of bed, was also burnt to death. Numbers 20 and 21 Edwin's Place, Porter Street, were demolished and also the upper rooms of 19 and 22. Doors, windows and roofs of the remaining nineteen houses were more or less shattered. The back bedroom and scullery of 24 Lucy's

Place, Porter Street, were demolished and houses and shops in the vicinity were much shattered. At 154 Walker Street an incendiary fell on a partition wall and then through the ceiling of the landing setting fire to the wallpaper; Godfrey Scott and his wife extinguished the fire. A large hole was made in the High Street, outside the premises of John Good and Sons, some twenty feet across and seven to eight feet deep.

On the east side of Hull, in Bright Street, not far from the Hewetson timber yard, Palmer's grocer's shop was destroyed but no-one injured. All the houses were more or less seriously damaged in East Street, off Church Street, a short cul-de-sac consisting of sixteen houses, seven front houses and nine houses in the terrace. Numbers 11 and 12 were totally demolished, 13 partly demolished and the others had doors, roofs, and windows wrecked. Of the fourteen houses in Walters Terrace and two houses fronting Waller Street (near the railway line), all were more or less demolished. Turner notes on the back of a photograph of this site that 'when joists run towards the front windows the floors nearly always collapse when directly hit within the full blast of the bomb'.[25] A bomb also dropped in the middle of the terrace making a hole about eighteen feet in diameter at the surface and about seven feet deep in the centre.[26]

A contemporary account of someone on the receiving end of the raid, written just a few days afterwards, is in a letter post-marked 10 June.[27] It was sent, to her brother and sister in Sheffield, by the wife of Martin Rowson, a yeast dealer, at 32 Coltman Street:[28]

Dear Bro and Sis,

We received your kind letter this morning – am thankful to tell you that we are unhurt although it has been a dreadful affair. It happened about midnight on Sunday. We were in bed and asleep. Mart heard them and waked me. I only heard about two. I saw one fall, at least I saw the blue light attached which causes the explosion.[29] One dropped in an empty house in this street but did not explode and in the backyard of a short street that runs out of Coltman St. There were some terraces absolutely wrecked and a great many people killed.

Do you remember going to the East Park when you and Gerty were here, that end of the City suffered the most. A large shop in the town was completely burnt down. I imagine it was only about an hour from being struck to utter collapse. I should have said it was Edwin Davis's shop (well known) – a street know [sic] as Porter street was smashed in all directions. Of course they won't let us know all, but I should think there will be anywhere from 50 to and 100 deaths and I cannot say how many wounded. I cannot tell you any more now. Mart is going to post this as he goes out – it is quarter to 9 morning. We do not know what may happen if there are more raids—and we escape—will write you, but you know dear Sis we are no more than anyone else. We are in the hands of God and we have got to leave it there (there were thousands of people went out into the country lanes on Tuesday night (they, the Zeps were expected) some until two in the morning).

Love and all hoping you are well

M and C Rowson

(if they come to Shef and you alright—write)

Dr Mary Murdoch and a Dr Dowsing, manned one of the 'dressing stations', at the Higher Grade School, Brunswick Avenue, not far from the consulting rooms of the former.[30] She wrote the following description on 9 June:

> Sleeping and eating times were reduced to a minimum, life is so full, and it is long since I gave up even writing to friends. Now these wretched air-raids make it worse than ever. We have had many nights of watching. As soon as the alarm sounds I have to be on duty at my ambulance station, and have come to the conclusion that the street is the safest place when the bombs are falling.
>
> Our poor city had a wretched time on Sunday at midnight. The Zeppelin threw about a 100 bombs on us, some incendiary and some explosive. In an incredibly short time six fires were raging in the city, and we had over 30 killed and 100 injured, and many buildings razed to the ground.[31] The poor have suffered the most, in their crowded tenements,[32] and one big drapery establishment [Edwin Davis; see above] was entirely gutted. We had no casualties at our station, so I got out my car and drove about the town for some hours, without lights, to try and pick up the injured. Our school for Mothers had every window blown out, and several ceilings fell; but we got out the Sister-in-charge and the cook uninjured. I was in no danger myself, though I saw the bombs thrown out, and feared one had struck the Children's hospital. However they were all safe when I went to them.
>
> I have absolutely no fear myself, and simply feel that we are in God's hands. Earthly protection from our fiendish enemies there is none. I have never felt hatred in my heart until Sunday night when I saw that wretched Zeppelin, like a cigar in the sky, throwing out its bombs. It must have been about 8,000 feet up. We had the alarm sounded five nights, and it always means hours in the streets until the danger is over. Last night the police ordered whole families into the open country, and it was a pitiful sight to see the exodus and the return of the people. The Zepp. was on the outskirts, but threw no bombs.[33]

The last remark indicates an abortive raid on 8 June.

Mary Charlotte Murdoch (1864–1916) was a formidable woman who had exhibited a strong will and determination since childhood. She gained a medical qualification when women were still regarded with suspicion and often downright hostility by their male colleagues. In Hull she was not only an industrious general practitioner,[34] particularly devoted to the needs of women and children, but also a campaigner for housing reform, creches for working mothers, schools for mothers, girls' clubs and women patrols (see below). She was also active in the women's suffrage movement and president of the local branch of the National Union of Women Workers. At the start of the war she immediately began a series of courses of Red Cross first-aid lectures, given three nights a week at the end of an already long working day.

When she first arrived in the city a bicycle was all she had on which to reach her patients, but this was subsequently replaced by a dog cart, then an electric landau, which proved too expensive. Finally she purchased a De Dion motor car in which she had many scrapes and knocks, often accompanied by a dog, at first a collie and then a succession of Yorkshire terriers.

The Lord Mayor J. H. Hargreaves was in touch with the Chief Constable throughout the night of the first raid and the next morning obtained:

> —details as to the raid, and as to the reception of the wounded, Mrs Hargreaves[35] visited each of the institutions where the injured were being treated—the Infirmary, the Victoria Children's Hospital and the Naval Hospital—where everything possible was done. Proper clothing was provided for them on discharge, for many of the injured were taken to the hospital in their night attire. Alderman Hargreaves, with the Town Clerk and the Chief Constable, drove round after each raid [four during the mayor's term of office] to inspect the damage.
>
> Upon returning to the Guildhall after the first raid, the then Lord Mayor communicated with the late Mr. Winter (clerk of the Hull Guardians) and Mr. Wild (the clerk of the Sculcoates Guardians) that in no circumstances were victims of Zeppelin raids to be buried by the Poor Law authorities, but any application which might be made was to be referred to him. As a matter of fact the then Lord Mayor came to the rescue and provided the funds for the burial of the Zeppelin victims in Hull, with one or two exceptions.[36]

Burials seem to have been done on an individual family basis, a combined public burial was probably avoided as potentially bad for morale. However in Sunderland, after a raid on 1 April 1916, on the Tuesday following, all twenty-two victims were conveyed to the cemetery, many thousands lining the streets. The coffins were borne on motor wagons, followed by representatives of public bodies and contingents from the army and navy. Thousands more waited at the burial site and the whole ceremony lasted some two hours.[37]

Hargreaves also contacted the vicar of each parish in which damage had been done and they in turn got in touch with the Nonconformist ministers and Catholic clergy and relevant councillors to form a committee to assess the needs of the victims to whom assistance was given from the Lord Mayor's Fund. In addition a leading local furniture firm was asked to provide a detailed list of prices for furnishing a working man's home and the Property Owners Association a list of suitable houses of the same class that had been destroyed that were available to let in the relevant districts. This was done in the space of three days and:

> ...the women in the houses destroyed or partially destroyed had the pleasure of themselves acquiring their new homes. The people were at liberty to purchase where they liked, and they were not bound to buy articles from the list, though in no cases must the prices be exceeded.

In retrospect there were occasional lighter moments:

> My brother was 14 at the time and worked at the Pavilion Picture Palace.[38] He had to take the films from one cinema to another, once they had been shown. We were watching a film one night when the buzzers blew and everybody panicked, my brother was supposed to show the King and Queen and play the National Anthem, in his panic he showed the films upside down and lost his job because of it.[39]

CHAPTER ·6

The First Women Police and Self Help by the Citizenry

Though there were no female specials, a band of forty women Voluntary Patrollers were active in Hull by 1915. These Voluntary Patrols were established first of all in London during 1914, monitoring the streets, parks and open spaces, mainly out of concern over the moral welfare of young women in this new world filled with men in khaki. At the same time the Women Police Volunteers were also founded, by Miss Nina Boyle and Miss Margaret Damer Dawson,[1] with the aim of providing a full-time body of uniformed policewomen that might eventually become a permanent and integral part of the nation's police forces. In 1915 the name was changed to the Women Police Service headed by Margaret Dawson and Mary Sophia Allen as her deputy. Both groups were recruited from women of good education and social background.

Miss Allen, a prominent suffragette, had been one of the earliest recruits of the WPS and in late 1914 she (the sub-commandant), and Miss E. F. Harburn[2] were invited to help in the provinces, first of all in Grantham, Lincs. The following year Hull invited the two women to supervise and give police training to the existing Voluntary Patrollers.[3] They arrived in the May just in time for the first air raid:

> It is impossible to exaggerate the courage and fortitude needed by both men and women police for this nerve-racking and unprecedented test. Before long, the population in general became more or less inured to these grim and terrible aerial visitants, with their unheard of and devastating weapons; accepting them in the end with the dogged sang-froid which never ceased to be an astonishment to our foreign friends. On these first occasions, however, the horror and bewilderment of the utter surprise caused a panic, especially in the crowded slum areas, where a single bomb created appalling havoc, and the loss of life was accompanied by such ghastly mutilations.
>
> The first air-raid naturally found no arrangements to meet it. A cordon of police blocked the way to the damaged part of the town, and panic-stricken crowds surged around the forbidden area. At the first alarm Commandant Damer Dawson, Inspector Harburn, and I[4] rushed out, and the cry 'Women police' was

enough to make it possible for us to circulate freely. We at once busied ourselves in locating and picking up the wounded, and in carrying them to given points, where cars conveyed them to the nearest hospital. The late Dr. Mary Murdoch was one of the first to answer the call for help, and could be seen at many subsequent air-raids calmly giving first aid, or collecting victims in her car for their prompt removal to hospital.[5]

The Hull corporation minutes for 19 October 1914 record a resolution:

> That four patrol women officers be appointed to act in cooperation with the police and under the direction of the Chief Constable, at a salary of 15s per week each and that such appointments be left in the hands of the Chief Constable.[6]

On 10 March 1915, the council minutes record that a number of women patrols (i.e. volunteer patrols) had been working in Hull under the supervision of an organiser of the National Union of Women Workers and the original resolution was rescinded at the suggestion of the Bishop of Hull. Instead he advised that a woman organiser be appointed at a weekly wage of £2 and two patrol officers at 15s.[7] The compilation of a report on the progress of the appointees is minuted, but its contents were not published and are not now discoverable. The chief constable informed the Watch Committee that 'the authority in London who supplied the Women Police[8] has found great difficulty in getting women to act because the pay was not equal to that paid in other places, and one of the women was leaving',[9] and he suggested that the salary of Miss Sandilands should be increased to 35s a week, which would be an increase of 10s per week upon the amount now paid to the two women'[10] On 9 January, it had been resolved that they were all to be given a war bonus of 5s a week and on 8 May 1918 it was proposed that Sandilands be placed on the same pay rate as constables of the same length of service. The Chief Constable was asked to obtain information on the rates paid to women police assistants elsewhere.[11] On 12 June Miss Sandilands pay was raised by 5s a week.[12]

The Bishop of Hull, Francis Gurdon,[13] had been the prime mover behind the invitation to the WPS, chiefly concerned with the moral welfare of the female population in time of war. In so doing he had clearly helped in the development of the Voluntary Patrollers into an organisation of women who would make a significant contribution both to maintaining order and helping the bomb victims to safety. By permission of the Chief Constable, Inspector Harburn occasionally undertook public house duty 'in order to induce publicans to keep youths and young girls out of bars where soldiers were served'; and, though not sworn-in, policewomen were permitted to arrest drunken and disorderly women, as well as 'making the charge, signing the charge sheet, and giving evidence when the case appeared in court the next day'.[14]

The status of women officers varied from town to town but in Hull members of the WPS were not sworn-in as full members of the force. They were paid from £2 5s for constables to £2 15s for inspectors, with a 5s bonus and uniform provided.[15]

Miss Sandilands is recorded as one of the original members of the Women Police Service, serving at Hull from August 1915, and in Allen's account of the origins of women police given the rank of sergeant.[16] This would have been her rank in the WPS, in the Hull force she was a Women Police Assistant.

Clarke, historian of the Hull City Police, tells us that two years later, in 1917, she is the first woman officially enrolled into the Hull force, named as Woman Police Assistant Sandilands. He says that she was employed part-time, taking witness statements and not used on street patrols, though that was after the war, and as an acknowledged member of the local police.[17] Allen says that 'Until 1918 five policewomen continued to serve in Hull; but in the next year, owing to a plea for public economy, it was considered advisable to call them 'police matrons',[18] and in this capacity they are still working there'.[19]

A week after the Armistice, George Morley, chief constable, requested permission to employ three women police but because the pay on offer was much less than that received by the Munitions Police and those in similar posts he could not find recruits of the right calibre.[20] He asks for Miss Sandilands 'who was in charge of Voluntary Women's Patrols, and would be in charge of any Women Police appointed' pay be to be raised from the current £2 5s a week to 60s. Other police assistants should be paid 50s.'[21]

Because of the appalling numbers of casualties, killed and injured, during the offensives which punctuated the long stalemate of trench warfare, ever more men were sent to the front. At home, in factories, public transport, and on the land women learned new skills and successfully filled the gaps. The nurses of the Voluntary Aid Detachment,[22] participants in the Voluntary Patrols and the nascent women's police force were from 'good families'. In contrast the 'munitionettes' and other factory workers, tram drivers and conductors, and women of the Women's Forestry Corps, Women's Forage Corps and Women's Land Army came from all kinds of backgrounds. Though most returned to looking after the home and family after the war was over there was now a broad spectrum of women who could see the possibility of full time paid work, or even a career, outside the domestic environment.

The need to organise huge armies and keep them supplied with armaments and food resulted in state control of the economy. The increasing intervention of the government in the lives of every citizen led to a greater involvement in public welfare. To support people working in the munition industries, and generally to sustain the war effort, people had to be fed and looked after. In addition, the soldier at the front needed to be reassured that his family left at home was being supported. Following the Second World War this 'contract' between government and citizen became more explicit and was enshrined in the National Health Service and the development of the welfare state.

To offer support during and after a raid it seems that at least some of the citizens of Hull organised themselves into patrols on a street by street basis. A picture shows a total of eighty-six males, including a handful of youths fourteen to sixteen years old and the oldest in their sixties and seventies. One of the young men on the front row holds a board painted with the inscription Courtney St Voly/Night. Patrol. 1915. The company must be pretty much the entire population of able-bodied males from this street in east Hull. Courtney Street comes off the north side of Holderness Road and leads into Dansom Lane,[23] part of a commercial and industrial area dominated by Reckitts & Sons Ltd,[24] a famous manufacturer of household products, at that time noted particularly for their Robin Starch, Zebra Black Lead,[25] and Reckitt's Blue.[26]

One imagines the patrol was established immediately following the first raid and the picture was probably taken either at the end of the war, or at a time after 1916 when the airship threat had largely vanished. For the camera everyone is dressed in his 'Sunday best', with collar and tie (including one man with a bow-tie), and an occasional 'muffler', a few of them sporting flowers in their buttonholes. There is also a dog, a Jack Russell terrier! Precisely what duties they undertook is not clear. Presumably they acted like the 'fire watchers' and air raid wardens of the 1939–45, and after a warning 'buzzer' sounded watched for where bombs and incendiaries had landed. They would no doubt keep an eye on the women and children and help the police and fire brigade if houses in their locality were hit.

CHAPTER 7

Counting the Losses, and those Seeking Advantage from the Raid

The Hull Royal Infirmary, Prospect Street, in the heart of the city and not far from the main railway station, received four dead and eleven admitted to the wards, three of them subsequently dying. Thirty or forty casualties were attended to and about fifteen of these were sent on to the Naval Hospital (Anlaby Road) for further treatment.[1]

Thirteen high explosive bombs and thirty-nine incendiaries (German sources give the figures as ten high explosive and fifty incendiaries) were dropped without any means of retaliation. When the airship headed for home it rose to an estimated 10,000 feet, well beyond the range of any of the batteries. Fog at the mouth of the Humber prevented aircraft being sent up from the RNAS station at Killingholme and neither was the cruiser squadron, intended to provide a vigorous response to raids, able to set sail.

The *Hull Daily Mail*, 7 June 1915, simply states it cannot publish details of the Zeppelin raids so as not to give away information which might enable the enemy to assess the effectiveness of its attacks. There was no confirmation of which towns had been hit, information that might have aided their navigation on future occasions.

Censorship was imposed on reports of all the raids after the attack on London in May 1915. Official bulletins supplied from the Press Bureau,[2] were brief and generalised, the names of individual towns being omitted. The *Eastern Morning News*, 7 June 1915, published the following at the head of the front page:

> During last night hostile airships visited the East and South-East coast of England. Bombs were dropped at various places, but little material damage was done.
>
> The casualties so far reported are few.

This was followed by an equally brief note of the effects of the raid on London the previous Monday.

William Henry Willatt, a captain in the Territorial Army, describes his own experiences:

> I happened to be at home in Newland Park, Hull, in 1915, on 24 hours leave from Sunk Island Battery when the first bombing took place; I have now in my

possession an incendiary bomb which fell through the roof of the house into a W.C. (it hit the target and the water put it out of action!).³

Though censorship had an otherwise tight grip on the material that could be published the names and ages of the fatal casualties appeared on 19 June as a result of the coroner's inquests into their deaths. This was on the front page, and the top of the column is headed 'RAID VICTIMS. The East Coast Affair. Names of the killed. Sunday week's dead.' Eighteen of the deaths were ruled to be due to 'injuries sustained by the explosion of a bomb discharged from a German Zeppelin airship' and the remaining five 'from syncope produced by shock' (see casualty lists below).⁴

Whatever catastrophic event occurs it always provides a commercial opportunity for someone. The same issue of the newspaper includes an advertisement headed, 'Be ready for the next Zeppelin raid' which proclaims the virtues of a domestic fire extinguisher, the Kyl-fire. This was a small cylinder containing dry powder, priced at 5s 6d, which was thrown at the base of the flames to smother them.⁵

Kyl-fire had been on the market some time before but a new product, or more likely something renamed to emphasise its usefulness against incendiary bombs, was offered for sale. This was a hand grenade, probably a spherical glass container, called Antizep, offered at 5s 3d, carriage paid, by Sanelak Ltd. Manufacturing Chemists, Clerkenwell, London E.C.⁶

This advertisement is inserted in a column on the back page of the newspaper, without any illustration, and masquerades as normal piece of journalistic copy giving advice on how to deal with fire caused by a bombing raid. The price would have put it beyond the pockets of most individuals.⁷

On the day after the attack, Messrs Muir Beddall & Co. Ltd were advertising bomb insurance, twenty shillings for £1,000 cover, clearly only affordable to wealthy property owners or businessmen.⁸ An example of an insurance policy against damage by 'aerial craft', for a year from 18 October 1915, issued by the Royal Insurance Co. to a client in Worthing, was recently sold at auction.⁹ A maximum of £3,000 was payable for a premium of £10. Most national and local newspapers offered their readers' protection. The *Sunday Herald*, a free policy which gave £1,000 for death of husband, wife and every adult member of the family as well 'a sum varying from £1,000' for injury to any of them. The *Daily Chronicle* published a striking image by the notable artist Frank Brangwyn, of a 'Tommy' shaking his fist at a Zeppelin flying overhead, while a mother comforts a small child, and a body lies prone between them. It is headed 'The Zeppelin Raids: the vow of Vengeance', and with the legend 'Daily Chronicle readers are covered against risks of bombardment by Zeppelin or aeroplane'.¹⁰

The *Hull Daily Mail*, promised up to a maximum total of £10,000, according to whether the victim had died, had lost limbs or suffered damage to their house and furnishings.¹¹

Following an official report, 9 July 1915, HM Government offered cover for war damage from aircraft and other sources of bombardment, for which purposes property was divided, 'into five classifications, roughly into divisions of private, agricultural and varied commercial specifications'.[12] The premium of the Government Aircraft and Bombardment Insurance for private citizens was £1 16s a year for which the government would, 'pay or make good within 30 days' to a sum not exceeding £1,200.

There was a ready sale for postcards of the effects of the bombing especially the ruins of the Edwin Davis store in Church Side, but no artist's impression of this first airship attack on Hull has been discovered. Actual pictures of the Zeppelins would have been impossible because the raid was at night and the photographic emulsions then available could not satisfactorily capture an image in such low-level light conditions.[13]

The bombing and civilian deaths had a marked effect on recruitment for the armed forces as Captain Willatt confirms:

> The Zeppelin raids caused the recruits to crowd out Recruiting Stations, many country people could not realise we were at war, until the Zepps came and made them aware of it!!! So from the point of view of German Militarism, the Zeppelin airship bombing raids were a bad policy.[14]

The 133rd Annual Report of the Hull Royal Infirmary, 1915, includes a thank you from the Managing Committee to all those who gave their services during the first air raid, 6 June:[15]

> The Committee of Management desire to express their high appreciation of the satisfactory manner in which the casualties resulting from the recent Zeppelin Raid were attended to, and to return their sincere thanks for the invaluable services rendered by Drs A. E. Francis, Ed. Harrison, E. M. Hainworth [sic], F. C. Eve, G. P. Hartley and Jos. Nelson, Mr. W. H. Jennison, The Matron and Nurses, The Housekeeper and Domestics, Dispensers and Porters on that memorable occasion.
>
> The Committee of Management wish to express their high appreciation of the satisfactory manner in which the casualties resulting from the recent Zeppelin Raid were dealt with, both at the dressing stations and by the stretcher bearers, and also for their voluntary offer of help inside the Infirmary, and to return sincere thanks for the valuable services rendered by the Ambulance Corps on that occasion.

There is no further mention of the raids in any subsequent Annual Report for the remainder of the war.

On 9/10 October 1915, *L9* headed towards the Humber and Hull but owing to ground mist obscuring his intended target, Kapitänleutnant Loewe instead found himself at Goole where his bombs resulted in sixteen deaths, the destruction of ten dwellings and damage to warehouses.[16]

CHAPTER 8

Public Reaction to the Bombing

After the first raid whenever there was fear of attack streams of women and children passed along the main roads of the city to the parks and surrounding fields to spend the night in the open. This phenomenon was also witnessed in 1939–45, when it was dubbed 'trekking'.[1] The testimony of Dr Murdoch (above), a reliable witness and someone in public service who had close contacts with the authorities, indicates that the temporary exodus when under threat was originally instigated by the police.

The Lord Mayor Alderman Hargreaves:[2]

> through Mr. McCombe, approached the tramwaymen with a suggestion that when the relief buzzer sounded they should take the cars to the various termini and bring in the women and children; also that if they should give their services, he would arrange with the Tramway Committee to bring them in free of charge.[3]

The tramwaymen did indeed offer their services free, so saving many women and children a long, weary walk home. As part of the 'black-out' trams had their windows painted over to prevent light showing through; it was an offence to attempt to remove this covering. Mary Allen of the WPS tells us that 'a man on top of a tram was badly mauled for inadvertently lighting a cigar'.

It was a perpetual struggle for the 'Specials' to ensure lights in homes, offices and factories were switched off or rendered invisible from the outside. Sometimes they were the guilty party:

> The 'lighting order' (which should have been called the 'darkness order'), being rigorously enforced, added suspicion and terror to the general atmosphere of bewilderment. Upon one occasion a special constable rushed from his room to answer a call for help, leaving his gas jet full on. An angry crowd at once collected, and as no one answered the door, a ladder was procured, a window smashed in, and the light put out...[4]

The responses to the buzzer varied according to where the families lived and what personal resources they had. Some families found refuge in the nearest public park:

> There were 7 children in our family and when the buzzers went, we had to go to the Anlaby road park [West Park], as we lived nearby, down Bean street, we had to save seats[5] for my mother and father, as my father only had one leg and mother had to get the insurance policies and brought food, because we did not know how long the raid would last.[6]

It is mentioned by several of those who provided reminiscences for Steven Suddaby, and is a constant refrain from the Second World War too, that mother would gather up the bank books, insurance policies, and such essential documents, before seeking shelter.

Mary Allen of the WPS gives further testimony of the response to the sirens or to some rumour of impending attack:

> Too distraught to make any sensible preparations for the emergency, the unfortunate inhabitants of the poorer districts, would seize the first objects at hand – piling up their possessions in the family perambulator, from under which it was sometimes necessary to rescue half-smothered babies. As a consequence the parks were littered with large framed pictures, birds in cages, huge vases, sea-shells, bundles of clothing, bedding, and the most incongruous and astonishing articles.
>
> As the raids, or the sounding of warnings, multiplied in frequency, the habit grew upon many, at the first hint of danger, to take refuge in the open: and sleeping in crowds in this haphazard fashion inevitably led to disorderly conduct.[7]

Elsewhere she states:

> The duty of the women police was, in general terms, to 'keep order'—a difficult task in the Stygian darkness, where often the returning crowds after the air raids, in the gaiety of their relief after terror, could only be heralded by the sense of smell or hearing.[8]

Percy Cook recalled that they stayed in the house until someone shouted that the Zepps were coming: 'Then we used to flee to a field at the back of the houses, mother used to cover us up with a large black shawl.'

While G. S. Clark, at the age of eighty-three, recorded:

> I was taken downstairs and put under the table on which my mum and auntie brought the feather bed and pillows down and placed them on the table.

I remember in an air raid my Dad wrapping me up in a shawl and taking me into the front garden to see the Jerry Zepp which was caught in the searchlights- it looked like a silver cigar.[9]

Another responder to Suddaby's request for memories of the raids was someone only referred to as Freda, who clearly was from a more affluent family:

When the buzzers blew for a Zeppelin raid alert I remember working by candlelight in the living room, with the big bay window shrouded in heavy black-out curtaining. Yet in many ways life went on as usual I continued with dancing, singing, and piano lessons. We went out in the evening to the library, lectures, and the cinema as usual, in spite of darkened streets. The word 'mugging' was never even heard.[10]

Despite the commotion resulting from a raid many seem to have slept through the event and were oblivious to the effects until the following morning when returning to their everyday activities:

It was remarkable how many people who had gone to bed were unaware of the happenings. It sounds like a fairy tale, but it is perfectly true that on the morning following one raid, in which the damage was done in the Old Town, we were on duty at Mytongate corner, when the men were going to work. When they saw us and the damage, several of them asked 'What's up. Has there been a fire?' When we told them what had happened they actually stared at us with open mouths.[11]

Though attendance at school was inevitably affected as a result of the upset of normal routines many pupils still made the effort to turn up for lessons. The logbook of Boulevard Junior School records on 11 June, 1915, 'The attendance was poor on Monday morning after the air-raid of the 6th, but on Wednesday morning after the alarm, it was much worse. Only 185 out of 268 children being present.'[12] Marion Large seems to have had some very sympathetic teachers in her primary school whose type of approach, illustrating the scenes they had witnessed, is nowadays strongly advocated by those caring for children exposed to the trauma of war and disaster:

We were also encouraged to draw pictures of our experiences and many small masterpieces of these silver cigars in converging searchlights decorated the class room walls.[13]

Because the Zeppelins were large and a highly visible presence across the city the disruption of everyday activities was the same whether near to where the bombs actually landed, or not. At Stepney school, some way north of the city centre, off the Beverley Road:

> 7 June 1915. Attendance very poor. 252 present out of 306. Zeppelin raid of previous night disturbed and alarmed children.
>
> 9 June 1915. Attendance very bad owing to Zeppelin panic last night. Notice of danger sounded at 10 p.m. after which time many went to the fields and did not return till 2 a.m. 123 absent.[14]

The war had its effect on the cultural life of the city too and on 24 June the Property Committee authorised the removal of the paintings from the walls of the art gallery, which since 1910 had occupied part of the City Hall, in the centre of Hull.[15] They remained in storage for two years until the curator, Mr Procter, expressed concern over their condition after this lengthy incarceration in the basement. By January 1918, councillors were able to see the gallery fully open again.[16] Thomas Sheppard, curator of museums, was given permission to do whatever necessary to protect the collections and at the request of its owner, the Earle collection of Staffordshire pottery, on loan to the city, was crated and placed in the cellar. Though the museum was situated close to the centre of the city (in Albion Street) the curator evidently considered the danger of damage and destruction was not great, and the gaps left in display by the removal of the ceramics were filled with other items from store.[17]

T. R. Ferens, MP for East Hull, raised the question in parliament concerning compensation for losses due to the bombing, who might be eligible and how it would be paid.[18] Born near Bishop Auckland, he was a member of parliament and privy counsellor and the head of Reckitt & Sons who gave generously to the city of Hull, including the art gallery named after him.[19]

CHAPTER 9

Attacks on the German Community

From the outbreak of war, all German citizens were obliged to register themselves at the nearest police station and were later transferred to internment camps. As in other places those at Hull of military age, from seventeen to forty-two years, and liable to call up by their native country were taken into custody:

> Fully 300 of our German residents have been arrested and put on board the Wilson liner 'Borodino'. The majority are reservists and several are well known in Hull. This ship is guarded by regular troops but those on board are being well cared for and treated with every courtesy.[1]

British women married to German citizens were regarded has having taken the nationality of their spouse and also had to register, even if their husbands were abroad or dead. The children were also treated as German nationals and were no longer allowed to proceed with the process of naturalisation. An individual might escape internment if he could prove that he was exempt from military service, but no German was allowed to leave the country without a special permit of the Secretary of State. The fear of sabotage and a 'fifth column' resulted in telegrams being sent to all chief constables, warning them:

> Keep special watch to prevent aliens travelling by night by motor car for purpose of committing outrages. Motor cars belonging to Germans may be seized, as by order in council passed today no German may possess motor car without written permission of police. Motor car garages should be warned not to hire out cars to aliens.[2]

Large areas of the country, embracing vital naval and military sites, became 'prohibited areas' accessible to citizens with proper identification but completely forbidden to aliens and suspect persons. These included the east coast, much of the south coast and a greater part of Scotland, and the problems of negotiating one's way into and out of these areas without a passport or identity papers is featured in the Richard Hannay story, *Mr Standfast*.[3]

Then came the bombardment of the east coast ports (Hartlepool, Scarborough, and Whitby) on 16 December 1914, and the sinking of the *Lusitania*, 7 May 1915. The latter with a large loss of civilian life, including many women and children, was the spark for the first serious attacks on 'Germans' living in Britain, which occurred 10 May, in Liverpool, the home port of the torpedoed liner. The *Eastern Morning News* for Saturday 8 May gave news of the sinking and the next day there was a strong denunciation of the German attitude to war from the pulpit of Holy Trinity church, the hub of the Anglican community in Hull and the vicar, Revd L. G. Buchanan, accused the Kaiser of:

> outNeroing Nero himself ... [but] ... prayed this country would never descend to the methods of barbarity adopted against it. It was worthwhile losing any amount of temporary battles in order that when it was all over we might have a clear conscience before God and man.

A sermon by the Revd J. G. Patton, at the Newland Congregational church, was also reported in the same newspaper the front page of which was filled with the latest information on the *Lusitania*, including eyewitness accounts. He attributed the new 'total war' to:

> A steady and accepted indoctrination of the ideas of Nietzsche,[4] and he claimed that the Kaiser had, by his own statements and actions, proved himself to be a convert of the teacher who sought to entirely reverse the morals and religion of mankind. Certainly the Kaiser had wonderfully fulfilled the dreams of the man who looked for a conqueror who would mercilessly destroy all his foes, stopping at no savagery, however devilish, to effect his will to power.[5]

The congregation of German Lutherans dated from 1848 and had opened a new church in 1911, serving both the resident community and the transient population of German speaking seamen. It closed at the outbreak of war since many of its adherents had been interned and it was politic for the remainder not to gather together in significant numbers. Antagonism against the German community persisted a long time after hostilities had ceased. Remarkably the church did not open again till 1935, just four years before the outbreak of the Second World War. After that conflict there was a more sympathetic response and the doors were reopened in 1951.[6]

There had been growing anti-German feeling in Britain since the beginning of the war when stories had circulated claiming atrocities committed against the civilian population in the German advance through Belgium. Then there had been the east coast bombardment, the sinking of an ocean liner with the loss of nearly 1,200 lives, and at Ypres, 22 April 1915, with the use of poison gas against the allied troops for the first time.

Despite the increasing anger there were no disturbances until 14 May 1915, when stones were thrown, breaking the windows of a German woman's home, and the following day five pork butcher's shops were targeted. Owned by German nationals or their descendants, they were situated on the Hessle Road, a working-class area which was home to the local fishing community. Windows were broken but there was no looting and there were no further incidents until the first air raid in June. The main reason for these first desultory attacks may have been mostly frustration at the effects of the war on local employment. Large numbers of trawlers had been requisitioned by the Admiralty for use as mine-sweepers and patrol boats thus significantly reducing the size of the fishing fleet. The limited reaction in Hull contrasted markedly with that of Liverpool where, over the course of three days, some two hundred German shops were targeted and the anti-German feeling soon became a general antipathy to all foreigners.[7]

It was the first air-raid, 6/7 June, that sparked off serious riots in Hull. Incidents may even have occurred before the first bombs were dropped as a reaction to the mere presence and impending threat of the Zeppelins. Their arrival no doubt crystallised thoughts about a 'fifth column' who would be trying to help the invaders. This idea of the 'enemy within' was not restricted to the poor and uneducated and is a fear expressed in Turner's report of the raid (Appendix II).

As noted in the introduction William Le Queux had promoted the idea that a vast 'army of German spies' were actively at work in England before the war, an 'advance guard' preparing for invasion. His *Spies of the Kaiser*, published in 1909, begins: 'No sane person can deny that England is in grave danger of invasion by Germany at a date not too far distant.' He continued hammering home his prediction, already set out in detail in *The Invasion of 1910*. Hull had featured prominently in his account of the German landings and in the later publication is also one of the towns where agents are sent to gather intelligence for the Kaiser's war ministry. Two men are described buying tickets for Hull at King's Cross Station:

> That same night I found myself in the smoke-grimed Station Hotel in Hull, where the two foreigners had also put up. Next day they called at a solicitor's office at the end of Whitefriargate, and thence, accompanied by a man who was apparently the lawyer's clerk, they went in a cab along the Docks, where at a spot close to the Queen's Dock, they pulled up before an empty factory, a place which was not very large, but which possessed a very high chimney.[8]

In this fictional story they rented the factory in order to install a wireless station, linked to another in Sydenham, London. This would have enabled them to tap into the Admiralty communications in Whitehall, thereby obtaining a comprehensive knowledge of the movements and intentions of the Grand Fleet.

Another agent resident in the town was making notes of the topography of the coast, and any military installations:

He had once lived for a whole summer in Withernsea not far from Spurn Head [...] he took a train from Hull to Hornsea, where the railway ends at the sea, and walked along the shore for several miles ... when he suddenly halted near the little village of Barmston, and producing a neat pocket-camera took a long series of snap-shots of the flat coast, where I saw there were several places which would afford an easy landing for the invader.

Each chapter of Le Queux's book concerns a different spy or group of spies, each trying to obtain valuable secrets concerning armour plating, details of a submarine, a new aircraft, a gun, an improved Dreadnought, plans of the Rosyth naval base, and the like. These tales combine to make a 'dossier' of Germany's plans to invade England and overthrow the Empire.

Though there was much exaggeration and hyperbolae from Le Queux and a vocal minority a number of individuals were arrested who were clearly up to no good. These included Lt Siegfried Helm discovered making sketches of the defences around Portsmouth in 1910. As a serving German officer he was regarded as doing his patriotic duty and the court dealt with him leniently. He was bound over and discharged. Later it became clear that he was not part of the German intelligence service and that what he had done was entirely on his own initiative.[9]

There certainly were agents active in Britain but the network run by Steinhauer was not more than forty individuals, and most of those were probably giving him low grade material. This was a tiny number among a community of many thousands of German nationals and those of German descent nationwide. What they supplied was mostly public opinion and generalised information they picked up in their daily work. It is difficult to determine whether any were actively penetrating into the heart of government and the military. One of his agents was a Dr Max Schultz who, in 1912, used his houseboat at Portsmouth for regular parties during which he hoped some of his guests would let slip important naval or military secrets. His amateurish attempts were fruitless, quickly drew the attention of our security services and he was arrested. The new Official Secrets Act was now in force and Schultz was jailed for twenty-one months.[10]

Steinhauer's most important source was Frederick Adolphus Schroeder, alias Gould, licensee of the Queen Charlotte public house, at Rochester, on the Medway, conveniently placed near to Chatham dockyard. He was the last spy to be convicted before the outbreak of war, after Mrs Gould was apprehended trying to leave the country with a gunnery drill book, charts of Spithead and plans of cruisers. In April 1914, Schroeder was sentenced to six years' hard labour.[11]

Whatever the quality of intelligence being gathered all of the agents were bagged as soon as war was declared, only one escaped abroad, and that was Weigels the Hull fruit trader.[12] All significant contact between Britain and Germany was immediately severed, all the agents arrested, telegraph cables cut and all postal communications opened and examined. This sudden and complete shut-down meant that the German military were making their decisions in a vacuum. Initially 150,000 men of the regular army, well trained and experienced professional soldiers, later joined by an Indian corps and some Territorials, were sent across the Channel to support the French. Unaware of this rapid build-up of allied forces, substantial numbers of German soldiers were moved to the eastern front, who might well have made the difference at the Battle of the Marne, 5–12 September 1914. Casualties on both sides during the first battle of Ypres in the October and November were immense and the ranks were soon to be filled with some half million volunteers raised by Kitchener's recruiting campaign. Von Moltke's offensive, aimed at taking Paris followed by a drive to the coast, was brought to a halt by the allies, and thereafter the opposing sides settled into their trenches for the next four years.

Carl Lody, posing as an American citizen and hence a neutral, was one of a small number of spies the Germans managed to infiltrate into Britain after the outbreak of war. He could not use the telegraph because as soon as war began the underwater telegraph cables to Germany had been cut. Though intelligent and resourceful he was compromised immediately he forwarded his first report. Sent to a contact in Sweden, his description of coastal fortifications and naval armaments was not in code. Since all letters were opened and examined before being sent to their destination, Lody was immediately exposed as a spy, arrested, and executed by firing squad only ten weeks after his arrival in England. As well as attempting to discover the movements of the Royal Navy he tried to:

> find out whether Buckingham Palace was strongly protected against Zeppelin bombs, for in his ardour—and ignorance—he apparently thought that the Kaiser would be so angry at what he described as English perfidy as to try and bomb his royal cousin![13]

A wire cage had been constructed on the roof of Buckingham Palace in 1916 as a protection against Zeppelins but King George said he did not think it would be very effective, and added, 'Mary says we shall have to go down into the cellars'.[14] It was only with the Official Secrets Act of 1911 that the passing of information to a foreign power had become an indictable offence. Introduction of the Defence of the Realm Act on the outbreak of war made espionage a military offence to be tried by court martial, and those found guilty were faced with the death penalty. All of the would-be spies were arrested by officers of the Special Branch of the Metropolitan Police[15] and a total of eleven were executed in the Tower of London.[16] One of these, Carl Frederick Muller, arrived at Hull, on 11 January, from Rotterdam aboard the Hull and Netherland Steamship Co. steamer *Whitby Abbey*, and on 23 June was facing a firing squad.

The port of Hull was a gateway to and from western Europe and Scandinavia, and was the route into and out of England for other agents. H. P. M. Janssen arrived in Hull aboard the SS *Estrom* and made his way to York. In his interrogation he claimed to have a friend (also named Janssen), living at the York Hotel, Anlaby Road, Hull, though apparently not involved in espionage. Irving Guy Ries, his real name is unknown, arrived in Britain from New York, 4 July 1915, and during his time here visited Copenhagen sailing from the port of Hull. Like all the others he was quickly apprehended and after only four months at large met his end in the Tower of London.

One of the first anti-German attacks, sometime between 12.10 and 2 a.m. on 7 June, was on the Holderness Road, east Hull, at the premises of J. F. Ott, pork butcher. He had been interned and the business was being run by his wife. In west Hull, between 12.15 and 1 a.m., the shops' of Robert Brehm, Caroline Street, and Gottlieb Lang, Charles Street, and, in the east of the city John Hanneman's premises, were attacked and looted. The latter's shop was at the junction of Hedon Road and Woodhouse Street not far from Hewetson's sawmill. These were all pork butchers but a clothier's belonging to Gus Adler next to Hanneman's was also a victim. In Spyvee Street the home of an internee was assaulted by some four hundred men and women. Thankfully, a lone constable was able to take the woman and her children to safety at the local police station. There were eighteen separate attacks between midnight and 5 a.m. scattered across the city at a time when the police and fire brigade were fully occupied dealing with burning buildings and rescuing people from the wreckage of their homes.

At the height of the unrest assemblies of up to seven hundred and sometimes maybe even a thousand people smashed shops and stole the property of 'aliens' many of whom were naturalised or had been born in Britain.[17] German-speakers were well-established in the meat trade, especially pork butchery, and this section of the immigrant community bore the brunt of the assaults. Many of the younger officers had been called up so the police were sorely overstretched, even with the help of small contingents from the army. They found it impossible to protect property from such large scale assaults but successfully kept safe the threatened shopkeepers and their families.

Wrecking and looting continued until the late afternoon of 7 June and there were further sporadic outbreaks in the evening from 7 p.m. till 12 midnight. There was rioting on Tuesday 8 June in the Waller Street and Craven Street area of east Hull. In the afternoon the only reported case of violent assault against the person was perpetrated against the sister-in-law of Alderman Feldman. She was rescued by the military and the *Eastern Morning News* lamented:

> Those who remembered the valuable services which Alderman Feldman rendered to the city would think it a great pity that the mob could not discriminate a little more than they seemed inclined to do.[18]

There were in all sixteen separate incidents but by the next day, 9 June, the police and military were in control, though there were two isolated incidents in the evening. The first dozen or so individuals involved in these fracas to be dealt with by the bench were found guilty of stealing goods from the shops of 'alien tradesmen' and, depending on the gravity of each offence, fined one, two or five guineas with the option of fifteen or twenty-nine days in prison.

The compensation for the effects of the bombing was ultimately paid for by the government but damage from public riot fell on the local police authority and hence on the ratepayer. The Corporation tried to minimise the depletion of the city treasury and many of those who had suffered loss failed to meet the deadline of fourteen days in which to make their claim. A total of £3,652 19s 10d was asked for but many of the figures submitted were disputed and knocked down as far as possible so that only £2,510 19s 2d was actually paid out in compensation.[19] Damage claims amounted to £42,000 for what had been the worst air raid experienced in England up till that time.

Though individuals of German origin survived physically unscathed on this occasion, the livelihoods of a great number of victims were destroyed and many moved to other towns.[20] One has only to compare the listings of pork butchers in the trade directories for 1914 and 1916 to see the impact on this once thriving part of the community. The former had Baeurle, Beck, Brehm, Deerolf, Dimler, Gaiser, Heinzmann, Hohenrein, Houfe, Kress and Wagner, Lang, Sallmann, Schellenberg, Schmeig, Schumm, Stabeler, Steeg, Stelzle, Uebel, Wenterhoff, Wieland and Zeigler, but the latter only Houfe, Kress and Wagner, Stabeler and Hohenrein, though the last had now changed his name and is recorded as Ross.[21] Only this handful had the resilience, or the respect and standing among the people of Hull, as well as the financial resources to overcome the effects of this cataclysm.

The story of the Hohenreins one of the supposed 'alien' families can be followed in some detail thanks to a collection of papers deposited in the Hull archives, summarised by John Markham.[22] Originally from Swabia, Georg Friedrich Hohenrein arrived in Hull in the middle of the nineteenth century. Of two sons born in Hull, one, George William, married a German wife and went back to live in the 'old country' while the other, Charles Henry, married a local girl and stayed to run the prize-winning pork butchers business.[23]

At the outbreak of war, George and his son were interned in Ruhleben camp, Berlin, held in equal suspicion as an 'enemy alien' by the Germans as Charles was in England.[24]

Attempts were made to prevent German butchers from buying pigs at local auctions and on 20 May the Hull Master Butchers Association sent a circular letter requesting that all members of German or Austrian descent should resign. Ironically the letter heading was blazoned with the name of C. H. Hohenrein as Vice President![25] The *Eastern Morning News* for 15 June carries the following statement:

£500 G. E. Hohenrein & Son Owing to the erroneous opinion of the public that we are either Germans or naturalised English and our consequent unpleasant position we have decided to close until the government interns[26] all aliens, so that we may reopen our 65 year old business without being subject to unjust threats, insults and much inconvenience. We are prepared to pay £500 to any local charity if anyone can prove we are not ENGLISH.

Chas. H. Hohenrein

The fear of possible attack or apprehension by overzealous officials is indicated by a 'letter of protection' given to him and signed, on behalf of the Chief Constable by W. Bailey, Superintendent and Chief Clerk, 7 July 1915:

Chief Constables' Office The bearer Mr. C. H. Hohenrein is a British born subject who I have known since his youth. He is a man of the highest integrity and honour, and I have the most implicit confidence and reliance in him.
He is well known to most of the leading citizens in this district.[27]

The Chief Constable was a personal friend of Hohenrein's and according to the latter's son he was given prior warning of impending raids by telephone, the code being 'Please deliver the usual order of sausages'![28] Head of one of the most successful pork butchers[29] in Hull, whose family had been in the city for over sixty-five years, he decided to change his name to Charles H. Ross, duly registered 15 July 1915.[30] The family were well respected and two letters, sent anonymously, to warn of attacks being planned are preserved in the Hohenrein papers. One, written in capitals 'TAKE A GOOD TIP, DON'T BE ON THE PREMISES MAY 13–15 OR MAY 20–26.'[31] In another, posted without a stamp and on which 2*d* postage due had been paid, the writer says 'your shop is going to be broken up' in revenge for the *Lusitania*, but he was giving a warning because Hohenrein's parents had been good to him as a boy 'when I was hungry and needed bread.'[32] Charles, though a member of the Yorkshire Imperial Yeomanry since 1907,[33] was declared exempt from call up until 1917 (when he was aged thirty-four), and when ruled as unfit for active service he became a sergeant in the East Yorks Motor Volunteer Co.[34] A photograph shows him in uniform standing outside the air raid shelter he had built at the family home, Derringham Cottage, adjacent to 2 Victoria Street, off Derringham Street.

Piled with sandbags over the thick concrete roof it was known as the 'dugout' and held 'about ten people on comfortable benches and was heated by a solid fuel stove'.[35]

Anyone of foreign extraction was liable to be accused of spying and there were stories of signals being made to the Zeppelins flying overhead. Needless to say none of these tales, certainly in Hull, were ever substantiated. However, one local man, Max Schultz,[36] was recruited by our own espionage services before the war started, either by the Naval Intelligence Department or by Commander Mansfield Cumming (known as C) to gather information on the German navy during his trips to Germany as a broker buying and selling yachts.[37] According to Judd he was a 'Southampton shipbroker' and he no doubt had contacts in that town essential to his buying and selling of yachts, so near to the Solent and Cowes, home of the Royal Yacht Club. Schultz's home was however in Hull. He was the son of a shoemaker from Pomerania,[38] had previously worked at Earle's shipyard in Hull and so had a good grasp of the technical detail of ship construction. Arrested at a hotel in Hamburg in 1911, he and several of his German contacts were tried. Schultz was sentenced to seven years imprisonment and was only released at the end of the war. Ironically, at home, his wife like so many others, fearing for her own safety and that of her children, had in the meantime discarded his patronymic and used her maiden name of Hilton.[39]

An event the following year, 1916, would have helped maintain the local hostility to 'aliens' when, on 3 May, in the battle of Oppy Wood more local men were lost in one day than in any other engagement in the war.

CHAPTER 10

An Organised Defence

In December 1916, Major General Sir Stanley Brenton von Donop[1] took over as General Officer Commanding the Humber Garrison, replacing Major General Ferrier who went into retirement. A distinguished ordnance expert, he had been Master General of Ordnance from 1913 to 1916, and helped develop the integrated system intended to intercept the Zeppelins with aircraft, as they came over the east coast, or harass the raiders with searchlights and anti-aircraft fire as they sought their target. Spotting the airships as soon as they crossed the coast relied on picking up German radio traffic, direct observation, the use of Direction Finding[2] and sound mirrors. Once directions had been received the aircraft were sent in pursuit but they were generally underpowered. The time needed to climb to the altitude of their intended prey usually meant the Zeppelins were too far ahead to engage, or were already heading back over the sea to base often without a sighting being made. Guns and searchlights provided the main response as the airships passed from the coast, across the countryside and toward Hull and other conurbations in the Humber region.

Throughout his tenure von Donop seems to have kept away from the public eye as much as possible, which is not surprising. Given the public reaction to supposed 'aliens' after the first raid one can only imagine the response of some citizens to the appointment of this army officer, no matter how distinguished and experienced, with such an obviously German name. At the beginning of the war Prince Louis of Battenberg (scion of a Hessian family with a long history of supporting the British), after forty years' service in the Royal Navy, was forced to resign as First Sea Lord, due to rising anti-German feeling stirred up by the 'popular' press.

In July 1917, he was persuaded to anglicise his name from Battenberg to Mountbatten and in the same month, by decree of King George V, the Royal Family changed its dynastic name from Saxe-Coburg Gotha to Windsor.[3]

From the beginning of the war, air defence had been arbitrarily divided between the Admiralty and the War Office, and had resulted in a less than satisfactory intelligence and warning organisation. The public, especially since the large raid on the Midlands in January 1916, had become very nervous and alarms were rapidly spread across the country. The report of a Zeppelin over Scarborough, on

10 February, had plunged great tracts of the country into darkness and brought about a widespread cessation of work. Two government factories, as far remote from the source of the scare as Gloucester, had temporarily closed down.[4]

As a result, from May 1916, the military were put in sole charge of the warning system and the country was divided into 'warning districts' each 30 to 35 miles square, and each under the command of a 'warning controller'. When the enemy were fifteen to twenty miles from the district boundary the controller, using the telephone system, informed the appropriate persons in his area to take air raid action:

> In some provincial towns where public warnings [buzzers, maroons, etc.] had been tried, the effect was to bring excited crowds into the streets and, after a time the system had been abandoned. In others, for example Hull, the system was continued because the public had become accustomed to it. Writing in October 1915, the Constable of Hull stated that he would have hesitated to introduce sound signals had he known at the beginning what the effect would be, 'The buzzer was intended,' he said, 'and in theory is still used, for the purpose of extinguishing lights rapidly, for calling out the Special Constables, and for assembling the ambulance workers—but in practice it is regarded as a warning to the population. It has been opposed by a good many of the upper classes, but there is an almost unanimous desire for it among the other classes, and I have insisted on it being kept, having once started it, because (1) it gets all lights out in from 10 to 20 minutes: (2) the result of it is that on ordinary nights the people are perfectly 'careless and secure' […] But the result of it is that when it sounds great numbers of people leave their houses and troop out with their children into the country, and in some cases stay there for hours in the fields […] They are perfectly orderly and show no signs of panic, but it must be a very harassing thing for the women and children, and as a matter of fact the schools do not open the morning after. Sick people, old people, others who cannot leave their houses, and many of the better classes, who prefer to stay at home, are always greatly upset on 'buzzer' nights.[5]

In the Old Town area, during the first raid, there seems to have been panic among many citizens but for those 'trekking' out of town the flow of people was controlled at the roadblocks, or Motor Halts, and the Specials and women of the Volunteer Patrols were able to give reassurance and impose a certain amount of discipline:

> On the night of another raid I was at Beverley road motor halt. It was pitiable to see the hundreds of old people seeking shelter in the open country. Old men and women, infirm and children. There was some panic, but we subdued it by forcing some of the noisy elements to lie down, and this calmed the rest.[6]

The description by an anonymous special (see Appendix V) indicates large numbers of people coming onto the streets in the Old Town area of Hull, and his rather oblique remarks implies not only panic but also violence perpetrated by a mob against other citizens, presumably attacks on members of the German-speaking community. Clearly however there was never a wholesale breakdown of morale or law and order.

It is easy to regard trekking itself as a sign of panic but a more realistic view is that it was a positive and deliberate attempt to seek a safer place away from the bombing. It was a release from the stress and immediate threat of death by fire and explosion, far better to be up and moving than staying near the danger zone and being overwhelmed by terror.

An interesting witness of the phenomenon was the soldier and military historian Basil Liddell Hart who, after convalescing from the blast effects of a shell in France, was posted to Hull to join the 3rd KOYLI (King's Own Yorkshire Light Infantry):

> An early experience here was a Zeppelin raid which did a lot of damage by the standards of the time. As there was no defence, the two airships hovered low over the city, and one could see the gleam of light each time a trapdoor opened to drop a bomb. The moral effect of the undisturbed attack was so great that every time the sirens sounded, in the weeks that followed, thousands of the population streamed out into the surrounding countryside – and must have suffered far more casualties from exposure to the wintry wind than they would have done from bombs if they had stayed at home.[7]

This reference to wintry weather indicates he was in Hull at the time of the second raid in March 1916. Though no doubt a cold and miserable experience at any time other than the height of summer, there are no reports of serious health problems as a result of trekking.

There was however one victim at least of that bitterly cold snowy night, the indefatigable Dr Mary Murdoch, known as 'Murdie' to all her friends. She with her fellow medical officer had trudged to their station, often up to their knees in snow. She caught a chill which developed into influenza, which on top of a lifetime of overwork, and problems suffered over many years with a gastric ulcer proved fatal. Despite the ministrations of her medical colleagues and a consultant from London, she died early on the morning of 20 March. At her bedside was her devoted friend Dr Martindale,[8] her first practice partner, and Dr Stacey[9] who had succeeded her.

The coffin was placed in her consulting rooms, 102 Beverley Road,[10] surrounded by flowers and the Bishop of Hull held a short service in the presence of her closest friends The Bishop of Hull officiated at the funeral service in her neighbourhood church, All Saints (Margaret Street), and the chief mourners were members of her family, friends and medical colleagues, representatives of the National Union of Women Workers, staff of the Victoria Hospital, and members of the St Johns Ambulance Association. There was a long cortège of fifteen coaches, preceded by her faithful De Dion motor car. The Right Honourable T. R. Ferens, President of the Victoria Children's Hospital was prevented by his parliamentary duties from being there. Thousands came onto the streets and men of the Ambulance Corps, many of whom she had taught in her lessons to the Red Cross were coffin bearers. Early the same day there was a requiem held in the St Francis Mission Church again presided over by the Bishop of Hull, and Father England. After cremation there was another service in the evening, again conducted by the Bishop of Hull and an urn with her ashes was placed in the lady chapel of All Saints church.[11]

In 1914, the Babies Ward at the Victoria Hospital had been closed through lack of funds. It reopened in March 1915 when Dr Murdoch promised to raise £250. After her death, £962 was raised, enough to cover this and also endow a cot in her name.

For the defence of Leeds and Hull, 33 Squadron was moved from Bristol to Bramham Moor, and, specifically to cover Hull, 47 Squadron was formed at Beverley, on 1 March 1916, strengthened by a detachment from Bramham Moor.[12] Additional air protection for the Humber and East Yorkshire came from the RNAS stations at Killingholme and Atwick (Hornsea).

In 1915, six light cruisers each with one 6-pounder and one 2-pounder anti-aircraft guns had been assembled at Immingham for intercepting Zeppelins cruising over the North Sea on reconnaissance or on their way to raid England.[13] These were not as useful as might have been expected because it was difficult to provide warning far enough in advance for them to reach a point of interception. Also weather conditions, especially fog in the days before radar, would often prevent them from sailing. They might already be at sea, chasing minelayers for example, or on the look-out for raiders but wrongly positioned, and unable to respond in time when given more precise information. The regular patrols of armed trawlers with their 1-pounder anti-aircraft guns were of more use. Though unable to inflict significant damage on the airships their response was usually enough to disrupt the raider's flight path and cause them to alter course or rapidly gain height.[14]

The raids were largely conducted by men of the Kaiserliche Marine, the Imperial German navy, and the results could have been vastly more destructive than they had been if more airships and more time had been given to the bombing campaign. There were many thousands of scouting missions compared with only scores of bombing flights over Britain. Priority was always given to aerial reconnaissance, to plot the movements of the British fleet and the activities of mine-laying submarines and surface vessels. It was vital to the Germans to detect the movements of the Royal Navy and the location of mines laid with the intention of destroying their shipping and preventing free movement in the North Sea.

Eventually the blockade of Germany was to be so effective that food and other essential supplies were reduced to a trickle. After the winter of 1916/17 shortages were so severe that an increasing number of staples were being substituted by ersatz products: 'meat' made of grain and mushrooms, 'coffee' of barley and dandelion roots, and 'tea' from raspberry leaves. Fats, butter, margarine and lard were all in short supply and soap was added to the list of what became many thousands of items, including cloth made of a mixture of paper and textile fibres. Coal a basic domestic fuel was increasingly diverted to manufacturing industry for the war effort, and away from the ordinary citizen who was frequently hungry and cold. It has been estimated that there were some 700,000 German civilian deaths from malnutrition during 1914–18.

According to Jacob Ser, a prisoner of war, repatriated in 1917:

> ...the German working class are on the verge of starvation. The four-pound loaf of bread weekly has only one pound of flour in it, the rest is straw or bad potatoes, and the supply is not expected to last till next month. They have eighty grammes a week of butter. The milk is kept only for the sick and children on a doctor's certificate. They have no beef, but there is some smuggling of geese and chickens at twenty-five marks apiece, and 150 marks are got by Holland [a neutral country] from rich people. Fish from Norway is no longer obtainable.[15]

There had been an abortive attack on Hull, 4 June 1915, by an army Schütte-Lanz airship,[16] the *SL3*:

> ...first reported eighty-five miles east of the Humber at 7.30 p.m., but she cruised about and did not come inland until 11.45 p.m., when she crossed at Ulrome. She went out again almost at once, apparently undecided as to her position, and turned north to Flamborough Head, which was recognised from the breaking of the waves against the headland.[17] She turned inland again at 12.30 a.m. and made for Hull, the distant lights of which could be plainly seen. As the airship approached Hull the city was plunged in darkness, and this fact, together with an increase in head wind, induced her commander[18] to give up the raid and return. He dropped only three bombs which did no damage.[19]

CHAPTER 11

Raids in 1916

Buttlar-Brandenfels describes the usual preparations for a Zeppelin bombing mission:

> From the time of receiving the order to that of leaving the ground, about two hours elapse, in which to make final preparations. As far as possible, everything has already been done. The shed doors are open, the handling party are standing by and the airship itself is ready for flight. The necessary petrol, machine guns, oxygen breathing apparatus [only with the advent of the height climbers, see below], and whatever else is needed during the flight are in the ship. The bombs must now be hung in position. These are brought out from the munitions depôt on small hand carts, and placed under the ship. The light calibre bombs are carried into position in the corridor by men belonging to the ship's care and maintenance party. The medium and heavy calibre bombs must be hoisted into position with the aid of tackles, and suspended by hooks to the bomb frames.
>
> The work is willingly performed, and each bomb is accompanied with a hearty wish that it will not be released from the ship in vain.
>
> The crew now put on warm clothing, eat their mid-day meal, and bring further supplies on board for the flight.[1]

The airships flew low over the Heligoland Bight and often steered close to the Dutch coast to accurately determine position before heading over the North Sea. The maximum duration of a return voyage was thirty hours, more usually between eighteen and twenty-five hours, depending on fog and contrary winds.[2]

For the second raid, 5/6 March 1916, the Zeppelin *L11*, Korvettenkapitän Schütze, passed over the coast near Tunstall, north of Spurn, at 9.45 p.m. and made its appearance over a snow-covered countryside. The airship flew toward Lincoln before turning back to the Humber and moved about the sky at leisure before any bombs were dropped, at about 1 a.m., prior to departing over Spurn. *L14* (Kptlt Böcker) had preceded him, dropping 'six bombs that fell in fields near Beverley. Seven explosives and thirteen incendiaries then followed as *L14* crossed Hull at 9,500 feet', mostly landing on houses near the docks, soon after midnight.[3]

In Queen Street a public house,[4] café,[5] a Co-operative, and several other shops were totally destroyed. The Holy Trinity windows suffered further damage and there was a hole some twenty feet deep nearby. The airship was seen to hover over Paragon Station but this was relatively unscathed except for the northern end near Collier Street. Anlaby Road was also hit, three sisters were killed when a bomb dropped on a house in the Avenue, Linnaeus Street. At Earle's shipyard a bomb caused the collapse of the framework of a steamship under construction and there was some damage to the Riverside Quay.

The gun on the roof of Rose, Downs & Thompsons foundry, Cannon Street, which with its military guard had seemed so reassuring, proved to be a wooden 'quaker'. This angered the people of Hull even more and they demanded some real protection. It is not clear when the public at large first knew of this deception but Sir Alfred Gelder, a Hull alderman and MP for Brigg (Lincs.), revealed in the House of Commons the existence of the dummy gun and the lack of any anti-aircraft defences for the city.[6]

The gun had been installed on 5 July 1915, a month after the first raid, a desperate attempt to convince the people of Hull that something was being done to protect them. It was set up over lunchtime at a time when few staff were about. A yard foreman apparently witnessed the installation and realised that the way the weapon was being handled it could not possibly be a real piece of metal ordnance.

The gun was manned from 8 p.m. until 5 a.m. and the man not on night duty made a show of cleaning it and then replacing the cover before reporting to his superiors that 'all is well'. The plan was that following a signal, the firing of a gun from a ship in the docks, that three rockets would be discharged near the gun and then cease fire. Charles Downs[7] the managing director of Rose, Downs and Thompson had not been informed of its nature by the military authorities but it quickly became apparent and the military admitted the deception. He was very concerned of the effect on the morale of the citizens of Hull if the whole charade were to become known and he did all he could to see that it was removed.

In the 1930s, Arthur Tidman, a reporter for the *Hull Daily Mail*, claims it was taken away on 23 January 1916, a little over six months after it was installed and before the second raid in March that year.[8]

A letter sent in 1934 by Major General J. A. Ferrier (G.O.C. till 1917) to William Hurst, former chief of staff of the Humber Garrison, was paraphrased by Tidman:

> ...the original idea was to use rocket bombs & make a noise in the vicinity of the dummy gun when the navy opened fire with their guns, as on the first attack in June 1915; until he could get some one pound signal rockets of which the supply was short and did not appear until the big attack on Spurn Head.[9]

The naval guns were presumably the large ordnance pieces at Spurn, though smaller guns aboard vessels on the Humber may have been intended. Perhaps it was no accident that crew were available to man the guns of HMS *Adventure*, then being worked on in Earle's yard, but had been directed there to offer the only firepower then available.

Ferrier apparently claimed that the rocket bombs launched from the site of the dummy did have some effect:

> It is stated that the Germans themselves were deceived and regarded the gun as some sort of secret weapon, which it was wise to give a wide berth. A German account describes the rockets as very formidable and added that they were avoided as much as possible by the Zeppelins.[10]

This cannot be the case because the dummy had not been installed until after the first raid, and although the buzzer sounded another nineteen times, these were false alarms and no Zeppelin appeared over Hull again until March 1916. The rockets may have been fired (after a false alarm) to give the impression of effective action but there were no Zeppelins to see them! According to Tidman the gun had already been removed in January 1916, though its existence is only acknowledged in the press after the second raid and Gelder's revelation in parliament during his demands for defences to be provided for Hull against the airships.

Six houses in Collier Street, fourteen in James Place, Collier Street, were demolished or damaged beyond repair; though fourteen of the twenty-two houses were unoccupied at the time. Mr Naylor lost an eye and his right arm was injured and Maggie Ellen Barnes, 2 James Place, Collier Street, was blinded. James Gallagher, 24 Collier Street, was also slightly injured, Annie Beatty of 24 Collier Street had cuts and bruises, and Fred Beatty of the same address received an injury to his left leg. Frank Johnson, 22 Collier Street, was cut in two places by shrapnel and Mrs Rees cut in two places on the body and had a laceration on the head. Capt. Edward Leadner, very old and deaf, did not respond to the buzzer and would not be persuaded to leave his room in the master mariners' almshouses of the Hull Trinity House in Carr Lane. He was burnt to death when an incendiary dropped through the roof and ceiling. The bomb made 'a depression in the concrete floor about the size of the saucer of a breakfast cup. The whole of the furniture in the room and the interior fittings were burnt.'[11] A report of the inquest gives the age of the victims and circumstances of their death but not their names or addresses.[12]

George Thorp, architect and surveyor, who lived in Ella Street away from the main action, but had his office in Lowgate in the heart of the 'old town', gives us a telling report of the damage to the area around Holy Trinity church:[13]

> ...then to Posterngate destroying a Hardware Warehouse next to the Rating Offices. A huge high explosive at the S W angle of Holy Trinity Church tearing

up the pavement, crushing the massive stone coping and the railings,[14] breaking most of the windows in the Chancel from the South Transept to the West End of the Chancel, the beautiful West Window as far as the stained glass was concerned being almost entirely destroyed. King & Cos. windows were entirely destroyed in all the four stories of their large premises, the huge gashes scored in the stone and brickwork being awesome to behold. The Old Grammar School found by John Alcock Bishop of Ely in 1486 and rebuilt 1583 was much damaged by flying pieces of shell.[15]

The 'signal of safety' was given at 2.30 a.m. A newspaper photograph shows the incendiary bomb which fell on the Corn Exchange Hotel, North Church Side.[16] The infirmary received three dead, and admitted twenty-seven people, three of whom subsequently died. In addition, twenty-five casualties received treatment and some minor cases were dealt with in the Out Patients department by St John Ambulance personnel.[17]

Korvettenkapitän Viktor Schütze in L11[18] reported that:

The town, though very well darkened, showed up clearly under the starlit sky like a drawing, with streets, blocks of houses, quays and dock basins beneath the airship. A few lights were moving about the streets… During a period of twenty minutes incendiary and high explosive bombs were dropped on the harbours and docks—and the effects were carefully noted. The first H.E. bombs struck the quay, big portions of which went up, and another hit the lock-gate of one of the harbour basins. The burst was so directly on the gate that it might have been taken for a gun fired off there. Buildings collapsed like houses of cards. One hit had an especially far-reaching effect: radiating round the burst more and more houses collapsed and finally showed up, in the snow covered area, as a black and gigantic hole. A similar, bigger patch in the neighbourhood seemed to be due to the raid of L14 […] With binoculars it was possible to see people running hither and thither in the glare of the fires. In the harbour, where the lock-gates were hit, ships began to move.[19]

A Press Bureau bulletin was published in the *Eastern Morning News*:

A Zeppelin raid took place last night when two hostile airships crossed over the North-East Coast, but at the time of the report their movements have not been clearly defined. Some bombs were dropped which fell in the sea near the shore but information is not yet available as to whether any damage has been done on land.[20]

The *Hull Daily Mail*, 6 March, reports (on page 6!) 'Last Night's Raid' in the most perfunctory fashion along with the Press Bureau bulletin which tells us that two hostile airships passed over the northeast coast. On the Tuesday a brief note appears of damage to property and casualties in Yorkshire, but not specifying Hull. It tells us that a ninety-year-old was burnt to death in his bed while the injured were taken by ambulance to the Infirmary. Following this are a few details on what occurred in Lincolnshire, Cambridgeshire and Kent.[21] On the 8 March, the War Office Press Bureau stated that ninety bombs had been dropped and thirteen killed, and on the next day five more were added to the death toll.[22] Marion Large,[23] who was nine at the beginning of the war:

> I remember the famous 'snowy night raid'; the second severe one we had, when we wandered with countless families far up the Holderness road, getting colder and colder and tireder and tireder, and unable to find anywhere to rest. Another night we spent in the East Park crouching down in the shrubbery while the bombs fell in nearby streets. [...] After this raid, we decided on another plan and spent long periods in a field behind our house, where there were dips and hollows, and one could make a kind of dugout. We sat there for weary hours wrapped in coats and blankets and longing for warmth and sleep.[24]

Some felt individually persecuted by the raiders and Joseph Westoby, formerly a shipwright, recounted his experiences to a reporter of the *Hull Times* of his all too frequent encounters with bombs. On 6 June 1915, living with his wife and daughter, at 5 St Pauls Avenue, Church Street, a bomb dropped four houses away breaking all the windows, bringing the ceilings down and throwing him out of bed. He decided to move to Withernsea, on the east coast, but had his pocket picked on his first walk around the town and so the family returned to Hull where he took a house in Regent Street. On 5 March 1916, a bomb landed a few yards away and so he decided to join the trek into the countryside whenever danger threatened. Visiting a friend in Arnold Street, 9 August 1916, a bomb dropped twenty yards away and damaged the house!

Others described the thrill of seeing the Zeppelins caught in the beams of the searchlights:

> On one occasion a Zeppelin approached from the west side of town. After remaining at a standstill for about five minutes a searchlight caught it, and the Zepp dropped a quantity of ballast on the football ground. Two star shells were seen to pass underneath the Zepp, and caught the balloon broadside, but it quickly turned, and calmly continued dropping messages of death from a great height.[25]

The impact on civilians is clear but details from British official sources of the damage to military objectives is lacking.[26] The above extract, from the airship commander's report, indicates some direct hits on the docks but inevitably any bombs not hitting the desired target landed on the mainly working class housing adjacent to the docks and railways. The photographs taken by Turner show Wade's timber yard, near Tower Street, Citadel Estate, Victoria Dock, where explosive and incendiary bombs landed buckling the rail line. An incendiary caused a dent in the concrete of the composition deck of the Swedish vessel SS *Igos* in the dock basin. At Alexandra dock, the cargo lighter *Crocus* was damaged by an explosive bomb and a pile of pit props scattered when a bomb landed 250 yards north of the coal conveyor.

The effect of an air raid for the survivors could be a loss of their homes, their means of making a living, or death of family and friends. Among a collection in the Hull archives of letters received from his constituents by Lt Col. Sir Mark Sykes MP,[27] was one from A. W. Ford, owner of the cafe in Queen Street:

> I have to ask that you will pardon me writing to you but my reason in doing so is to ask whether you could get me any financial help.
>
> I have had a Cafe at Hull called 'The Mikado Cafe', being no.23 Queen street, which I am sorry to say was totally destroyed on the 5th instant by the German Zeppelin Raid on that City.
>
> My manager was killed and through the loss of the same my life savings have gone, and therefore have no means of support from the business.
>
> If you could recommend any payment by the Government I should be ever so grateful to you Thanking you in anticipation I remain Sir Your obedient Servant A. W. Ford[28]

Another letter offered ways of dealing with the Zeppelins:[29]

> 1 Spring street, Hull, Feb. 1916
>
> Sir, Seeing your speech in the Daily Mail re the Zeppelins, & also of M. Fokker[30] offering his machine to the war office, I beg to say that I had the same experience. I made a weapon that will destroy a Zeppelin at once. Last August I sent particulars & drawings of it to the Ministry of Munitions & about two months afterwards I received the same reply as M. Fokker, that it was no improvement on what was already in use.
>
> Now had the ministry have taken my invention up, made it, served it out to our flying men, we could have destroyed every Zepp that came over, & without the Germans knowing how it was being done, were it carried out by good tactical system.
>
> Firing from below is madness it is a 100 to 1 on hitting &, the falling shots do as much damage as the bombs from the Zeppelin, & if by chance we do hit, the Zepp can still travel. One of my weapons destroys it at once.
>
> I sent also at the same time a new rifle, for hitting moving objects, this they said was unpractical, I thought it was a good weapon for attacking [a]eroplanes.

They have also an Infantry shield from me, this I made & tested myself, though it is an Infantry shield it can be applied on aeroplane & armoured motors.

Your obedient servant

C. Scheck

The experience of those who suffered directly from the bombing is neatly summed up in the memories of Mrs Marion Large:

> The shock of this [the raid] is with me to this day. I remember being carried downstairs by my father while my mother brought down my little brother. My grandmother was collapsing with severe palpitations and incapable of controlling her panic. The devastating crunch of bombs falling, the shaking of the house and the clatter of glass as our back windows cracked and fell are unforgettable. It was long before we dare go back to bed – I doubt if my parents did all night. Our little world was shattered for me, my childhood was over. Here was something my parents couldn't protect us from; they themselves were shocked and distraught and couldn't conceal it.[31]

Great feeling was aroused by the attack and dismay that the Zeppelins should have been allowed to hover near the town for an hour without any attempt to attack them from land or air. In anger and frustration a Royal Flying Corps transport was attacked and damaged by a crowd in Hull and an RFC officer was mobbed in Beverley.[32]

The Lord Mayor, Lord Nunburnholme (the Lord Lieutenant)[33] along with a number of military officers had a meeting with the view of impressing on the authorities in London the necessity of providing some means of protection for the city. Because of the demands for munitions at the front this proved impossible but after the second raid there was strong local reaction and another demand for help. A conference in the council chamber led by the Lord Mayor received reports of the situation and a deputation was appointed to proceed to London for discussion with Lord French and General Shaw.

An unexpected source, giving us some idea of the level of public reaction in Hull to the lack of response to the raid, is the diary of Arnold Bennett, the novelist and chronicler of the 'Potteries':

Entry for 13 December 1916:

> Lieut. R. of a mobile A[nti] Aircraft unit stationed at Thorpe, came for tea. He said he carried £15000 worth of stores. He said that after a big raid at Hull end of last year about, when Mayor of Hull had been assured that Hull was one of

the most heavily defended places, and a Zep dropped 15 bombs in the town, the population afterwards mobbed officers, and A. A. officers coming into the town had to put on Tommies' clothes. Also that a Naval unit was telegraphed for and when it came with full authorised special lights, the population, angry at the lights, assaulted it with stones and bottles and put half of it in hospital, and had ultimately to be kept off by the military.[34]

The unidentified soldier also complained about the absurdly complicated administration of the unit and how they were forced to move a mobile gun away from an ideal site on a local golf course following complaints from the club officials.[35]

It is not clear exactly why the lights unit was mobbed, whether in frustration because of a lack of guns to sustain an active defence, or whether the population regarded the lights as a liability that might actually make it easier for the enemy to see the target. Buttlar-Brandenfels warns of the premature use of searchlights which made it easier for the airships to find their target:

> The English themselves make it fairly easy to find London, because they begin to get nervous at an attack. That can be seen by the searchlights which apparently sweep the sky in a purposeless way, and so one can see from far off where London lies, by the circle of searchlights which project their rays vertically into the air.[36]

T. R. Ferens MP was active in parliament seriously questioning whether enough was being done for the protection of the people of the East Coast. As we have seen the GOC Northern Command, Maj.-Gen. H. M. Lawson was deputed to meet with the Lord Mayor, local MPs and other prominent citizens who voiced their complaints with vigour.[37] They were assured that a defence scheme for Hull and the Humber had been settled and guns would be mounted as soon as available. In the meantime two 13-pounder guns of the Mobile Section were sent temporarily to Hull until the permanently allotted guns should arrive:

> By the end of May two 3 in., one 12 pounder, and one 6 pounder guns were in position at Hull, and the Humber defences had been strengthened by the placing of extra guns at Immingham, Killingholme, Waltham [near Grimsby], Spurn, and Hornsea.

This brought the total of anti-aircraft guns of the Humber Garrison to: Killingholme, two 12-pounders, two 6-pounders, two 1-pounders; Immingham, one 12-pounder, two 1-pounders; Waltham (near Grimsby), one 12-pounder, one 1-pounder; Spurn, one 3-pounder; Hornsea, one 3-pounder and Hull, two 3-inch, and one 6-pounder.[38] The shells of the 12-pounders reached up to 19,500 feet and the 18-pounder, slightly less at 18,000 feet, though whether any of the latter were used at Hull is not known.

Though the defences around the Humber had improved somewhat there were apparently only three guns (seemingly, two mobile and one fixed) for the entire city. The dummy gun which angered people so much when it was discovered had been removed on 23 January. Though some show of force would have helped to disturb the slow, deliberate movements of the Zeppelins the guns that were available early in the war had themselves the potential of doing a significant amount of damage to property and people: the shells had a very small bursting charge and so they returned to earth in the form of heavy missiles. Only by late 1915 and early 1916 was high-fragmentation ammunition available.[39] Even with improvements to the range of the guns and better shells anti-aircraft fire was very much hit and miss, most often the latter.

Two notebooks from 1916–17 belonging to Lt John Oswald Sibree, RE (T)[40] record the setting up of height-finding installations in Hull, East Yorkshire and Lincolnshire.

These appear to have involved setting up flags and ranging poles, their positions measured and aligned with surveyor's chains and theodolite, to be used in conjunction with the Bennett-Pleydell Height Finder.[41] The sites of the guns in Hull were four in number, Sutton, Marfleet, Harpins (north of the factory of the Radiator Co. and the Hull and Barnsley railway), and Hessle Priory.[42] It is not clear if the mobile guns were brought to these sites or whether they were only for fixed gun emplacements, and if the latter whether each of them ever accommodated more than one gun.

These locations are confirmed by Arthur Tidman in his jottings on the Rose, Downs dummy gun and he refers to one of the guns as being on Hessle road, near to Pickering Park. Together with Sibree's notes this gun can be more precisely placed, on the south side of the Hessle Road, opposite the park and adjacent to the railway and the important marshalling yard known as Priory Sidings. A searchlight was housed in Colonial Street and operated from Corporation Field but it is not known how many were eventually brought to Hull and deployed during each raid.[43]

Elsewhere in Yorkshire decoy fires were lit to mislead the attacking Zeppelins aiming for a major city and cause them to drop their bombs in the countryside, though there is no evidence of their use in the East Riding. Nine people had been killed at York in a raid on 2 May 1916, and a further twenty-three people on 25/26 September the same year. The history of the grammar school at Pocklington, some thirteen miles from York, records:

> In these days of lightning bomber raids it is strange to remember the threatening hum of the comparatively slow airship, faintly seen above like a colossal cigar, avoiding moonlit nights and cruising about to find a well-lighted town. Decoys

were lit then as later and a fire purposely made on Barmby Common saved York Minster but caused the demolition of a pig-sty. The airship's engines so alarmed the Pocklington townsfolk that they sent a message to the headmaster asking him to quieten the boys' voices for fear they should guide the Zeppelin crew into dropping their load![44]

In addition to the Turner photographs a series of pictures were taken for the City Engineers department of the Hull Corporation, recording the results of the first attack. Some of these survive along with two maps of the city on which the sites where the bombs landed are recorded for both the first and second raids

Upon the occasion of the second Zeppelin raid in the following March, twenty-four people rendered homeless were housed for a time in Thornton Hall, and the accommodation, provided by the Revd C. H. Hulbert, was greatly appreciated.

A similar procedure for looking after the homeless was adopted after each of the Hull raids, and the people were also supplied with food.[45]

Despite the trauma and anxiety caused by loss of one's home or indeed the death of family members and friends there were humorous incidents. These also reveal the now familiar phenomenon of what we now call 'disaster tourism' as well as the ways in which people can take personal advantage of the situation. A supplier of second-hand furniture remonstrated with for his slowness of delivery, replied:

> No, I am not likely to get on quickly with the job. The people come into town in order to see the damage done by the Zeppelin, and there are old women at the doors sir, who tell the tale- with the result that they get plenty of tips. In fact I know one woman who got 22s in one day.[46]

In another case:

> Two men made an appeal to the Lord Mayor, and one man said that he lived in Collier-street and was injured in the Zeppelin raid. He called also on a generous resident, who was told by the man, who limped badly, that he had the previous day been discharged from the Infirmary. Mr. — telephoned the Infirmary and said: 'You had a man named — admitted from Collier street?' 'Yes', replied the head of the Infirmary. 'Was he discharged yesterday?' 'No' came the answer; 'nor is he likely to be for weeks, because his leg is broken.'
>
> The caller, who was soon told that he was fortunate not being in the hands of the police, made hasty retreat, and then there were no signs of limping.[47]

As the chief constable stated:

> The buzzer was intended and in theory is still used, for the purpose of extinguishing lights rapidly, for calling out the Special Constables, and for

assembling the ambulance workers—but in practice it is regarded as a warning to the population.[48]

It was announced in the local press, starting 5 April 1916, that all the Hull Street lights 'will be extinguished at midnight. This will be continued throughout the summer months'.[49]

More than one person recalls as a youngster shinning up the lamp-posts to put out the gas lights. Alf Dee recalls:

> Another lad used to climb up the lamp posts when the buzzers blew—and when we got to the top pulled a lever to put out the light before they were put out from the source of supply.[50]

In the third raid, 5 April 1916, by *L11* (Korvettenkapitän Schütze again[51]), the first bomb landed in Portobello Street; there were no direct casualties though a woman died of shock. Originally bound for the Firth of Forth he was driven south by rain squalls and made landfall at Hornsea Mere 9.10 p.m. and proceeded inland at a height estimated at about 12,000 feet. Approaching Hull the airship was picked up by searchlights and came under immediate anti-aircraft attack when it dropped its height to about 6,000 feet suggesting it had been hit. This was not to be the leisurely cruise of Schütze's previous visit and after dropping four bombs he retreated out to sea again and headed home. Attracted by the furnaces of the Skinningrove iron works he dropped nine high explosive bombs and twenty incendiaries before turning east for Germany.[52] RAF aircraft from Beverley and an RNAS plane from Scarborough went in pursuit but failed to intercept their target.[53]

The local newspaper was allowed to give a full, morale boosting report, though the resulting account of the anti-aircraft barrage seems to be somewhat exaggerated. Because of censorship rules, the correspondent had to refer to Hull as a 'North-East coast town', a sobriquet which became very familiar during the 1939–45 war when the city was seldom identified by name in news bulletins and reports.

> Raiders last night. Received by brilliant gunnery. Magnificent spectacle. Searchlights and bursting shells.
>
> North-East coast town—last night a Zeppelin was discovered at a high altitude. Searchlights flashed across the sky. Two great beams met at the uppermost point of the arc they had stretched over the area beneath, immediately 'found' the visitor.
>
> Simultaneously guns were put in action, and shells were seen to burst with surprising rapidity all round the object, which, still held in the rays of the searchlights, gleamed like a yellow incandescent mantle.[54] Shells burst

with blinding flashes, and the Zepp crew appeared bewildered as to their whereabouts.

The airship descended quickly to a low altitude, rose again, and suddenly made out towards the sea.

The engagement was a magnificent spectacle. The population kept cool, and watched the firing with confidence.

In one part of the town every shot from our guns was greeted with a murmur of applause, which grew into a cheer as a missile from one of our guns appeared to slide up the beam of a searchlight, straight for the aerial marauder.

It was a beautiful, clear night; myriads of stars studded the sky, and all the time the action was in progress, the moon was shining brilliantly.

Meanwhile, the Zeppelin had become lost to sight. Overhead the whirr and drone of aeroplane engines sent the inhabitants to their firesides, knowing that the enemy had been driven away.[55]

No doubt the account had originally been written by a reporter of the *Hull Daily Mail* but it would then have to be vetted by government officials. So, bizarrely, a description of the event when published in the local newspaper had to be printed without directly identifying Hull as the scene of the events featured in the article though the residents would know it to be the subject of the report anyway!

George Thorp has the following entry in his diary:

I saw that the [searchlight] beams of different localities, Endike Lane, Liverpool Street and Marfleet[56] had caught Herr Zeppelin in one common focus and were hammering at him with the long range guns as hard as they could go. The scream of the missiles as they tore through the air exploding above and below and on each side some seeming to burst very near, but I don't think it was hit, but the Monster which I saw very clearly did not appreciate his very warm reception, for it made off very rapidly in a North Easterly direction.[57]

A bland and generalised bulletin from the Press Bureau states:

a Zeppelin attacked the North-East Coast about 9.50 last night, and was driven off by the fire of the anti-aircraft defence. Some bombs were dropped, but no information has yet been received as to casualties or damage.[58]

The ack-ack guns[59] apparently used small balloons for target practice and a label was attached to each so that if found by a member of the public he was directed to take it to his local police station. From there it would be sent to the local commander of the Anti-Aircraft Defence[60] and a half-crown reward, a considerable amount, was given to each finder.

It is difficult to imagine it was particularly necessary to retrieve these balloons and I think we can conclude it was mainly a means of engaging with the public and to encourage positive thinking about the anti-aircraft batteries.

Commercial interests were still trading on the airship threat and Kings of Hull, a notable ironmongers (whose premises adjacent to Edwin Davis' store had been damaged in the second raid), advertised Milner's safes as Zeppelin proof!

The fourth raid, 8/9 August 1916, by *L24* (Kapitänleutnant Robert Koch) took place on a dark and cloudy Tuesday night.[61] There was little response to the buzzers because the public were now convinced that there was an adequate defence. The attack commenced at 1.15 a.m., the airship was apparently returning to Germany from a raid further inland but found Hull a convenient target on which to unload its bombs. This was a commonplace of the 1939–45 war when Hull, so often a primary target also received the bombs of aircraft which had failed to reach industrial sites in west Yorkshire and Lancashire. Even without navigational aids Hull, at the confluence of two rivers, was easy to find. The expanse of water in the several docks was highly visible and the railway lines, if not obscured by low cloud, could easily be followed into the heart of the city from the east coast, from Leeds in the west, or Beverley in the north.[62]

In the same way Buttlar-Brandenfels describes finding his way to London:

> The Thames has such a peculiar formation that it forms a splendid means of learning one's position. I have only therefore, to proceed on a southwesterly course until I see the Thames, and then start upstream until I reach the capital. For the same reason, I have also often kept near the Dutch coast, until somewhere in the vicinity of the North Hinter Lightship, which lies approximately due east of the mouth of the Thames, and then steered west, until I reached the mouth of the river, and so go upstream.[63]

Bombs were dropped in Selby Street damaging several houses and a part of the railway wall at the bottom of a footbridge. At the other side of the railway lines a fried fish shop was destroyed and Emma Evers (Brunswick Avenue, St George's Road) hearing the airship ran into Walliker Street and was killed:

> Mrs Evers was killed while taking shelter in the doorway of no. 61 Walliker Street, where she and her sister had been pushed by a man for protection from a bomb which dropped on the road in the centre of Walliker Street (opposite no. 61 and 63). Her sister, who stood behind her in the doorway, was uninjured. The bomb demolished nos.42 and 43 Brunswick avenue, St. Georges road (this property adjoins Walliker Street). Nos. 61 and 63 Walliker Street were wrecked also a great number of houses in the vicinity were more or less shattered.[64]

Mr and Mrs Broadby of Roland Avenue, Arthur Street, were injured and their three-year-old child was killed:

...the above family left their home and proceeded down the back way between Sandringham street and Granville street for protection, when a bomb dropped in this backway killing the child John Charles whilst in his push cart.

Sandringham street had a terrifying time and the Naval Hospital, Argyle street, had a narrow escape. The last of a batch of incendiaries fell into the front bedroom of a semi-detached villa, Victoria Avenue.[65]

Mr. and Mrs. Jones ascribed their escape to being in the garden at the rear, watching the effects if the raid. The incendiary fell with a prodigious clatter of slates right through the roof and ceiling, and damaged the floor. The bedroom was wrecked and fired, and the flames mounted fiercely, but were put out by willing 'specials', two plucky youngsters from school, and neighbours generally.[66]

Under the headlines 'More Zeppelin murders—Raid on East Coast and Scotland—The casualty list' came another official announcement which stated that in some places the airships were met with anti-aircraft guns and that three women and one child were dead and fourteen others injured. There was no damage of 'military importance'. Further brief and generalised descriptions of attacks on several towns in the South East and Scotland are given, then a more detailed piece allowed through by the censor. The target is not specified, only that it is the North East, but the subject is quite definitely Hull and the surrounding rural district:

North East Victims: It was a clear starlight night and when about 1.30 the engines of a Zeppelin were heard the inhabitants had difficulty discerning the shape of the enemy airship against the starry background. A few minutes later thuds caused by the dropping of bombs in a country district had been heard. The only damage caused was the ploughing up of a grass field and the smashing of a gate.

A fourth bomb was dropped near a village. The Zeppelin was travelling from a westerly direction and dropped three incendiary bombs in rapid succession in playing fields. The Zeppelin then altered course slightly to the south, and explosive bombs were dropped. Some of the projectile which dropped in the locality are described by the residents as aerial torpedoes:

Explosive bombs Further explosive bombs fell, one making a big hole in the roadway and demolishing hoardings in the neighbourhood. It was at this point that the greatest damage was done and the loss of life occurred.

The raider dropped several explosive bombs on each side of the railway [ie. in the Selby street area], for which they were apparently aimed. Two persons were killed in a shop and a woman running for safety was buried in the debris. Another woman was killed by flying fragments, and her husband and son were injured.

A woman aged 44, was killed, and her fourteen-year-old daughter succumbed to her injuries in hospital. In another instance a man and wife were proceeding along a street with their three-year-old child in a go-cart[67] when they were struck by splinters of shell, and the child was killed.

A single woman, aged 46, was killed when taking shelter, and a retired minister died from shock. Incendiary bombs created several fires but these were quickly extinguished. A number of people were treated at dressing stations for injuries, and about a dozen were admitted to the Infirmary in a more or less serious condition.[68]

While no mention of any individual town is made in the official bulletins or other news reports it is clear that the censor was now allowing the readership of local newspapers to be given at least a summary account of damage and casualties inflicted on their particular town. The overseas press would receive the official reports with their generalised references to the North East, the East Coast, South East etc. They were unlikely to light upon the local newspaper stories which would have given the German High Command more precise indications as to precisely where and with what effect bombs had landed. If there were any undetected German agents at large in Britain it is doubtful that they had any effective means of communication back to Germany.

Forty-four bombs had fallen on the town which had killed eleven people but despite all the assurances made in advance the response was described as one searchlight and a 'pop-gun', an opinion repeated by George Thorp:

> Soon the sound of engines was heard, growing louder and louder, firing continuously at intervals. Then we saw the 'thing' dark and ominous at a great height, then a fire started due south and few minutes later, another in the south-east. The Zeppelin then came right over Newland passed over our row of houses[69] and a search light – one which never found it, more firing and then apparent retreat and silence.[70]

He later states that the sounds he had imagined 'as of shells exploding' were mostly high explosive bombs going off and that there had been 'one solitary gun and a search light'. The assurance of improved defences were, as he quotes from Shakespeare, 'a promise kept to the ear, but broken in the hope'.

The feeble reaction from the ground defences again resulted in the temporary exodus of large numbers of people which occurred whenever danger threatened. Patches of ground mist had effectively blinded the Hull anti-aircraft gunners, and only eight rounds were fired and the ground mist which hampered the anti-aircraft defenders, also prevented aeroplanes from going up.[71] The Infirmary received thirteen cases, nine were admitted and one of them, a woman, later died.[72]

After the death toll from the Selby Street area became apparent the Mayor and Civic authorities came in for a great deal of criticism. Alderman Hargreaves received five deputations from around the city and it was explained to them that the allocation and distribution of anti-aircraft guns was beyond the control of the civil authorities. One of the deputations, comprising leaders of the Trade Unions, responded with the shaking of hands and 'Cheer up, old man! We will put this matter right with our people!' As a result Hargreaves arranged with General Ferrier for three leaders of the Trades Unions to pay periodical visits to the gun sites and report as to whether the pieces of ordnance were at their appointed stations.[73]

The Sheriff of Hull and T. R. Ferens MP conveyed to the editor of the *Eastern Morning News* a report of a long interview with the Air Board and the General Headquarters of the Home Forces. More powerful anti-aircraft guns were promised but the two men to the best of their understanding believed that everything had been done as far as was humanly possible. A few days later inspection of the defences confirmed that the dispositions shown to them by the planners were a reality.[74] This must have been a great relief because before this last raid guns had actually been taken away to be used elsewhere. An eyewitness account was collected by Suddaby, from Mrs M. E. Hall, a survivor of the raid:

> ...when the buzzers went ... we were outside my mother's front door having a cup of tea, when all at once this Zeppelin came in from the River Humber. We lived in Selby street and a railway line ran in front of our houses, a train came along and stopped opposite, it was bombed. I ran and stood beside a family called Bearpark who were huddled together on a piece of waste ground... The bomb dropped only the width of the road away from us. My life was saved, although badly injured, the result of the killed and injured being thrown on top of me... I was in hospital for weeks, the doctors said I would never walk again, but I did. I married the boy [see Casualties; below] who was also injured [...] he had shrapnel in his head to the day he died four years ago. He saw his mother and two sisters killed, but a baby six months old was saved; she died at the end of last year, age 78. I shall be 90 in November [1994]—I was a girl of nearly twelve when this raid happened.

By 1916 a systematised response to air raids had been developed and a pocket manual entitled *Anti-aircraft Attack on Airships, Home Defence (Provisional)* was being supplied to anti-aircraft batteries. It was recommended that fixed guns should open fire at long ranges and maintain a continuous fire so long as the target remained in range. Mobile guns should not open fire till the aircraft was within medium range and maintain continuous rapid fire while it was within range. If the aircraft was crossing in front of the mobile guns and clearly not going to come within medium range then fire was to be opened at long range.

No less than nine types of guns, with calibres of 3, 4, 4.7 inch, and 75 mm, as well as 6-pounder, 12-pounder and 13-pounder[75] are listed. This variety along with numbers of different fuses must have caused real logistical problems in supplying the right shells and fuses to the various batteries, especially when guns were frequently being moved from town to town to meet the perceived threat. According to which gun was in use the printed tables show medium range to be 4,000 to 4,500 yards and long range 5,000 to 6,000 yards. The maximum height of the airship to be targeted is recorded as 14,000 feet.

For stationary, slowly drifting, or distant crossing targets the echelon system was recommended when two rounds were fired with three different fuses each shorter than the last. When targets were approaching or receding, either directly or obliquely, the zone system was used. The object being to put up a barrier of fire so that the aircraft if it continued on its course must inevitably fly into the gun fire.

Flank observers, at three locations ideally, but at least one, were necessary to indicate whether shells were exploding in front of or beyond the aircraft. The observers, situated 2,000 to 3,000 yards away signalled to the gunners using an electric light system, the telephone, or a lamp.[76] Without such observers the guns were effectively shooting blind.

If physical protection was unreliable there was recourse to spiritual help and a prayer for 'Protection against the Zeppelins', first issued 30 October 1916, was circulated as a small hand bill, printed locally.[77] The mutual support of the members of church congregations and the help provided by neighbours in one's local community was vital to maintaining morale in those stressful times.

In west Hull the Thornton Hall, Thornton Street, an active site of Methodist evangelism, under the leadership of the Revd Charles Hulbert, became a place of refuge from the bombing. A large and impressive building it was designed and built by Alfred Gelder, MP and architect ,one of a number of prominent and influential Methodist laymen in the city, including Thomas Ferens MP and C. D. Holmes, founder of a major local engineering firm. The hall seated two thousand, and rather than pews, was furnished with tip-up chairs like a theatre or cinema, an innovation at the time. Situated between the Hessle and Anlaby roads, not far from the main railway station (Hull Paragon), it was in the centre of a large working-class population. A reminiscence by Kenneth Hulbert, younger son of the Charles Hulbert is worth quoting in full, and ends with another account of trekking:

> Thornton Hall soon became a centre for the reception of air-raid casualties. The roof lights were blacked out, and curtains were hung over the windows. The danger of panic was ever-present during crowded services because the air-raid alarm made an unpleasantly eerie sound readily heard in the hall. The possibility of two thousand people wildly alarmed by the siren and all struggling to get away was to be feared. As it happened, the employee who sounded the siren, a member of Thornton Hall, arranged to give advance warning so that a steward at

the back of the hall could flash a torch to the minister on the platform. Whenever that happened a hymn was sung to drown the noise, after which the people would be invited to go quietly home.

When a bomb fell one night on a row of small houses not far from the hall, two small boys were blown out of bed. They landed in the street wearing nothing except their shirt neckbands and wristbands. Taken to the hall, they were found to be as black as coal, and when the missioner saw them he turned to one of his workers—Charlie Russell, a converted coal trimmer—and said: 'Charlie, light a fire under that copper'. In that bath, the minister of the hall bathed the two boys, afterwards allowing them to run about in front of the fire until they were dry. Next day Hull was talking about the practical parson, and Charles Hulbert was pointed out as 'the parson that bathed the kids'. The effect was remarkable. It broke down any barrier between him and the people—and more and more flocked to hear him preach.

Another night the siren sounded when Charles was going to his station at the Hall. Unnumbered people were flocking to the open country with as many belongings as they could carry on carts and in prams. One woman, a member of the Hall, was seen running along the road with her caged parrot in one hand and a photograph in the other. Asked what she was doing, she said her old man would not go with her so she was talking his photo, just in case! [78]

The two boys were probably victims of the first raid when Porter Street, further east from Thornton Street and nearer the railway station, was badly damaged. Thornton Hall was itself destroyed in the Second World War.

As well as the threat to life at home there was the ever growing toll on the Western Front and the constant fear which affected every family directly or indirectly, of receiving an official telegram announcing death, injury or 'missing in action'.

CHAPTER 12

Success in the South

In the south of England there had been some successes, *L15* was brought down off Margate, 31 March 1916, (see below), and, with the aid of the new incendiary bullet,[1] the army airship *Schütte-Lanz SL II* was shot down in flames over Cuffley, Herts., 3 September the same year. Flying his B.E.2c Lieutenant William Leefe Robinson emptied several drums of ammunition into the envelope and the airship fell from the skies in flames. He became a national hero, was awarded the Victoria Cross but subsequently died in the influenza epidemic of 1919.[2]

The B.E.2c, designed by Geoffrey de Havilland (also designer of the versatile 'Mosquito' in the 1939–45 war) was the most effective airship-killer of the war destroying nine out of the total of twenty-one brought down by British aeroplanes. The loss of the *SL 11* resulted in the Germany army withdrawing their airships from the bombing campaign to concentrate on reconnaissance work.

The pursuit by anti-aircraft batteries across London and its final destruction was witnessed by thousands and Sir Mark Sykes, the Hull MP, was one of the excited spectators. He subsequently drove to Cuffley where crowds had gathered to see the wreck and later wrote home 'sending each of the children a piece of Zep'.[3]

This highly visible success led to the sale of large numbers of postcards many of them produced far from London and the Home Counties. One produced in Hull shows the airship breaking up in flames and is entitled 'HIS LAST TRIP ZEPP IN FLAMES Sept. 2, 1916, Copyright Cartledge, Brook Street, Hull.' This was evidently produced by enterprising newsagent Fred Carriss Cartledge of 34 Brook Street in central Hull. Though referred to as a Zepp this craft of course was an army Schütte-Lanz, but to the population at large all enemy airships were Zeppelins. Probably due to the influence of the censors determined to demonstrate that we were beating the 'Zepps' a large proportion of cards produced across Britain seem to be of downed airships. Many were of the Cuffley airship, since its path to destruction had been watched across London and the Home Counties by countless bystanders, making it perfect propaganda for the government press agency. This was the last Schütte-Lanz airship to appear over England and the efforts of the German army had always been hampered by the restricted payload of a craft with a heavy wooden frame. In addition, the army had made a grave mistake by dissipating 'their force by erecting large numbers of single sheds all over Germany, and so required an inordinate personnel for handling parties'.[4]

More often the cards show the raider being sought by the searchlights or held in their beams and often bear the inscription 'Publication sanctioned by the Official Press Bureau, (Copyright) Publicity Office, 19 St. Andrew Hill EC' indicating perhaps that the image in some instances has not only been permitted by, but also devised and provided by government sources.[5]

On 23 September 1916 an airship was forced down at Little Wigborough and its crew captured. Two more airships were shot down over England in November 1916.

As the numbers of airships brought down over England and the continent increased so our knowledge of their construction and equipment was advanced. This resulted in publication by the Admiralty War Staff, in February 1917, of a large, foolscap size manual, entitled *German Rigid Airships*, illustrated throughout with line drawings and photographs.[6]

The downing of one Zeppelin led to some doggerel verse, printed on a postcard and sold for 1*d*, which could be sung to the tune of 'Back home in Tennessee'. It implies, incorrectly, that an airship had been shot down over Hull:

His home in Germany, that Zep will never see, The British gunnery did bring it down you see. All he could think of that night was of setting Hull alight—[7]

Policemen spend a lot of time waiting around involved in hum-drum routine punctuated by bursts of activity which may, especially in wartime, be accompanied by life-threatening danger. During the quiet times on duty there would be plenty of time to think and perhaps compose some verse. A special constable produced the following while on duty at Walton Street, Spring Bank West, waiting for an attack:

Guarding still in days of ill
This port from Zeppelin raids;
The Threatening foes we dare oppose
Our Constable Volunteers

The Huns may come at beat of drum
Across yon rolling main;
They'll cross the waves to find their graves,
Nor 'tempt this shore again

This ancient port defies the shock,
No German aircraft fears
While on the streets undaunted stand
Our Constable Volunteers [8]

Various organisations were happy to support the Specials who had volunteered to do their bit, including the Dairycoates Air Rifle Club. They offered free use of their 7-10 and 22 yard ranges, along with their BSA rifles, to all Special Constables, charging only for the pellets at ten for a penny.[9]

CHAPTER 13

Further Raids in 1917 and a Royal Visit

There was evidently serious concern about public morale in the north of England and in June 1917 King George V and Queen Mary did a whistle stop tour of the North East, starting at Middlesbrough on the fourteenth of the month, followed by Newcastle and ending at Hull on the 18 June before returning south.[1] The royal couple arrived 10 a.m. by train at Paragon station and were greeted by the Lord Lieutenant of the East Riding, Lord Nunburnholme, the Lord Mayor, Francis Askew, and a variety of other civic dignitaries and their wives, including the High Steward of Hull, T. R. Ferens, and a rare appearance by Major General Sir Stanley Brenton von Donop KCB, KCMG, General Officer Commanding, of the Hull Garrison.[2]

The King and Queen were driven via Waterworks Street, Clarence Street and Hedon Road to Earle's shipyard which over the years had built everything from Nile boats, royal yachts, and trawlers to ocean liners and warships. Returning to west Hull the engineering works of C. D. Holmes was the next place on the itinerary, before meeting local worthies at the Guildhall, followed by the VAD Hospital, Cottingham, where the dowager Lady Nunburnholme was the Commandant. Next stop was the Royal Naval hospital, Argyle Street, and then to the Hull City football ground where the King, received by Major General von Donop and his staff, and presented medals and decorations to officers, NCOs and men of the Humber and neighbouring garrisons.[3] After this busy schedule the King and his consort departed from Paragon station at 4.30 p.m.

On 21 August 1917, a raider passed over the Holderness coast and advanced towards Hull. The airship was from a group despatched across the North Sea comprising *L35, 41, 42, 44, 45, 46, 47* and *51*, a force which returned with only meagre results. Only *L41* was actually spotted over England and her commander, Hauptmann Manger, attempted an attack on Hull. Evidently loath to face the guns and searchlights its load was dropped east of the city, on Paull, Hedon, Preston and Thorngumbald. Damage was confined to Hedon: a Methodist Chapel was destroyed,[4] and some cottages, a Roman Catholic building, and a YMCA hut were damaged. In addition one man was injured.[5]

Lt H. P. Soloman, 33 Squadron, flying from Scampton, Lincolnshire, encountered the airship over Beverley and pursued it some twenty miles out to sea before returning to base.⁶ He fired bursts at long range but could not get near enough for his guns to have any effect. The pilot estimated that his quarry was some 5,000 feet higher than himself, and at an altitude of 20,000 feet, far higher than he could hope to reach.

The alarm for the fifth raid was heard at 10.25 p.m., Saturday 2 September 1917, and the Zeppelin (its identity has not been established) was sighted at about 12.40 a.m.

Demonstrating the effectiveness of von Donop's improvement of the defences there was a hot reception from guns guided by searchlights, no bombs were dropped and the airship quickly departed.

Because of the demands for manpower on the Western Front more and more experienced soldiers were taken from home defence. Eventually the guns at each site were in charge of a regular soldier but otherwise manned by anti-aircraft volunteers, a mixture of working men and local businessmen, mainly from National Radiator Works, Premier Oil Works, British Oil and Cake Mills, Hull Oil Mills Co. and members of the local business fraternity from the Pacific Club.⁷ According to Arthur Tidman the guns were not put in the hands of volunteers until after April 1918, when all available regulars were rushed to France, and the replacements were trained by the 27th Company of the Royal Garrison Artillery.⁸

On a calm Monday night, 24 September, for the sixth raid, obeying instructions the public got well under cover. The Zeppelin *L41* arrived at 02.50 a.m. and bombs fell once again in South Parade as well as St James Street, Lansdowne Street and Fountain Street. No one was seriously injured thanks to some providential escapes, especially as the bombs were reckoned to be three times the weight of those used in the early attacks. A number of these larger bombs, popularly referred to as 'aerial torpedoes', failed to explode.

In the neighbourhood of the workhouse and Naval Hospital, Argyle Street:

> At the rear of a row of old houses an aerial torpedo fell with terrific explosion. The back portions of the houses were demolished and a few feet from one backyard a crater eight feet deep and twenty feet wide was made. The missile was heard whistling through the air before it fell and had evidently been fired obliquely from a Zeppelin two or more miles away.⁹ It is miracle that practically all occupants escaped, the exception being a woman and her daughter, who were cut with glass. A man and wife with their four children were in bed in one of these houses at that time, but escaped. Outhouses and rear of houses were smashed and bricks piled in heaps, and debris was scattered, round an area of 200 yards. As showing the force of the explosion, part of a mangle was blown from a yard into the workhouse grounds 250 yards away. As soon as daylight came some patients from the hospital turned out in search of souvenirs.
>
> In another part of the city a fruiterer's shop and adjacent property was damaged, a great quantity of glass being smashed by the vibrations. The occupier of the shop and his wife were sitting by the fire when the aerial torpedo fell on the yard, only separated from them by a brick wall. The explosion was

outward, otherwise they and a neighbour who had called in might have been killed. It should be borne in mind that is very doubtful whether aerial torpedoes ever were used, that is bombs with a mechanically propelled screw. The story of aerial torpedoes may have arisen from the fact that the German bombs had large flanges at the upper ends to guide the missile through the air.

In the same area an old man lying on a couch on the ground floor was partly covered with a shower of glass and splinters, and escaped with a few scratches. The concussion shattered many windows of the Hull Workhouse Infirmary. This place adjoins the Naval Hospital, and the inmates, a large number of wounded seamen felt the force of the explosion. Here one of the special constables picked up the bronze 'dud' with two blades intact.[10] St Stephens Parish Church, which is not many yards from the rails leading out of Paragon Station had several stone pinnacles injured, and several roads were thickly strewn with broken bricks, mortar, tiles, and glass. The property damaged was of the poorest type.[11]

The portion of a mangle referred to was one of the large wooden rollers, blown out of 55 Lansdowne Street and right over the Naval Hospital finally landing in the bedroom of Mrs Drewitt, at 18 Argyle Street![12]

Another account comes from the pen of George Thorp:

...the backs of some fairly new and well built small houses at the corner of Crystal Street and Derringham Sreet, at the end of Lansdowne Street a considerable amount of damage had been done to front houses and a terrace called May Terrace on the left hand side. On the other side backing up to the grounds of the Workhouse Infirmary a huge hole had been made, the back yard wall destroyed and the whole of the infirmary windows fronting in that direction were smashed. In South Parade Melrose Terrace has been damaged to some extent.[13]

A photograph by Turner shows a range of bombs that had been recovered and deactivated; the small early types, were mostly 50 kg, but in later raids bombs of up to 300 kg were used and the total loads carried by a Zeppelin varied from less than a ton to some three-and-a-half tons. A 50 kg bomb, retrieved in unexploded condition, was displayed in the Hull Municipal Museum in Albion Street, with a plaque inscribed:

50 Kilo high explosive bomb dropped from a Zeppelin on Hull during the night of Sept. 24-25 1917. Recovered and emptied by Capt. W. R. S. Ladell, A. O. D. (100 M. G.), and presented to the Lord Mayor and Corporation of Hull by the General Headquarters Home Forces. The bomb passed through the roof of 40 Lister Street, through three floors and two chests of drawers, and after penetrating the basement, was found embedded in clay four feet from the surface. Various articles of clothing it collected during the flight, were found underneath the bomb undamaged.[14]

Further Raids in 1917 and a Royal Visit

A photograph of this is in the Turner Collection in the Hull Museum. Another 50-kilo bomb still in the museum collections is described in Appendix VIII. A plaque informs us that it also was deactivated by Capt. Ladell but does not have a description as to where and how it landed.

A Major Cooper-Key was chief inspector of explosives; he examined an incendiary which had dropped at Tonbridge Wells and had been taken to Duck Island (St James Park) to be opened up.[15]

Jones tells us the *L41* was part of another large force, consisting of *L35, 41, 42, 44, 45, 46, 47, 51, 52, 53* and *55*; it was as unsuccessful as the squadron despatched in August.[16]

The *L41* (Hauptmann Manger) 'came in over Hornsea at 01.27 a.m., crossed to Beverley, and then followed the railway to Hull, the usual way of approach to the city by the Zeppelins'.

The *L41* had crossed Hull at full speed, from northwest to east and, at 02.40 a.m., dropped sixteen bombs which caused injury to three women, but inflicted little damage. The airship passed over the river and came in again above the east side of the city, dropping four more bombs, in a field at Marfleet. She then went on towards Paull, where she came under fire, after which she turned off in a north-easterly direction. Four more bombs came from her as she passed over Preston.[17] Manger in his report says that Hull was clearly outlined, 'He dropped his bombs, one 300 kg, five 100 kg, ten 50 kg, and twenty incendiaries in two loads from 16,600 feet'.[18] Although thirty-seven aircraft were launched few made contact because the Zeppelins were flying at up to 20,000 feet, beyond the reach of most fighter aircraft.[19] The relief buzzer finally sounded at 05.50 a.m.

The official response from the Press Bureau stated 'Hostile airships appeared on the Lincolnshire and Yorkshire Coast early this morning. The raid is still in progress and details are not yet to hand'.[20] On a clear and starlit night, the airships were first visible at 11 p.m., searchlights and guns engaged at 02.30 a.m. There were possibly three casualties but militarily the attack was totally ineffective.

Generally there had been a marked improvement in search-light installations and anti- aircraft batteries in vulnerable towns. From late 1915, a network of home defence aircraft squadrons had developed. In East Yorkshire there was a base at Beverley Westwood, occupying part of the racecourse, and one at Atwick near Hornsea. On the south bank of the Humber at Killingholme a Royal Naval Air Service station for seaplanes and float planes had opened in 1914. The paddle steamers *Brocklesby* and *Killingholme*, cross-Humber ferries requisitioned for war purposes, became operational in spring 1916, each carrying two Sopwith Baby seaplanes.

At various locations along the east coast sound mirrors were erected, concave, concrete structures fifteen feet in diameter which focused sounds from incoming 'hostiles'. A bearing could then be taken and local aircraft directed to intercept them. A good example survives at Kilnsea on the Holderness coast.

Despite all these efforts the military authorities were juggling with scarce resources and it seems that after the very successful response on 2 September they were confident enough to yet again withdraw anti-aircraft guns for use elsewhere. George Thorp in his diary:

> Rumours as to all our guns except one at Sutton having been removed are freely circulated. Though semi-officially denied: if the guns were there, why did they maintain (as St. Simon comically put it) such a 'furious silence'.[21]

Zeppelins were initially used for reconnaissance rather than in an offensive capacity and when they shifted to offence the German General Staff decided in September 1914 that all airships should be used 'at the dark of the moon', in the period some eight days before and after the new moon.[22] Though bright moonlight would have made it easier for the intruders to successfully navigate to their target, the Zeppelins were also more vulnerable being easier to pinpoint by British defences on the ground and in the air.

As Buttlar-Brandenfels puts it in a lecture he gave to the Marine Institute (Institut für Meerskunde) of Berlin University in January 1918 based on his personal experience of raids in Britain starting in 1915:

> There are roughly twelve days in the month, when this [practically no moon] is the case, i.e. from the last to the first quarter. We must also take into account the time when the moon rises and sets, as even at a great height an airship is a conspicuous target for anti-aircraft guns; for in the course of the war one has learnt to shoot accurately at aerial objects.—Besides this a defending aeroplane can much more readily sight an airship on a clear moonlight night, than when it is dark, and at great heights the air is very much clearer, and the range of vision is greater than it is close to the ground, where dust and smoke interfere with the horizontal view. Consequently, an airship must have the protection of darkness for an attack.[23]

Defensive measures involved details such as the supply of a chart showing the phases of the moon, and thereby indicating the most likely dates for an attack. Of course, in the summer when days were long, it was essential to arrive late in the evening, or very early in the morning while it was still dark.

The normal naval gyroscopic compass was too heavy to carry aboard the airships but the light liquid compass carried instead would often freeze and be rendered useless.[24] There was no radar, radio fixes were not reliable, and a clear view of the countryside to pick up landmarks was essential if the airship was to locate its target. Buttlar-Brandenfels commanded one of the three Zeppelins in an attack on Britain 15 April 1915. He flew over the east coast and dropped his bombs but had no idea where he was and only after his return, did he discover, 'from a newspaper in neutral Holland' that it was Maldon in Essex![25]

CHAPTER 14

1918: The Last Raids

On 12 March 1918, the seventh raid commenced on a dark, cloudy drizzly Tuesday; the attacker received a terrific barrage from below in the full glare of the searchlights. The *L63*: came in at Hornsea at 8.30 p.m and followed the railway back to Hull, where bombs began to fall about 9 p.m. Six exploded within the municipal area of the city and sixteen more in fields at Sutton and Swine. A few houses were damaged in Hull, where one woman died of shock, but otherwise the bombs exploded ineffectively.[1] Several landed in allotments in Southcoates Avenue and many windows were broken. Bombs were unloaded over Cottingham, at Sutton road, near the Isolation Hospital, and as far as Wawne, where a cow was killed. Weather conditions were unfavourable for the raiders, with low clouds and flying at a ceiling of 16,000–20,000 feet it was impossible for them to select their targets. From the ground the searchlights could not pierce the clouds and the anti-aircraft guns were directed according to the engine sounds of the attackers.

The alarm buzzer had sounded at 7.20 p.m. and there at first seemed to be nothing to fear. George Thorp decided to leave his house, but:

…at the bottom of the street, plop-plop-plop, out went the street lamps one by one. Got as far as the bridge over Newland Avenue, and couldn't tell foot path from road.

As he stumbled home he collided with two equally disoriented women. The 'all well signal' went at 12.50 a.m. He also tells us that three or four houses in Montrose Avenue had been badly damaged, a bomb had landed in the allotments beyond and the signals gantry over the Hull and Barnsley railway near Wilmington station was severely damaged.

The *Hull Daily Mail*, 14 March, reports a raid on Hartlepool and an official statement that one or two airships had crossed the northeast coast and about twenty bombs had fallen close to the coast but no reports of casualties or damage had yet been received. This is followed by a report of the inquest by the coroner Col. Thorney on the sole victim of the Hull raid during the Tuesday night. Sarah Masterman, wife of a 'core maker',[2] accompanied by her husband

and granddaughter had entered the street following the air raid alarm. Though previously she had enjoyed good health, Masterman was taken ill and died soon after. A post mortem revealed acute bronchitis, an enlarged and fatty heart as well as valvular disease of the heart and the verdict was given as death due to 'syncope accelerated by shock and nervousness'.[3]

A note following is perhaps indicative of the slackening of censorship in this late stage of the war when the allies were increasingly confident of a victory, not long to be deferred. It refers to a piece from the *Sheffield Telegraph* in which the correspondent revealed Hull as the target of the raid. This was apparently the first time a place where a Zeppelin had dropped its bombs had been revealed, except for London and those places where an airship had come down and was already known to the public at large.

Thorp remarks on this too:

> Wednesday 13 For the first time in the history of official announcements the authorities mentioned the locality and name of the place attacked; our Hull being boldly printed.[4]

Zeppelins *L61*[5] (Kapitänleutnant Ehrlich) and *L62*[6] (Hauptmann Manger) had apparently been looking for the RNAS (Royal Naval Air Service) station at Howden:

> One was unable to find them and gave up the search, going away with her bombs unexploded; the other, when within range of the Howden guns, dropped her full load six miles away and made off [L62]. Two others [L.53, L54] never came to land at all. Ten aeroplanes sought the airships in vain.[7]

Established in 1916, the Howden station by 1919 boasted the largest airship shed in the world. During 1926–9, it was the home of Barnes Wallis[8] and his team, which included the aeronautical engineer and author Nevil Shute Norway,[9] where they designed and constructed the *R100* airship.

CHAPTER 15

Measures and Countermeasures

Aeroplanes were now 'making things very hot for any aerial invaders, as well as our anti-aircraft guns'. The inflammable hydrogen in the gas bags made the airship particularly vulnerable to incendiary bullets (universally available from late 1916) and this caused them to be flown at ever greater operational altitudes, making accurate bombing even more difficult.

It was found that the most effective weapon was a mixture of .303 explosive, incendiary and tracer ammunition fired from the Lewis gun.[1] Before this was realised a variety of explosive and incendiary darts and bombs were tried.[2] The effect of numerous holes made even by ordinary bullets in the gas bags could be serious as appears from an attack on a group of British minelayers near Heligoland. The sailors had responded with rifle fire, which at the time had been regarded by the Zeppelin crew as a futile gesture, but on the journey back to Nordholz the airship suffered a significant loss of buoyancy. Inspection on the ground revealed more than six hundred holes in the gas bags and a loss of some three per cent of the gas which had increased to fifteen per cent by the following morning.[3] Similar losses on the long journey back from a raid on England might have been fatal, with the added danger of large amounts of the highly inflammable mixture produced by the escaping gas combining with the oxygen in the air. This 'oxyhydrogen' can be ignited, with explosive results, by lightning and other forms of static electricity (e.g. St Elmo's fire) as well as a naked flame of any kind.

Thanks to the highly effective incendiary bullet Zeppelins were now no longer the menacing threat they had once been and even the arrival of the six engine 'super Zeppelin', some 650 feet long, did not completely shift the balance away from the defenders, at least not in London which tended to receive the most effective ack-ack guns. Though faster and capable of carrying a bigger bomb load it flew at much the same altitude as its predecessors and was still in range of anti-aircraft guns and fighter attack. In an attempt to reduce their losses a new generation of airships was developed, dubbed the 'height climbers', which could reach a height of 16,000 to 20,000 feet. To achieve this the weight of the new Zeppelins was much reduced: the defensive armament removed,[4] the aluminium framework lightened, the control car made smaller, and the bomb load decreased.

The greatest problem with airships is that the bigger they are the more difficult it us to handle them on the ground, and a great many suffered serious damage or became a total loss after accidents manoeuvring them into and out of their hangars:

> a giant ship has, naturally, a high resistance to the wind, and cannot be held down by a large number of men, even in moderate winds of 12–15 metres per second (27–33 miles per hour), because the wind either tears it away from the men, or else breaks it in two on the ground.[5]

When the war ended Buttlar-Brandenfels was in command of the latest and biggest 'Super Zeppelin', the *L71*.

Flying in the sub-stratosphere brought with it the problems of altitude sickness, due to the reduction in oxygen levels which could also reduce engine power by a half. The extreme cold also introduced the danger of frost bite and tended to reduce both physical and mental agility though inhaling from flasks of oxygen, replaced in 1918 by cylinders of 'liquid air', counteracted the effects of oxygen starvation and the overall sensation of fatigue.

Butlar-Brandenfels tell us:

> It has been observed that most men must inhale oxygen when a height of 4,500 metres (14,800 feet) has been reached. The exact height, however, depends on the person, for I have got members of my crew who need no oxygen even at 6,000 metres (19,800 feet), although at this height the atmospheric pressure is only 0.49 of what it is at sea level.
>
> If one does not inhale oxygen when at a great height, a feeling of nausea and headache is experienced, and often vomiting follows. As a consequence, every man is provided with a flask of compressed oxygen, which must be used when the order is given by the commanding officer, after passing a height of about 4,500 metres (14,800 feet). No two men require the same amount, but it is necessary to use it very sparingly each time it is inhaled, to ensure having sufficient for the final stages of the flight.[6]

At a stroke they were now beyond the reach of the entire defence system. Staying at this height they were safe, but bombing with any accuracy was that much more difficult and whenever tempted to drop down lower the danger of air attack with incendiary bullets was ever present. Because they were bombing from such a high altitude only a large conurbation like London was a feasible target. As a result the initial successes were never repeated and the main effect of the Zeppelins throughout the remainder of the war was to divert personnel, guns and aircraft that could otherwise have been used on the Western Front:

By the end of 1916 there were specifically retained in Great Britain for home anti-aircraft defence 17,341 officers and men. There were twelve Royal Flying Corps squadrons, comprising approximately 200 officers, 2000 men, and 110 aeroplanes. The anti-aircraft guns and searchlights were served by 12,000 officers and men who would have had a ready place, with continuous work, in France or other war theatres.[7]

CHAPTER 16

Götterdämmerung

On the evening of 5 August 1918, the weather was bad, with poor visibility and rain. The progress of the Zeppelins was usually plotted on a grid as reports came in but the weather conditions prevented visual sightings over land and the fact that 'Not a single square message indicating position of enemy received through the night' meant that when a squadron received an 'airbandit' (the contemporary expression) call the aircraft were being sent up blind.

A Zeppelin had been reported off Spurn at 20.10 (8.10 p.m.) though it was afterwards disputed whether the message received had indicated that it was six or sixty miles distant. The Humber region, East Anglia and London were all potentially threatened and despite the conditions patrols were still being sent up. An F.E.2b aircraft, 2Lt A. J. Marsden, from A Flight of 38 Squadron,[1] Leadenham (Lincolnshire), took off at 9.55 p.m. heading north, reached a height of 12,000 feet over Lincoln, then turned south and east climbing to 14,800 feet, but with rain increasing and visibility to the ground nil, he returned to make a landing at 11.45 p.m. Aircraft of 33 Squadron from the Lincolnshire airfields of Kirton Lindsey, Scampton and Elsham,[2] were also searching for the enemy. A BE2b from 76 Squadron at Ripon (Yorkshire) flew towards Flamborough and a Bristol fighter from Scampton[3] crash landed at Atwick (near Hornsea, East Yorkshire), the pilot, Lt F. A. Benitz, was killed and his observer seriously injured.

Apart from problems of visibility aircraft would often run desperately short of fuel. Capt. T. J. C. Martyn MC, of 51 Squadron,[4] flew his F.E.2b from Marham (Norfolk), and patrolled at 19,300 feet. He spotted what he thought was a Zeppelin a long way north, but running low on petrol he descended rapidly to 500 feet and found himself over the sea:

> I then climbed slowly with half throttle due west, engine overheated. On descending again I saw North Coates Fitties[5] Landing Ground, where I landed just as petrol supply was completely exhausted.[6]

The identity of the Zeppelin which reached Hull on the eighth and final raid has never been positively established[7] and nor has the airship of the fifth raid. It was 5 August, a bank holiday, and an alarm buzzer was heard at 9.40 p.m. and another ten minutes later. A little before 1 a.m. the Zeppelin, immediately pinpointed by the searchlights, dropped a smoke bomb but nothing else before departing.[8] This seems like an admission on the part of the commander that Germany could no longer win the war and that there was no point in inflicting further death and destruction. At the time it was stated in the newspaper, referring to Hull in the usual fashion as an 'East coast town', that 'No enemy aircraft got near this town' but also more ambiguously 'that the approach of the Zeppelins was distinctly heard in the neighbourhood last night' as well as 'Bombs were heard to explode a long distance away and it is thought one of the Zeppelins discharged part of its cargo over the ocean'. Perhaps this was the airship which had paid its fleeting visit to Hull. The overall headline was 'Paying the price. Zeppelin shot down in flames' – the latter was said to have been brought down forty miles out to sea and it was implied that the fleet of five airships had been intercepted over the sea by aircraft and forced to turn back without crossing the coast.[9]

George Thorp tells us:

...the Radiator [factory] and Liverpool Street searchlights are out.[10] 12.45 a.m. searchlights out all over and gunfire in the distance. Firing from gun stations near to, 12.50 a.m. star shells and heavy firing. Bright vivid flashes and heavy explosions. Sutton direction, it requires a very keen and expert ear to difference between the report of a heavy gun and the dropping of a high explosive shell [bomb]. But there was no ground vibration, but sounds of heavy engines similar to those of a Zeppelin from ten minutes to one, till one. At 1.17 p.m. [*sic*, clearly a.m. is intended] all quiet.[11]

Leading this first raid on Britain for four months was Peter Strasser, the Fregattenkapitän (Chief of the Naval Airship Division, Fuhrer der Luftschiffe), aboard *L70* the newest and largest Zeppelin. The new design had six engines, was 694 feet long with a gas capacity of over two million cubic feet, and could reach a height of 23,000 feet with an 8,000 lb payload of bombs. A DH.4 piloted by Major Egbert Cadbury[12] found her off the Norfolk coast and approached head on. A burst of Pomeroy explosive bullets blew a large hole in the fabric and fire quickly spread the whole length of the airship so that it was consumed in less than a minute. Strasser met his end 'while fighting at the head of his men in a last battle for a cause already lost'.[13] This proved to be the last Zeppelin raid and the war ended in November the same year.

During the war a total of seventy-eight airships, sixty-five of them Zeppelins had been in use, six of the total were for training or special purposes and never used aggressively:

In the course of hostilities we lost 26 of these ships at the hands of the enemy, 14 through bad weather conditions, and 12 through fire, explosions etc. Twenty-eight of these 52 ships that were lost were destroyed together with their crews. In addition, 17 airships were struck off the active list as obsolete. Thus on Armistice Day only 9 ships were still in commission.[14]

The following airships were lost during hostilities *L3* to *L10*, *L12*, *L15* to *24*, *L31* to *L34*, *L36*, *L38* to *L40*, *L43* to *L51*, *L53* to *L55*, *L57* to *L60*, *L62*, *L70*, *SL3*,[15] *SL4*, *SL9*, *SL12*, *SL20* and *PL19*.

The Parseval series were non-rigid and semi-rigid airships with wooden frames, designed by August von Parseval. *PL19* was intended for the Royal Navy but when war broke out was taken into the German navy and was brought down in Lithuania by Russian artillery, 25 January 1915. In the Government-issue recognition chart already referred to types of Parseval are illustrated in both the German and British sections.

Europe, after all the horrors of a protracted war, was also to suffer the effects of the most virulent pandemic of modern times. In July 1918, Britain began to feel the effects of the influenza epidemic or 'Spanish flu' which was highly infectious and quickly turned to pneumonia. Without modern drugs it was generally fatal, and by the end of 1920, when it finally subsided, had claimed more than 50 million, perhaps as many as 100 million, lives across the world.[16]

The logbook of Boulevard infants' school, 5 July 1918, records that it closed a week early for the summer holiday because of the epidemic.[17]

CHAPTER 17

Reactions to the Raids

At the beginning of the war the desperate need for guns on the Western Front deprived our cities of the weapons that could have defended them. Even so it took a while for the authorities to be convinced that active defence with anti-aircraft batteries and pursuit by aircraft was the real answer to the problem.[1] The passive defence, which was all that was originally offered, meant the attackers felt invulnerable and could cruise and manoeuvre at will so as to select the best targets. The airships needed to be constantly harassed, to prevent careful aiming and make them fearful of the constant danger of being shot down or seriously damaged.

The most devastating raid on Hull was the first one, in 1915, and the second, on the night of 5/6 March 1916, was almost as bad. In 1916 the city had three raids, more than in any other year, two of these resulted in a total of at least twenty-nine deaths, but there was one fatality in the third. As soon as positive action was taken to defend the city (before the third raid) casualties were dramatically reduced, and increased again during the fourth raid when ground mist prevented the gunners seeing their target. For the fifth raid there was a hot reception and only one further death until the end of the war. It must be said that there was a certain element of luck that there were no deaths resulting from the sixth attack, the Zeppelin commanders being fearful of defences more effective than actually was the case. In reality ack-ack guns had been withdrawn from Hull for use elsewhere. By this time the Zeppelin pilots were flying higher, out of range of gunfire both from the ground and of aircraft with their incendiary bullets, which also meant that the effectiveness of the bombing decreased.

One of the most experienced Zeppelin pilots speaking in January 1918 gives a considered opinion of anti-aircraft defences:

> Unless you have experienced it, you can have no idea of all that is fired at you. The defences in and around London are naturally by far the strongest to contend with, as they have the biggest object to protect, but in addition, other places, like Hull, and especially the inland industrial centres, like Liverpool, Manchester, Sheffield, Leeds, and so on, are now, after thee and a half years of war, provided

with quite a neat system of defence, which in many places is not inferior to London.[2]

In Yorkshire, and in the north of England as a whole, there never seem to have been sufficient aircraft, and certainly not of the most powerful types capable of reaching high altitudes at speed, to have really taken the fight to the Zeppelins. They were placed in the position of chasing their prey from a distance, some way behind and below. No record has been found by the author of a successful interception by an aircraft in the Humber region, resulting in any significant hits by machine gun fire, on either an incoming or outgoing airship. Over the entire north of England only one Zeppelin was destroyed, the *L34*, shot down over Hartlepool, 27/28 November 1916. Flying a BE.2c of 36 Squadron from Cramlington, Northumberland, 2Lt Ian Vernon Pyott set the raider on fire with incendiary ammunition, and was awarded a DSO for his action. The Zeppelin caught fire just after it had started dropping 16 HE bombs which caused considerable damage, two women died of shock, three men were injured, one of whom died later. A further six women were injured, one died later, and four children were injured.

There was a remarkable drop in the number of times the buzzers were heard in 1917. They sounded only four times, for the raids on the 2 September and 24/25 September, and two false alarms 21 August and 19 October. The number of Zeppelin flights had decreased but also the practice of ordering the buzzers to be blown as soon as the raiders crossed the east coast was discontinued. As a result the public were no longer being constantly put in fear by frequent and needless alarms.

At the start of the bombing campaign practically the only public evidence of government concern was the issue of wall posters with silhouettes (printed by HMSO, dated 1915, price 2*d*) to enable those on the ground to distinguish friendly and hostile aircraft. It was headed with a warning:

> Should hostile aircraft be seen, take shelter immediately in the nearest available house, preferably in the basement, and remain there until the aircraft have left the vicinity: do not stand about in crowds and do not touch unexploded bombs. In the event of HOSTILE aircraft being seen in country districts, the nearest Naval, Military or Police Authorities should if possible, be advised immediately by Telephone of the TIME OF APPEARANCE, the DIRECTION OF FLIGHT, and whether the aircraft is an AIRSHIP or an Aeroplane.

A chart of the phases of the moon has already been referred to, which, since the raids invariably took place at night, was a useful reminder of the level of illumination to be expected in clear weather and hence the most likely dates that an attack might occur. The example in the Hull museum collection was issued in the last year of the war and bears the (printed) names of George Morley, chief constable, January 1918, and M. Sabry, civil engineer, Leeds.

The public reaction to the raids varied no doubt according to how close one was to the scene of the action. There is an eyewitness[3] account, that of Mr A. Reed, captured by Suddaby in 1994:

> I did live through the Zeppelin raids, although I was only a very young child. At the time I was living on Southcoates avenue (next door to my uncle's bakery) where we used to shelter when the air raid alarm sounded. In 1916 (sic) the alarm sounded and we rushed into the bakery (a very strong building with concrete floors). The Zeppelin—was floating above the city with its engines switched off. After about half an hour there was a terrible rushing sound, and we thought it was a railway train on the Withernsea line—but it wasn't. It was a huge bomb, which exploded with a mighty roar, and shook the whole building and the table under which I was sheltering (it was on wheels) went half way across the floor!
>
> The bomb fell on allotments fortunately, otherwise, there would have been serious loss of life! The allotments were at the end of a small street called Whitworth Street, and every house in the street had its doors and windows blown in, and the occupants were covered in soot.
>
> The following morning, I went and looked at the crater the bomb had made, and it was about 6 metres deep and 10 metres long—The leaded lights in our front door were blown outwards[4] and there were large cracks in every ceiling and our house was about 300 yards from the crater!

The responses of a bored twenty-year-old separated from her friends and temporarily removed from her role as a VAD nurse was somewhat different. Dora Willatt, who had moved with her parents to the isolation of Silkstone Common, Barnsley, was writing to her soon-to-be fiancé in France, 27 December 1915: 'We miss the buzzers awfully—they were exciting and relieved monotony anyway.'[5]

She made occasional visits back to Hull: 'I went to Hull last Wednesday for my music lesson—the Zepps seem to have done more damage than last time but Nurse Waddington[6] said there were fewer casualties.'

This was in a letter dated 17 March 1916, referring to the raid on 5/6 March that had resulted in seventy-eight casualties. On 10 April she writes:

> We have been to Hull meanwhile and had a very Zeppy time – I expect you have heard all about Wednesday night when the Zepp came and we had guns and searchlights on it. It really was a beautiful sight – we had a beautiful view from Newland.[7]

On the 10 August, after an attack which resulted in thirty-three casualties:

> Mother came back from Hull suddenly last night – had enough of it with the Zepp raid of Tuesday night. She was in the house alone with one maid and they

dropped bombs on Westbourne Ave and Victoria Ave only half a mile away and then went over Newland Park – so poor old Ma felt a bit scared.[8]

Dora became formally engaged to Cecil Slack[9] on 11 December 1916 and they finally wed in 1919; the last mention of Zepps (or absence of!) is in a letter dated 25 July 1917:

> Our dug-outs an awful, slimy mess inside nowadays. The pump is out of it so consequently it's full of stagnant slimy water, and as there are no Zepps to relieve the peaceful monotony it really isn't much good except as a relic of Zeppy times.[10]

Stanley Duncan,[11] engineer with the North Eastern Railway and a keen wildfowler, hated to let a day slip by without him going down to the Humber shore to try his luck. He inserts references to the war and the Zeppelin raids in his pocket shooting diaries. Some are labelled 'MEMO BOOK North Eastern Railway'. The entries are brief recording the birds shot and the names of those who accompanied him.[12] The earliest reference to hostilities is 25 August 1914:

> We shot on the 25th until after 9-0 p.m. Heard about this hour a violent report – many miles from us but very loud. Never heard its equal before. War raging – gun boats (two off Grimsby) no interference with shooting on this shore.

> 21 September 1914: T. W. leaving on 22nd by car. He had seen a hydroplane [ie. a seaplane] drop a practice bomb off Grimsby.

A fortnight later, 5 September, he records the ominous news:

> <u>Shooting Prohibited</u> due to the War. Notice by the police, signed Major Dunlop.

There seems to have been an accommodation with the authorities and he and other shooters carried on, taking a bag which included rabbits and partridges. On 6 March 1916 at 12.05 a.m.:

> Zepps over Hull until 1.20 a.m. Second Raid. Saw Zeps on both occasions 'Frightful Machines'. Height probably 3 miles. Saw bombs drop. All the people terrified. 2 in. of snow on the ground, slight N. wind & before sunrise [an]other 2in. snow fell. Damage considerable.

> 5 April 1916: 9.00 p.m. Zepps – one on fringes of town – said to be another coming in on Lincs. side. Driven off splendidly by 8 or 9 search lights & hot gun fire. No one killed. Four bombs dropped on outskirt.

27 November 1916: Zepps over N. E. Coast. Two brought down in the N. Sea. Bravo. One off Durham coast the other off Norfolk.

14 March 1917: By an order of the Board of Agriculture & Fisheries – made 14th inst. Wildfowling shooting permitted till end of March-Birds may be sold until April 15th.

21 August 1917: Patrington. Zepp raid. Dropped bombs on Hedon. Kept out of gun ranges in attempting to reach Hull. Many shots were fired at it but she was 'out of shot'. I saw her in the lights. She was very high. Probably four miles. Home 3.0 a.m. into Paragon [station].

5 August 1918: (Bank Holiday) Air Raid alarm at night. One Zepp for certain brought down

11 November 1918: Date of Armistice Great European War.

The diaries thereafter continue solely with record of birds taken and names of some of his shooting companions.

All of these down to earth reactions can be compared with the fey and somewhat affected response of the novelist and poet D. H. Lawrence expressed in a letter to Ottoline Morrell, 9 September 1915:

…high up, like a bright golden finger, quite small, among a fragile incandescence of clouds. And underneath it were splashes of fire as the shells from earth burst— it was that small golden Zeppelin, like a long oval world, high up.

I cannot get over it, that the moon is not Queen of the sky by night, and the stars the lesser lights. It seems the Zeppelin is in the zenith of the night, golden like a moon, having taken control of the sky; and the bursting shells are the lesser lights.[13]

CHAPTER 18

Aftermath

There is some very perceptive comment in the post-war press on the psychological aspects of the raids, the fear engendered by the unknown and the ability to summon one's courage and respond constructively as soon as the nature of the threat is clear. The writer further remarks on the variety of response:

> There were members of the same family wholly diversified in their attitude—mothers who had kept quite calm, fathers extraordinarily agitated, thus showing that the guiding factor was the question of nerve control. Some men went to bed and slept tranquilly. Others sought refuge in the cupboards under the stairs. Some women fainted; others developed hysteria, whilst others were capable of soothing the whole household.[1]

The horrors of the raids seem to have been quickly forgotten by the population at large and no permanent memorial was ever erected in Hull to record the names of the casualties.[2]

As the threat of the Zeppelins began to recede there were children's games too. One entitled 'Sky pirates: A duel in the air', used a ball bearing which ran along a grooved track. There is a picture of a British bi-plane, bottom left, and a Zeppelin, top right, and the ball had to avoid eleven holes to reach and knock out the airship caught in the beam of a search light. This was probably inspired by the shooting down of *SL11* by Leefe Robinson, 3 September 1916. In a similar game entitled 'Trench football' the ball has to avoid the (shell) holes in the trenches and beat the German defenders, one of which is Count Zeppelin, and score a ball by dropping the ball into the Kaiser's mouth![3]

Zeppelina Williams, of Colchester, Essex, born in 1916, was named in commemoration of the Zeppelin that crashed at Little Wigborough the previous year, 24 September 1915. Many years later, in her eighties, she was invited to the reopening of the Zeppelin museum in Friedrichshafen, Germany.[4]

In Hull the only physical reminder now in public view, though not obvious to the casual visitor, is a small brass plaque in the south transept of Holy Trinity church recording not the human victims but the damage done to the stained glass in the second raid, 6 March 1916.[5]

1 Ferdinand von Zeppelin, (1838–1917). Zeppelin served as an observer with the Union Army during the American Civil War, and while in America he developed an interest in balloons. His first ascent in a balloon, made at Saint Paul, Minnesota—an inspiration for his later interest in aeronautics. After his resignation from the German army in 1891, Zeppelin devoted his full attention to airships.

2 The first Zeppelin airship, *LZ1* had its maiden flight at Bodensee (Lake Constance) on 2 July 1900. The airship rose from the ground and remained in the air for twenty minutes, but was damaged on landing. After repairs and some modifications two further flights were made by *LZ1* in October 1900.

3 By 1908 considerable development had taken place, but a Government purchase of an airship was made conditional on the successful completion of a 24-hour trial flight. The *LZ4* first flew on 20 June 1908, but was destroyed by fire at Echterdingen near Stuttgart after breaking free of its moorings during a storm. Notwithstanding this disaster, following the successful onward development the German Government finally supported the programme, and the operational life of the Zeppelins commenced.

4 The Dock Office, Wilberforce monument and the Prince's Dock, 1903. (*Paul Gibson collection*)

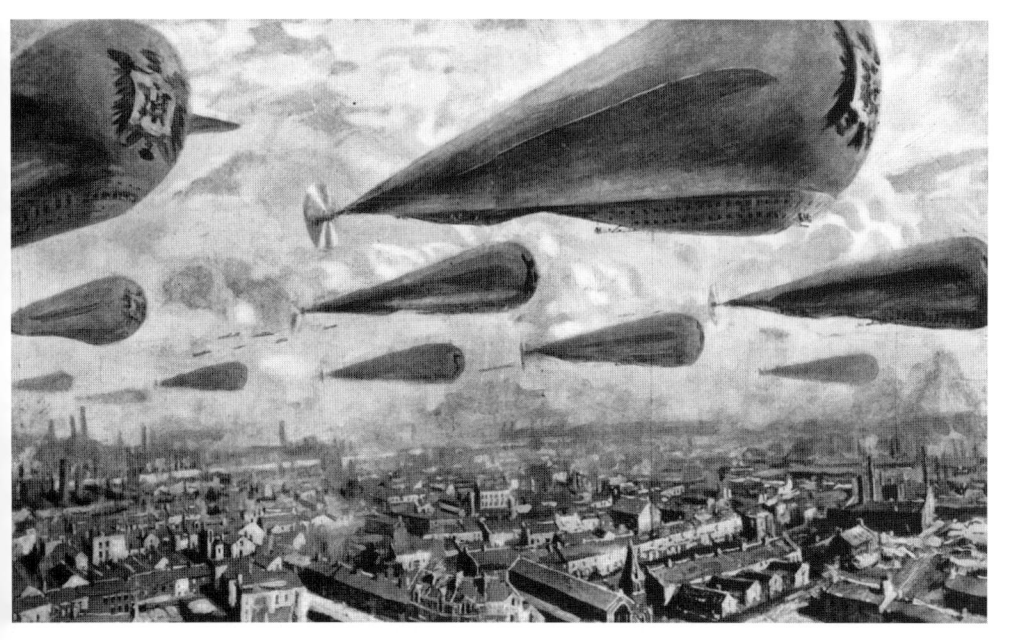

5 The German battle fleet of airships, flying over London; depicted by A. C. Michael in H. G. Wells' *War in the Air* 1908.

Above left: 6 *Punch* magazine; drawing by Bernard Partridge.

Above righr: 7 25 St Peters Plain, Great Yarmouth. (Author's photograph, 1980s)

Above left: 8 The Blundell and Spence 'buzzer'; used in both World Wars. (*Hull Museums*)

Above right: 9 Chief Constable George Morley in ceremonial dress, whilst in charge of the Durham constabulary. (*Durham County Archive*)

10 Lancashire fusiliers; washing hung out in Baker Street, Hull. (*Hull History Centre*)

Above left: 11 Portrait of T. C. Turner; from obituary in the *Hull News*.

Above right: 12 '*Gegen England*', watercolour of Zeppelin *en route* to England, a rather romanticised image from *Deutschlands Eroberungen der Luft* 1915. (*Derek Grindell*)

13 Regent House, Anlaby Road, far left, with galleries and pagoda top; 1908. (*Paul Gibson Collection*)

14 The rubble of Edwin Davis' store, King's, ironmongers and tool suppliers in the background. South side of Holy Trinity Church to the right, 7 June 1915. (*Turner photographs; Hull Museums*)

15 J. A. Hewetson & Co. Ltd., Saw Mill, Dansom Lane; the band or jigsaw in the right foreground bears the maker's name T. ROBINSON & SONS LIMITED/ROCHDALE ENGLAND, 7 June 1915. (*Turner photograph; Hull Museums*)

16 The destruction of Edwin Davis' store, after 7 June 1915; a contemporary postcard photograph by Marcus Barnard.

17 Smoking ruins of Edwin Davis' store from roof of Holy Trinity church, 7 June 1915. (*Turner photograph; Hull Museums*).

18 23 St Thomas Terrace, Campbell street; church in background, 7 June 1915. (*Turner photograph; Hull Museums*)

19 St Thomas Terrace, Campbell Street; Alice Walker was blown across the terrace walk way onto the aisle roof of the church and fell from there with mattress to the ground. (*Turner photograph; Hull Museums*)

20 Edwin's Place, Porter Street, 6–7 June 1915. (*Turner photograph; Hull Museums*)

21 Mr and Mrs Scott viewing the damage, 154 Walker Street, 7 June 1915. (*Turner photograph; Hull Museums*)

Above left: 22 North corner Grimsby Lane, High Street. (*Turner photograph*)

Above right: 23 High Street, corner of Grimsby Lane; police constable in the foreground, 7 June 1915. (*Turner photograph; Hull Museums*)

24 Walter's Terrace, Waller Street; a single HE bomb resulted in one death and fourteen houses destroyed, 7 June 1915. (*Turner photograph; Hull Museums*)

25 Courtney Street Volunteer Night Patrol, 1915. (*Paul Gibson collection*)

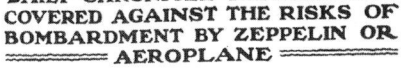

Above left: 26 *Daily Chronicle* offering insurance cover against aerial attack.

Above right: 27 Rt Hon. T. R. Ferens MP.

Above left: 28 Advertisement for G. F. Hohenrein, pork butcher, 1914.

Above right: 29 Charles Ross (Hohenrein) East Yorkshire Volunteer Motor Service; outside his garden air-raid shelter, 1917. (*Hull History Centre*)

30 Hohenrein, pork butchers, 7 Waterworks Street, 1911; note the medals won at the international exhibitions of 1910–11 displayed in the window. (*Paul Gibson collection*)

Above left: 31 Max Schultz (Hilton) 1875–1924, a British spy in the Kaiser's Germany.

Above right: 32 Major-General Sir Stanley Brenton von Donop, commander of the Hull Garrison.

33 Dr Mary Murdoch in 1901.

34 Zeppelin *L11*; note the two gondolas and, directly above the forward one, perched on top of the envelope is the very exposed gunner's position. (*Zeppelin Museum, Friedrichshafen*)

35 Zeppelin *L11*; the commander (Schütze?) and two of his crew in the control gondola. (*Zeppelin Museum, Friedrichshafen*)

36 Queen Street; the severely damaged Moors and Robson's public house is the 'Golden Lion', after raid of 6 March 1916. (*Turner photograph; Hull Museums*)

37 Folder with photographs from the Hull City Engineers' Department, raid of 6/7 June 1915. (*Hull History Centre*)

Above left: 38 Prayer for protection against Zeppelins; first issued 30 October 1915. (*Hull Museums*)

Above right: 39 Poem on the downing of Zeppelin *L15 (LZ48).*

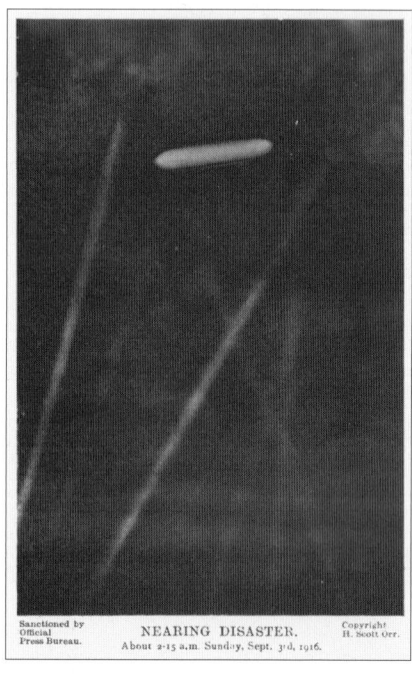

Above left: 40 Postcard titled 'The Raider'. (*Hull Museums*)

Above right: 41 Postcard titled 'Nearing Disaster'; London 3 September 1916. (*Hull Museums*)

42 Postcard titled 'His last trip', London 2 September, 1916; published by a Hull newsagent. (*Hull Museums*)

43 Mrs Drewitt holding the mangle roller which had been thrown hundreds of feet by an exploding bomb (25 September 1917).

44 *LZ38* Achieved its first bombing raid on London on 31 May 1915 killing seven and injuring 35 people. Five successful raids followed on Ipswich, Ramsgate, Southend (twice) and London, dropping a total of 8,360 kg of bombs. Destroyed by British bombing in its hangar at Evere on 7 June 1915.

45 A graphic depiction of the demise of Zeppelin *L7 (LZ32),* brought down off the coast of Germany on 4 May 1916 by gunfire from the Royal Navy cruisers HMS *Galatea* and HMS *Phaeton*. Its wreck was finally destroyed by the submarine *E31. L7* made 77 reconnaissance missions over the North Sea and several unsuccessful attempts to attack English coast.

46 An array of intact but deactivated bombs and parts of exploded bombs; 50 kilo, extreme right and left, 300 kilo in the centre, flanked by two 100-kilo bombs. Bottom left, rope wound core of an incendiary. (*Turner photograph; Hull Museums*)

Above left: 47 A classic Bruce Bairnsfather cartoon, from 1918; Tommy occupying a 'shell 'ole' at the front, but thinking about the folks at home.

Above right: 48 A boy scout tackling the enemy! Sent from Hedon to Hull, October 1914. (*Hull Museums*)

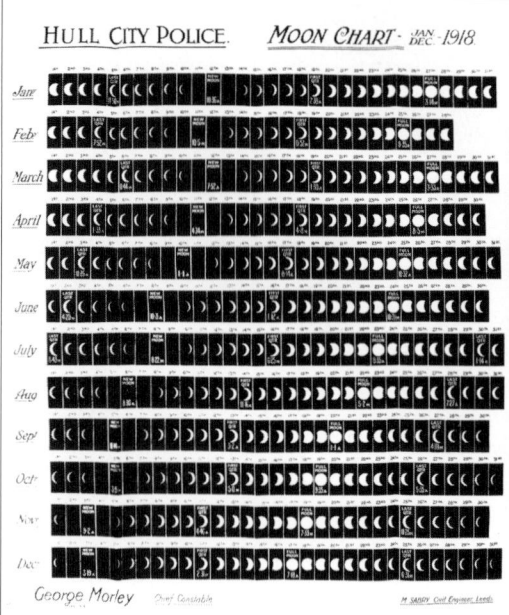

Above left: 49 Airship and aircraft recognition chart; 1915, HMSO. (*Hull Museums*)

Above right: 50 Hull City Police; moon chart, January–December 1918. (*Hull Museums*)

51 Brass plaque commemorating destruction of stained glass window, Holy Trinity church; 6 March 1916. (*author's photograph*)

Above left: 52 Alderman J. H. Hargreaves, Lord Mayor of Hull 1915–7.

Above right: 53 'Hints for specials' a cartoon, by Ern Shaw, in the *Special Constables' Gazette*. (*Hull History Centre*)

54 102 Great Thornton Street, home of the Needler family. Five boys were sleeping in the room, two in the bed stuck by an incendiary which penetrated the floor, landing on bed occupied by Mrs Needler who was seriously burned, 6/7 June 1915. (*Turner photograph; Hull Museums*)

55 The ultimate development of the 'Zeppelin', the *LZ 127 Graf Zeppelin*; a successful round the world passenger airship, landing at Friedrichshafen *c.* 1930.

56 Downing of *L15 (LZ48)*; signed J. S. Riches, 1916. (*Hull Museums*)

57 A. T. Hiller's shop, 18 Great Passage Street, 6–7 June 1915. (*Turner photograph; Hull Museums*)

Above left:
58 Zeppelin bomb from the raid of 24–25 September 1917. (*Hull Museums*)

Above right:
59 Sectional drawing of typical carbonite bomb: A. bomb suspension bar B. cylindrical tail fin C. firing bolt and ignition charge D. detonator E. explosive charge F. smoke capsule.

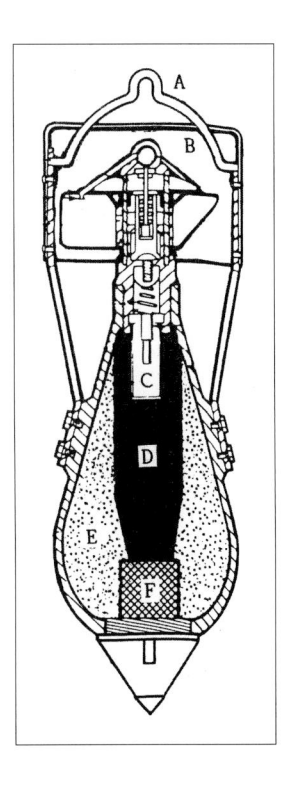

60 Incendiary bomb. (*Moyses Hall Museum, Bury St Edmunds*)

61 Incendiary bombs collected after the raid on Bury St. Edmunds, 30 April 1915. (*West Suffolk Record Office*)

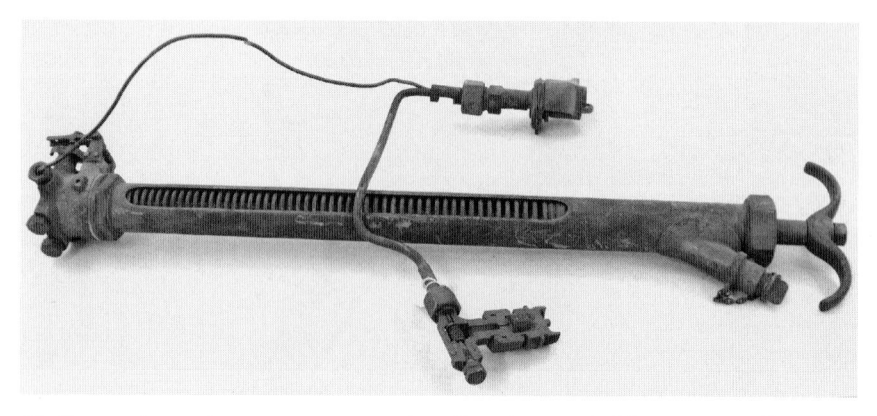

62 Constantinescu interrupter gear; made at Rose, Downs & Thompson, Hull. (*Hull Museums*)

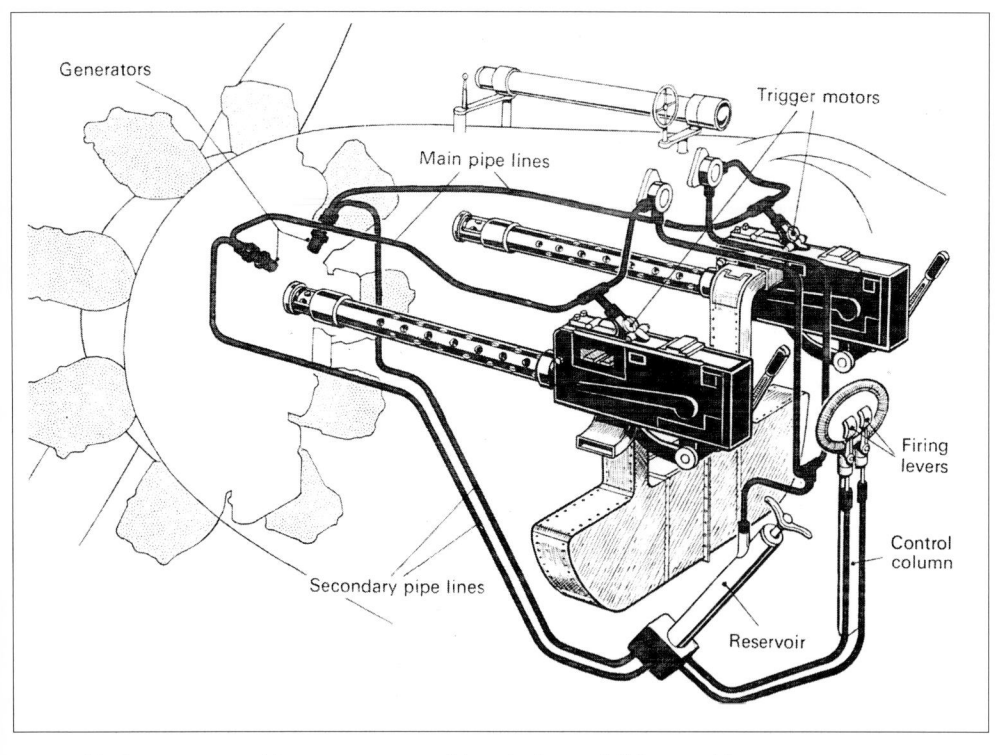

63 Arrangement of interrupter gear with twin forward-firing machine guns.

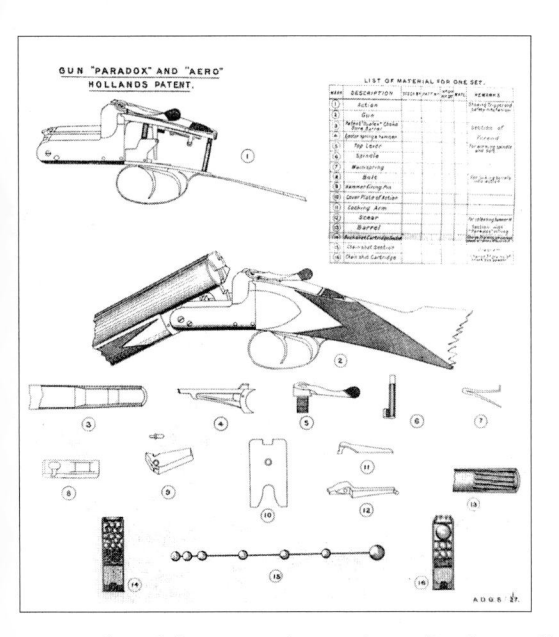

Above left: 64 Specification for Holland & Holland's 'Paradox' choke and the 'Aero Gun'; see chain shot at bottom of sheet (15) and section through cartridge (16); (14) section through buckshot cartridge. (*By permission of Messrs. Holland and Holland*)

Above right: 65 The 'anti-war memorial', Woodford Green, Essex (*author's photograph*).

R   I

66 *Fryer's map of Hull showing where bombs landed, 6 June 1915.*
A copy of a map of the city, updated by George Fryer FSI and published in 1914 by Harland & Son, Hull, is marked with red dots indicating where bombs landed, numbered in sequence 1–30, whether HE or incendiary is not indicated. The date of the first raid, June 1915 is pencilled in the lower right corner of the map. Across a roughly west-east line, south of the Anlaby Road, from Selby Street, eastwards to Cholmley Street, between Linneaus and Walker Street, to Porter Street and Great Passage Street to Castle Street, and then on the east side of the Town Docks (into the Old Town) and Blanket Row, and Market Place, then east of the river Hull into the timber yards and then northwards to Clarence Street, Holderness Road, Bright Street and finally Waller Street. *(Hull History Centre)*

CEMETERY
HYMERS' COLLEGE
WEST PARK
HULL CRICKET GROUND
HULL CITY FOOTBALL GROUND
LEONARD STREET
NORFOLK STREET
LONGSBOROUGH STREET
Corporation Field
ST STEPHEN'S ST
COLLIER STREET
WEST STREET
JAMESON ST
ALBION ST
PARAGON STATION
PARAGON STREET
ANLABY ROAD
CARR LANE
OSBORNE STREET
CAMBRIDGE ST
ST LUKE STREET
ADELAIDE STREET
WALKER STREET
NILE STREET
WILLIAM STREET
MORTUARY
RAILWAY DOCK
WAVERLEY STREET
KINGSTON STREET
LISTER STREET
CENTRAL GOODS STN
WELLINGTON ST
ENGLISH STREET
ST JAMES ST
HESSLE ROAD
JACKSON STREET
GOULTON STREET
ALBERT DOCK
RIVERSIDE QUAY STATION N.E.R.
WILLIAM WRIGHT DOCK
R
I

67 *Fryer's map showing where bombs landed, 5-6 March 1916.*
A second copy of Fryer's map, of 1914, is preserved in the Hull archives, and printed in the top left hand corner AIR RAID MAR. 5th 6th 1916, and marked with the landing places of high explosive bombs (dots) and incendiaries (circle, a cross within), following an arc from the north west towards the river and into the Old Town. (Hull History Centre)

HIGH EXPLOSIVE: a series of bombs fell in the grounds of Hymers College and north of the Hull City football ground (north of the Anlaby Road), south of the football ground (near Arnold Street), the north end of Bean Street, the middle of Linnaeus Street, and the south end of Walker Street. In the Old Town there was a heavy concentration between Blanket Row and Humber Street; others fell on the Corporation Pier and both incendiaries and HE on the Riverside Quay Station, and several dropped into the waters of the Humber.

INCENDIARIES: south of Paragon Station and Carr Lane, between Midland and Anne Street, also Waterhouse Lane, Castle Street (west of Princes Dock).

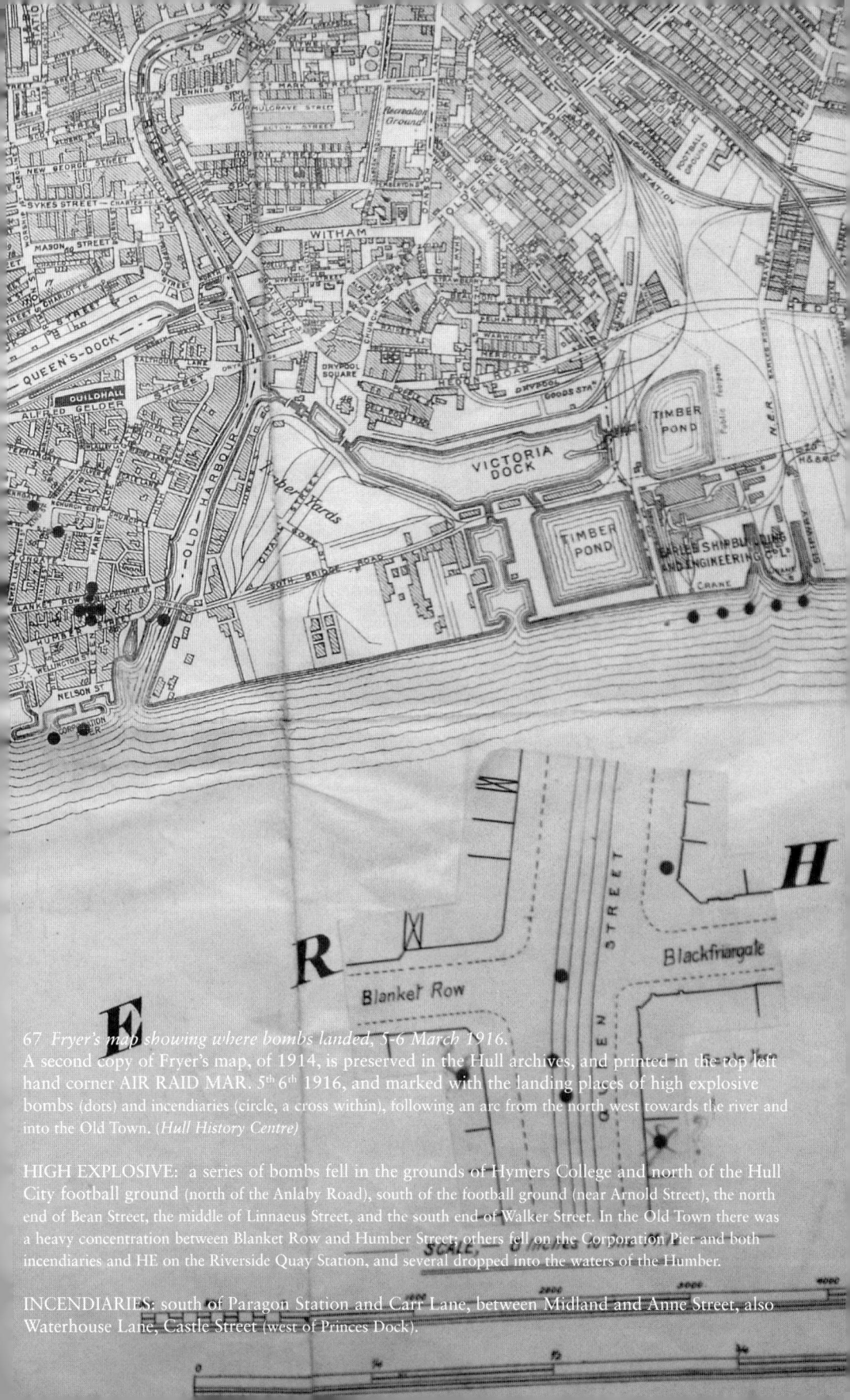

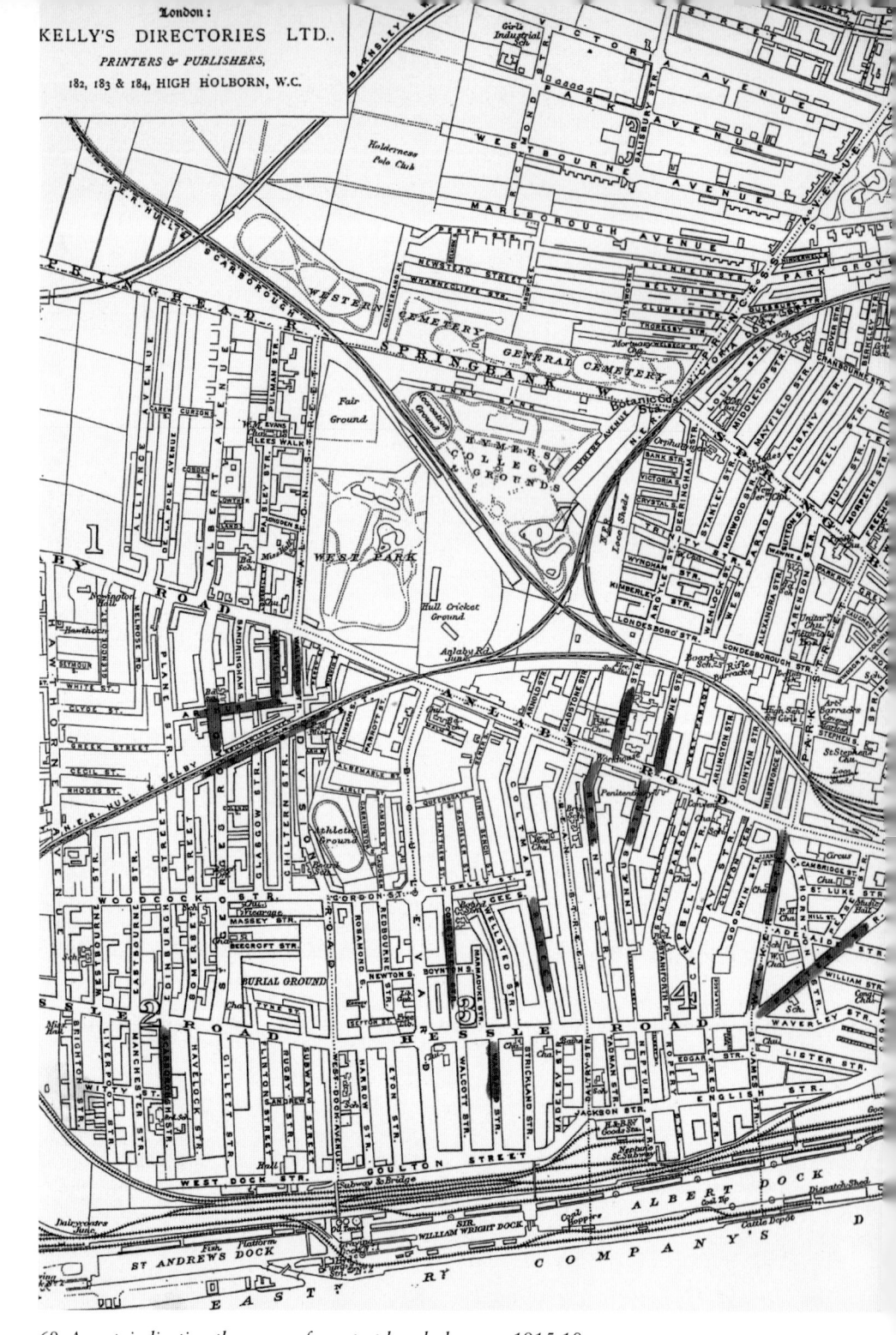

68 *A map indicating the areas of greatest bomb damage, 1915-18.*
The major concentrations of bombs landed on central Hull and in the area of the docks, and an overall pattern for the eight raids, three of which resulted in large scale damage and significant casualties, is indicated by the shaded areas: **LEFT** *Upper register, west to east* straddling the main railway line (Selby Street etc.), also adjacent to line and Paragon Station.

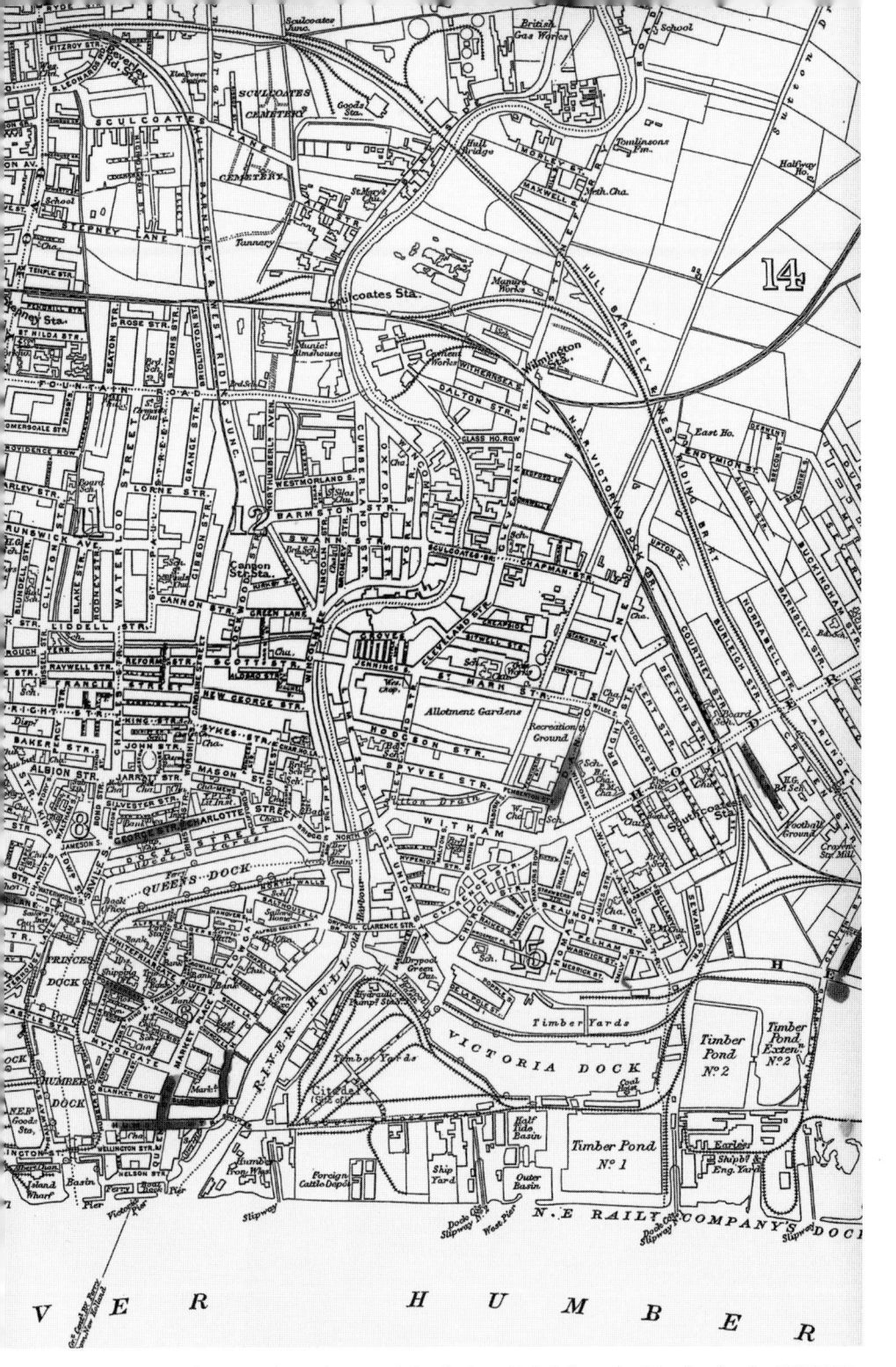

Lower register between the railway and the docks which follow the Humber bank. **CENTRE** the old dock system between the river Hull and the Humber surrounds the 'old town' which suffered significant damage. **RIGHT** the Drypool district east of the river Hull included a major dock, extensive timber yards and shipyards and their associated rail systems. Earle's shipyard was east of Victoria Dock, just outside the bounds of the map.

69 *L49 (LZ96)*, 13 June 1917. L49 made two reconnaissance missions around the North Sea and one raid on England dropping 2,100 kilograms of bombs; while returning it was forced to land near Bourbonne-les-Bains on 20 October 1917 and captured almost undamaged by French forces. Plans derived from *LZ96* were later used in the United States for construction of the first US "zeppelin", the USS *Shenandoah* (*ZR-1*), also used for the design of the British *R38*.

70 *LZ127, Graf Zeppelin,* a civilian was launched 18 September 1928, was the most successful airship in history. It made regular flights to North and South America; world tour in 1929, Arctic trip in 1931. It was dismantled in 1940 upon the orders of Hermann Goering.

Aftermath

Many of those who suffered directly from the attacks lived to experience another world war, and the 'blitz' beginning in 1940, becoming the victims of bigger bombs, and wholesale area bombing. Gas, initially considered the greatest threat, was thankfully never used but towards the end of the war the age dawned of the 'guided missile' in the form of the V1 'buzz bomb' as well as the V2 rocket, the world's first 'intercontinental ballistic missile'.[6] So within the first half of the twentieth century aerial weapons developed from bombs thrown from the cockpits of aircraft, those released from all too visible airships and aeroplanes, to missiles delivered from hundreds of miles away and which destroyed their target before anyone was aware of the danger.

The images of the Great War preserved in photograph and film and within the memoirs and poetry of the participants, recall the mud, death and destruction on the Western Front. A realisation of the magnitude of these losses, followed by the influenza pandemic, may make the suffering of the civilian population, at least in numbers killed and injured, seem insignificant. The sheer terror of the aerial bombing experienced by the people of Britain for the first time during the Great War should not however be underestimated.

In addition to the cost in lives the war raised the National Debt to an unprecedented £7 billion and in 1916 maintaining our troops and the whole apparatus of offence and defence resulted in an expenditure of £5 million a day. The national determination to carry on and conquer the foe is highlighted by the five per cent War Loan announced in January 1917, which quickly raised no less than £2 billion. Post-war the worldwide financial system was weakened by Britain's massive debt burden and, combined with the crippling reparations bill imposed on Germany, led to instability, inflation and the Great Depression. Another world war was followed by the dismantling of the British Empire, starting with the granting of independence to India in 1947.

Other than reports from the special Zeppelin issues of the *Hull Times*, 1919, there are relatively few contemporary records which give the personal reactions of those most directly affected by the raids. Censorship while the war continued prevented publication of individual responses or anything which might have engendered further fear and distress. Surviving hospital records only give numbers of people treated but no detail of the nature and extent of the injuries suffered. The council minutes include the occasional reference to measures undertaken by various committees in response to the threat of attack, decisions which are almost lost amidst all the routine business of running a large town.

There is a lack of a private written record, the diaries of Georg Thorp being an exception, and the 'Memories of a Special' and its sequel (see Appendix V) are the best sources for the effect of the raids and public reaction, from the point of view of those charged with offering help and protection to the ordinary citizens of Hull. Wherever possible the contemporary voices of those involved have been allowed to speak for themselves rather than being summarised in the words of the present author. Many comments and reminiscences were only recorded many years after the events described but none-the-less they are usually vivid and convincing.

Only a single letter has been discovered from someone recording their experience within days of the bombs landing. One would not expect diaries from the working class areas affected but there is likely to have been quite a number of postcards and letters, now lost or destroyed. Telegrams were expensive and only those in business or individuals who were comfortably off could afford a telephone. Urgent contact with friends and relations outside Hull or in some distant part of the city would have been by a hastily scribbled letter or postcard. In the early twentieth century, indeed up till about 1960, local post was very efficiently delivered. A communication posted in the morning would arrive at its destination in the same town on the afternoon of the same day. In a private collection of local ephemera is a postcard of Albert Dock, Hull, the half penny stamp post-marked 10 September 1916. Addressed to a Mr W. Hall, 113 Brook Street, Chester there is a brief note:

Dear Bill,

Very sorry I forgot your address. Excellent weather here. Zep alarm Wednesday night, Walt.[7]

CHAPTER 19

A Consideration

From the sources available it appears that the responses of the local authority and all those involved in preparing for enemy attack were practical and phlegmatic, with no evidence of sensational pronouncements or alarmist reactions. There had been some forward planning as indicated by the installation of warning 'buzzers' by the municipal authorities which started early in 1915. In response to the destruction and the civilian deaths the Hull Corporation, the police (which was part of that authority, as was the fire brigade), and the hospitals made concerted plans so as to be ready for any future attack.[1] Clearly Morley, the Chief Constable, in charge of police, the special constables, and the fire brigade, was a key figure in co-ordinating the response to the raids. The Lord Mayor was certainly the man who was the focus of public reaction, receiving their plaudits or brickbats.

Morley as head of a municipal force was also directly answerable to the Hull Corporation and was central to the organising of the means to protect citizens threatened by the air raids. Also answerable to the elected members were council officials, both technical and administrative but we cannot identify those individuals who made the biggest contribution to planning and executing that response. Herbert A. Learoyd was Town Clerk, Thomas G. Milner, City Treasurer, F. W. Bricknell, City Engineer, and J. H. Hirst, City Architect for the duration of the war. Any record made at that time of the planning meetings seems to have been destroyed. His experience in Hull was probably the reason that Morley, while Chief Constable of Co. Durham, was appointed county organiser for Air Raid Precautions for County Durham in 1939; he was then aged 66 and died three years later after an operation.

After the war special praise is given for the leadership of the then Lord Mayor Alderman J. H. Hargreaves 'and those acting with him'. Hargreaves served for three successive terms and had worked ceaselessly to help all those who had suffered from the bombing as well as raising funds for a wide variety of war charities. His activities, and the contribution made by his wife, responding to the injured and dispossessed is recorded above. Not surprisingly considering the demands of his civic duties, and as a businessman involved in the coal trade, his health broke down.[2] He was unable to accept a fourth term in office and was succeeded as Lord Mayor by Francis Askew.[3] In 1916, recognising his services to the city, he was elected Alderman and appointed C. B. E.[4] Shortly before the end of the war, 18 September, he was given the freedom of the city.[5]

The Hull City Police and fire brigade,[6] the Special Constabulary and contingents of soldiers from the Humber garrison had provided the personnel to secure the streets, deal with the effects of bombs, and help casualties when an air-raid took place. Also one should not forget the contribution of the youths and young men of the boy scout organisation created by Baden-Powell in 1908. Even with the war barely begun a young boy scout is depicted on an amusing contemporary postcard 'DOING HIS LITTLE BIT'. He is shown, a grin on his face, with a Zeppelin on a string like a toy balloon, and in the other hand dragging three German servicemen on a lead behind him.[7] It was posted 3 October 1914, from 'George' in Hedon (near Hull) to Mrs Isabelle Cartlidge, 194 New Bridge Road, Hull.

Germany had embarked on an all-out U-boat campaign against allied and neutral shipping in 1915 which resulted in the sinking of the *Lusitania* and the loss of hundreds of civilian lives including many Americans. Britain expected the USA to join in the war but the American president Woodrow Wilson was determined that his country should stay out of the conflict. The Germans were equally anxious for this industrial powerhouse to remain neutral and in the face of the strongest protests the unrestricted submarine campaign was suspended.

Determined to bring Britain to its knees the Imperial Government once again determined that the way to achieve this was by the destruction of merchant shipping and hence starving us of foodstuffs and war materials. This decision was announced to the Mexican government in the infamous Zimmerman telegram:

> We intend to begin on 1 February unrestricted submarine warfare. We shall endeavour in spite of this to keep the USA neutral. In the event of his not succeeding we make Mexico a proposal of alliance:-to make war together. Make peace together. Generous financial support and an undertaking on our part that Mexico is to reconquer the lost territory in Texas, New Mexico, and Arizona etc.[8]

Intercepted by British naval intelligence when the text was revealed to President Wilson he could no longer maintain a neutral stance and war was declared on Germany 6 April 1917. This was good news for the Triple Entente nations[9] but the losses of shipping in April that year reached a staggering 869,000 tons, 90 per cent sunk by German U-boats. This led belatedly to the introduction of the convoy system in which large numbers of transport vessels sailed under the protection of naval escorts. Up till May that year convoys had only been used for the protection of troop ships. There was an immediate drop in the numbers of vessels lost but despite this a great many ships were still left to sail by themselves unprotected and totally exposed to U-boat attack.[10] By October 1918 nine out of ten sailings were under convoy and throughout the last year of the war only 134 unescorted merchantmen were sunk.

The *Special Constables' Gazette,* the Specials very own 'newspaper', is the major source for determining details of how men and equipment were deployed and the control of food stuffs.[11] The content changes significantly in 1917 and 1918. More and more space is taken up with amendments to the Defence of the Realm Act referring to the control of the prices and supply of foodstuffs, for humans, horses and cattle, culminating in a limited and belated rationing. The government had taken overall control of food supplies at the end of 1916 and in early 1918 owing to the severe reduction of food supplies from the effects of the U-boat campaign personal rationing was finally introduced.

On 7 June 1917 a public meeting was held, at the Queen's Hall in Hull to debate the proposal: that no food stuffs of any kind should be used for the manufacture of intoxicating liquor, either beer or spirits.

This was carried unanimously and Francis Askew (the Lord Mayor), chairman of the meeting, wrote to Sir Mark Sykes MP with a call to press the government: to prohibit manufacture of strong drink during the shortage of food and shipping.[12]

Earlier in the war the brewing of heavy beers such as stout and porter had been banned, public house opening hours had been reduced, and in October 1915, under the 'no treating' order, it became illegal to buy a round of drinks. By 1918 these measures had reduced consumption over forty per cent.

The reminiscence of 'Freda', shows us that shortages affected everyone, including quite well off families:

The shortage of meat led to experimenting with vegetarian dishes, hitherto rather frowned upon as favoured only by cranks. These recipes were published in regular dailies such as the Daily Mirror, then a very sober paper much read by women. There was something called lentil paste, made of cooked lentils, pounded and mixed with Oxo cubes. It approximated to potted meat and was quite good on toast. Offal was obtainable at shops that sold tripe and both this and pig's trotters were cooked in onion or white sauce. One winter there was a potato famine -this was serious as potatoes were a good 'filler'. I seem to remember we had chestnuts instead. There was no shortage of bread but butter was a real problem. My role in the family seems to be that of shopper, and I recall standing in queue on a cold day hoping for some margarine. Report had it that if one skimmed the cream off milk, put it in a bottle with a sixpenny piece, and shook it violently for a long time, a small piece of butter would result. I think I tried it once, but I don't believe anything happened!—a school friend, who lived nearby, and who was a great scrounger—knew I know not how, of an egg warehouse near the docks, where the importer sold cracked eggs, which shops would not accept. They were cheap and excellent for cooking, when they would be cracked in any case. So armed with basins, we would present ourselves.[13]

The pages of the *Special Constables' Gazette* demonstrate an 'esprit de corps' developing among these volunteers through the period of hostilities and it may be noted that the first issue appeared on 18 June 1915, only a fortnight after the first Zeppelin attack on Hull.[14] This was what, in retrospect, we can identify as the worst raid in terms of fatalities and destruction of property but the decision to print the Gazette at this time seems to suggest a body of men who were confident of their ability to cope with aerial attack and its aftermath. They would have been well prepared for the second raid which was a major one too with almost the same number of dead and injured. The fourth attack, 8–9 August 1916, resulted in eleven dead and twenty-two injured but for the other five, the last 5–6 August 1918, there was a total of two dead and a handful of casualties. There were three raids in 1916 with a total of twenty-nine deaths but after 9 August that year and until the end of the war there was only a single fatality.

It is probable that, at the time the bombs were falling, all those who were in imminent danger simply tried to get away as quickly as possible, running, using horses and carts and whatever means of transport were available much as Winifred Holtby describes in her account of the shelling of Scarborough.[15] However the large numbers of specials deployed during a raid helped restrain any panic while the presence of manned road blocks ('motor halts') on the main roads to control the movement of all vehicles prevented or at least slowed down any attempts to make a mad rush out of the town. People would no doubt form into streams of refugees heading as fast as they could from fire, explosions and collapsing buildings and be joined by many others, who had heard the explosions or were simply frightened by the threatening presence of a Zeppelin in the sky. According to the Chief Constables testimony in October 1915 the large numbers of people leaving the town did so in an orderly fashion.

In October 1917 as a response to the Gotha attacks on London during daylight the Watch Committee resolved 'to at once take steps to ascertain what public and private buildings are available in which the public may shelter in the event of daylight air-raids, and that notices be posted on such buildings giving the necessary information and guidance'.[16] On 27 February 1918 it was decided that people should be advised to stay indoors or take shelter in the nearest available place and everyone was asked to offer shelter to those in need. It had been concluded that there would be great difficulty in deciding which buildings were safe to use and it would tend to encourage large numbers of individuals to congregate at any site so recommended.[17]

The terror was left largely unrecorded at the time and after the war no doubt those who had suffered wanted to forget their experiences. It was only some seventy years later, after the much more extensive devastation of the 1939–45 war, that anyone tried to capture memories of the Zeppelin attacks.

A contemporary account of an air raid on London albeit within a fictional story, one of the Richard Hannay novels, *Mr Standfast*, first published in 1918,[18] captures both the terror and the unreality:

There was a dull sound like the popping of the corks of flat soda-water bottles. There was a humming, too, from far up in the skies. People in the street were either staring at the heavens or running wildly for shelter—it took me a moment or two to realize the meaning of it all, and I had scarcely done this when I got very practical proof. A hundred yards away a bomb fell on a street island, shivering every window-pane in a wide radius, and sending splinters of stone flying about my head. I did what I had done a hundred times before at the Front, and dropped flat on my face.

The man who says he doesn't mind being bombed or shelled is either a liar or a maniac.

This London air raid seemed to me a singularly unpleasant business. I think it was the sight of the decent civilized life around one and the orderly streets, for what was perfectly natural in a rubble-heap like Ypres or Arras seemed an outrage here...

It was similarly outrageous to have shells from a long range gun rain down, on a billet in the Maire's house in a Flanders village, where he describes a room upholstered in cut velvet, wax flowers on the mantelpiece and oil paintings of the family on the wall:

> it was horrible to have dust and splinters blown into that smug, homely room, where if I had been in a ruined barn I wouldn't have given two thoughts. In the same way bombs dropping in central London seemed a grotesque indecency. I hated to see plump citizens with wild eyes, and nursemaids with scared children, and miserable women scuttling like rabbits in a warren.
>
> —Another bomb fell to the right, and presently bits of our own shrapnel [from the ack-ack guns] were clattering viciously around me. I thought it was about time to take cover, and ran shamelessly for the best place I could see, which was a tube station. —One stout lady fainted, and a girl had become hysterical, but on the whole people were behaving well. Oddly enough they did not seem inclined to go down the stairs to the complete security of the underground; but preferred rather to collect where they could still catch a glimpse at the upper world, as if they were torn between fear of their lives and interest in the spectacle.

The Special Constables played a vital role in the response of the civil authorities to the Zeppelin raids but it is now difficult to ascertain to what degree their contribution was recognised. A Special Constabulary Long Service Medal was instituted 30 August 1919 and though inscribed with the recipient's name, no date or place name is given.[19] There is no medal roll, and in the absence of any surviving list of local Specials it is only if the individual history of a medal is known (from members of the family, newspaper cuttings etc.) that we can identify with certainty the person whose name it bears. To qualify for war service the Special Constable must have served without pay for not less than three years, and have performed at least fifty duties a year, as well as be recommended by a chief officer of police as a person 'willing and competent to discharge the duties of special constable as required'.[20] The contribution of the women of the Voluntary Patrols and Britain's first women policemen and patrollers are unknown to the public at large and it is a great pity that we lack the names of most of them and any detail of the duty rosters of these brave and pioneering individuals.

The air raids of the Great War have been largely forgotten and it is the appalling casualties of trench warfare and the mass advances of infantry against a hail of machine gun fire that is still such a part of the public consciousness.[21] So much so that it is difficult to believe that this all took place nearly a century ago.

CHAPTER 20

Anti-War Propaganda and the Bolshevik Scare

So called 'Hostile leaflets', defeatist or anti-war publications regarded as likely to undermine the war effort, were put on official lists circulated to the police throughout the country, and in 1917–18 were included in the *Special Constables' Gazette*. When discovered such material was to be confiscated and destroyed.

It is interesting that Hostile Leaflets, Circular No. 10, specifically refers to 'A statement made by Second Lieutenant S. L. Sassoon to his commanding officer explaining the grounds for refusing to serve further in the army'. Siegfried Sassoon, the noted war poet, after being awarded an MC, and recommended for the VC, following a series of recklessly brave encounters with the enemy, became sickened by the destruction and waste of life and wrote his 'Finished with war- a soldier's declaration'. The full text of this was read in parliament by a sympathiser.

The Russian revolution and overthrow of the Tsar in October 1917[1] resulted in a fear of the spread of Bolshevism right across Europe. On 29 October 1918 Admiral von Hipper plans for a last ditch assault by the 'Hochseeflotte' was foiled by the mutiny of his battleship crews. Sick of war, poor food and lack of shore leave the men raised the red flag of revolution. This prevented a futile face-saving gesture by their officers which would have merely delayed the inevitable. A fortnight later the Armistice was signed and the war was finally over.

From late 1917 many of the proscribed titles listed in the Gazette are indicative of content of a more distinctly socialist, anti-establishment and anti-imperial nature and include literature advocating independence for India, the very symbol of the British Empire.

CHAPTER 21

Lessons Learned

After the Great War government officials and aviation experts certainly had not disregarded the impact of aerial bombing and thought deeply on how to ameliorate its effects and provide shelter for the civilian population. The central tenet of Giulio Douhet's influential *Command of the Air* (1921) was that 'the bomber will always get through', with potentially devastating results.[1] The planners concluded the population could be offered the protection of shelters combined with an effective warning system. These measures combined with trained personnel to enforce a blackout and guide threatened citizens to safety would enable morale to be maintained and air warfare against the civilian population successfully resisted.

There had been a degree panic and disorder, principally during the first raid on Hull, but this had never communicated itself to the city as a whole. When people became more convinced that anti-aircraft protection was in place, though on more than one occasion this conviction was proved to have been misplaced, their confidence grew. Despite this whenever the buzzers sounded it was a signal for an exodus to the parks and countryside. Given the relatively localised areas affected by bombing and the lack of proper shelters this was probably a sound reaction and took hundreds, even thousands, of individuals out of harm's way. Unlike the bombing in the 1939-45 when large swathes of a town were hit simultaneously and trekking became a dangerous response. Under these circumstances, unless they had set off long before the bombers arrived, people were likely to be exposed to severe danger and were much better off in a shelter.

The authorities during the Great War were however clearly worried about trekking and the dramatic decrease in the sounding of raid alarms after 1916 indicates that thereafter the buzzers were only blown when the threat was considered to be at a high level. While defences were under the control of General Ferrier[2] the alarm was blown as soon as an airship was sighted (usually as it crossed the coast of Holderness) but after General von Donop took command only when danger clearly threatened the town.[3]

In the early years, despite the great numbers of false alarms, no casualties are recorded as a direct result of a rush to safety unlike London in October 1917. Surprisingly there was no system of buzzers in the capital and rocket maroons were sent up as the alarm. On that occasion the maroons were mistaken for bombs and a stampede down into the 'underground' for shelter resulted in fourteen dead and as many injured, mostly women and children.[4]

It was very fortunate that up to the autumn of 1916 when the country was practically defenceless that the German's had not intensified their attacks, but instead they were long gaps of weeks or months between one raid and the next. Similarly, with the advent of the 'super Zeppelins', outside the capital there was a lack of aircraft powerful enough to pursue and reach their foe at the higher altitudes.

On 13 June 1917 fourteen Gothas dropped a hundred bombs on London, killing 162 and injuring 432. Most of the damage was in the heart of the city but in the East End an infant class was hit. The overall result was the highest number of casualties of any raid in the war. No Gothas were lost on this occasion, another indication of the inadequacy of the anti-aircraft defences, even in the capital.[5]

The Air Raid Precautions committee was established in 1924 in direct response to Douhet's doctrine and the huge civilian casualties which this and the experiences of the Zeppelin and Gotha attacks seemed to predict.[6]

Not until the advent of radar in the 1930s, which gave 'eyes' to the defenders, could a coordinated and effective combination of fighter aircraft and ant-aircraft batteries be created. The government pamphlets and posters to inform the public of the steps to take for personal protection, and which were to become so familiar at the outbreak of war, were already being circulated in 1935.[7] Under the Air Raid Precautions Act of 1937 committees were set up throughout the country to direct and coordinate the necessary measures to protect the civilian population in every locality. The provision of shelters was a vital part of the preparations. These were a mixture of communal shelters, individual family shelters constructed in back gardens, and the Morrison shelter, a steel topped table with mesh sides for use inside the house.

Hull suffered greatly and was described by the wartime Home Secretary as the most bombed northern city during the Second World War, 'It suffered eighty-two raids during which some 1,200 people were killed and 152,000 rendered temporarily homeless. Of the city's 92,660 houses only 5,945 were undamaged'.[8]

CHAPTER 22

Summary of the Hull Raids 1915–1918 and Lists of Casualties

After May 1915 and the attack on London censorship was imposed on all information relating to the Zeppelin raids. The main sources for numbers and names of casualties are the *Hull Times* (1919), the lists associated with the Turner photographs, as well as the *Eastern Morning News*, and the *Hull Daily Mail*, 1916–18.

In the secondary sources there are a number of discrepancies largely concerning the names of those who died subsequent to the attack. The Simmons list contains a number of obvious errors including names which are transcribed incorrectly.[1]

There is no complete list of the injured; the *Hull Times* as well as the typewritten sheets associated with the Turner photographs record names of only some of the injured, some of whom died later. Examination of death certificates and coroner's records would yield details of the latter, but the names of most of the injured were apparently not recorded at the time.

Descriptions of the raids and details of the airships and their commanders are given by Jones who gives an overview of the attacks across Britain accompanied by maps plotting the movements of the raiders. Rimell provides biographical details of many of the key combatants, both the Zeppelin commanders and the RNAS and RAF personnel who pursued them.[2] Robinson used the war diaries of all the German naval airships in compiling his volume. Morris provides the earliest overview of the raids, both by airships and aeroplanes, but his work was superseded by Jones' five volume *War in the Air* (esp. volume 3, 1931, for the Zeppelin raids).[3]

John Hook's *This Dear, Dear Land*, 5 vols. 1995, which gives a summary of the effects of the raids throughout Britain (as well as the coastal bombardment), uses the Home Forces Intelligence Bulletins, preserved in the Imperial War Museum. Regarding Hull and East Yorkshire his researches add little to the material in the sources already listed above.[4]

George Thorp, a Hull architect and surveyor, kept a diary throughout the war and is the source for many quotations above.

1. Sunday 6 June 1915 [*L95*, Kapitanleutnant Heinrich Mathy][5]; twenty-one killed (one of these unidentified), five died of shock, fifty-two injured; total of seventy-eight casualties; Jones (1935) says twenty-four killed and forty injured.

Summary of the Hull Raids 1915–1918 and Lists of Casualties

[13 (or 10) High Explosive and 39 (or 50) incendiary bombs were recorded] The following list is verified from the *Eastern Morning News* 19 June 1915, a report of the coroner's inquest providing all of the names of the dead. See illustrations.

50 South Parade; Maurice Richardson 11 years 4 months and Violet Richardson 8 years 10 months (incendiary in front bedroom, both burnt). Their father was a driver in the RFA 9th Scottish Division, BEF in France.

21 Edwins Place, Porter Street; William Watson 67 (painter, Hull Corporation) and his wife Ann(i)e Watson 68 (or 58).

22 Edwins Place, Porter Street; Mrs Georgina Cunningham 27 (elsewhere given as Canningham).

39 Blanket Row; Norman Mullins 10 and George Mullins 15.

6 Blanket Row; Tom Stamford (or Stanford) 46 (these last three all killed in vicinity of Edwin Davis' store).

12 East Street; Jane Hill 45 and George Hill 47 or 48.

11 East Street, off Clarence Street; Edward Jordan (or Jordon; father a school cleaner) 10 years 6 months.

4 Walter's Terrace, Waller Street; Elizabeth (or Eliza) Slade (widow) 54.

3 Walters Terrace, Waller Street; Florence White 30 and George (or Isaac) White 3 years 6 months.

11 Walter's Terrace, Waller Street; Alfred Matthews 50

2 St Thomas's Terrace, Campbell Street; William Walker (elsewhere given as George)

62 or 63 (tanners labourer) and Millicent Walker 17 (tailoress) and Alison Priscilla Walker 30

Mr. A. Johnson 273 Anlaby Road (presumably he was visiting Campbell Street).

2 Sarah's Terrace; Emma Pickering 68 (burnt in bed, could not escape owing to 'rheumatic stiffness'). The body of a woman, never identified, was discovered in the ruins of Edwin Davis' drapery store.

Five died from shock:

20 St John's or St James' Square; Ellen Temple 50.

37 or 39 Walker Street; Elizabeth Pickard Foreman 39.

5 Alexandra Terrace, Woodhouse Street;[6] Hanna (or Annie) Mitchell 42

8 The Poplars, Durham Street; Sarah Ann Scott 36

93 Arundel Street; Johanna Harman or Almond 67

Arthur Kitchen, 11 Walker Street, seriously injured by incendiary while in bed, taken to Naval Hospital by a group of soldiers.

See Appendix IIa, note 3, regarding Florence White, Maurice Richardson, Edward Jordan and Elizabeth Slade.

The House Committee Minutes (pp. 144-5) of the Hull Royal Infirmary, for the meeting Wednesday 9 June 1915:

The Secretary reported on the recent air-raid that four cases were brought to the Infirmary dead & that eleven were admitted to the wards of which three have since died & 30–40 casualty cases were attended to some of these (about fifteen) being sent on to the Naval Hospital for further treatment.

2. Sunday/Monday 5–6 March 1916 [*L14*[7] Kapitanleutnant Alois Böcker; *L11* Korvettenkapitan Viktor Schütze[8]]; 18 dead, including 2 of shock, 60 injured; total of 78 casualties; Jones (1935) says 17 killed and 52 injured; see also Simmons p. 96.

[Twenty-one explosive and two incendiaries dropped by *L14* and ten HE and fifteen incendiaries by *L11*].

8 The Avenue, Linnaeus Street; Mira Lottie Ingamells 28 (dressmaker), Martha Ingamells 35 (waitress) and Ethel Ingamells 33 (confectioners assistant), three sisters.   Refreshment House, 23 Queen Street; Edward Slip(p) 43 or 45.

50 Little Humber Street; Frank Cattle 8.

Carr Lane, Trinity House, Master Mariners Almshouses (completely destroyed in 1939–45); Edward Le(a)dner 89 (burnt).

14 John Place, Regent Street; James William Collinson 63 (labourer)

33 or 39c Regent Street; James Pattison 68.

4 Post Office Entry, High Street; George Henry Youell 40 labourer).

32 Collier Street; Charlotte Naylor 36 (husband a dock labourer), and her children Ruby 8, Annie 6, Edward 4, Jeffery 2.

2 Queens Alley, Blackfriargate; James or John Smith 30 (dock labourer) (ran into the Street).

Almshouses, Posterngate; William Jones 80. Two died from shock.

32 St Lukes Street; Edward Cook 38

6 Williams Place, Upper Union Street; John Longstaff 70 or 71.

The House Committee Minutes (pp. 187-8) of the Hull Royal Infirmary, Wednesday 8 March 1916:

The Secretary reported the result of the Air-raid 5 March as follows:- Cases admitted 27/Brought in dead; 3/Died after admission; 4/Casualties about 25. The St Johns Ambulance people treated several minor cases in the Out Patients Dept. The following were present: Doctors Howlett, Harrison, Francis, Hain(s)worth, Grieve, McKay & Eve. Messrs Palmer, Jennison, Grainger, Howes, Simpson, Smith, Pennington, J. Isaac, C. Rees, M. Hennerslye.

3. Wednesday 5 April 1916 [*L11* Korvettenkapitan Viktor Schűtze] Only one bomb was dropped, on a private house in Portobello Street.

Hull Times 1919 claims no one killed or injured, but one person died of shock; other sources give 5 injured.

11 Cotton Terrace, Barnsley Street; Jesse Matthews.

Summary of the Hull Raids 1915–1918 and Lists of Casualties

4. Tuesday/Wednesday 8–9 August 1916 [*L24*[9] Kapitanleutnant Robert Koch]; 11 dead, 22 injured; total 33 casualties; Jones (1935) says 10 killed and 11 injured; see Simmons p.97.
   [Twelve HE and thirty-one incendiaries recorded].
   35 Selby Street; Mary Louisa Bearpark 44 and Emma or Emmie Bearpark 14.
   61 Selby Street; Rose Alma Hall 31, Elizabeth Hall 9 and Mary Hall 7.
   61 Walliker Street; Charles Lingard 64
   25 Brunswick Avenue, St Georges Road; Emma Louise Evers 46; ran into Walliker Street.
   4 Rowland Avenue, Arthur Street; John Charles Broadby or Broadley 3.
   Three died from shock:
   6 Sydney Terrace, George Street; Elisabeth Jane Bond 76
   32 Granville Street; Revd Arthur Wilcockson 86
   13 Henley's Terrace, Wassand Street; Esther Stoppart or Stobbart 21.

The House Committee Minutes (p. 216) of the Hull Royal Infirmary, 9 August 1916:

> The Secretary reported that as a result of the air-raid, 13 cases had been attended to at the Institution of which 9 had been admitted & of these one, a woman, had since died.

5. Saturday 2 September 1917 [*L23*[10] has been suggested but this was shot down 21 August off Denmark]; no bombs dropped; no casualties.

6. Monday/Tuesday 24/25 September 1917 [*L41*[11] Hauptman Kuno Manger]; no casualties, [Rimell says three casualties] [Sixteen HE bombs and twenty incendiaries].

7. Tuesday 12 March 1918 [*L63*[12] Kapitanleutnant Michael von Freudenreich]; one dead, three injured.
   9 Humber Avenue, Scarborough Street; Sarah Masterman 58, died of shock.

8. Monday/Tuesday 5–6 August 1918 [probably *L56* Kapitanleutnant Walter Zaeschmar,[13] or *L63* Kptlt M. von Freudenreich[14]]; only a smoke bomb dropped. No casualties.

TOTAL 57 dead, 151 injured—Total casualties 208

There were certainly casualties who later died of their injuries, but we do not know how many, 1918 was not the last time a German airship flew over Hull and there is a photograph of *Graf Zeppelin* (*LZ 127*) over the Rialto cinema, Beverley road, in 1934.¹⁵ It flew round the world in 1929, a flight sponsored by William Randolph Hearst the American newspaper tycoon, which took twenty-one days flying a total of 22,000 miles from New York eastwards to Europe, across Russia and Japan and over the Pacific back to New York. By 1934 *LZ 127* had crossed the Atlantic more than fifty times carrying over 27,000 passengers covering a total of 620,000 miles in a flying time of 9,635 hours.

The Hindenburg (*LZ 129*[16]), commissioned March 1936, at 804 feet long was slightly bigger than the *LZ 127* and impressed the crowds gathered in Berlin for the opening of the 1936 Olympics. The following year, 6 May 1937, the Hindenburg caught fire while approaching Lakehurst, New Jersey, and crashed in flames with the loss of thirty-five lives. After carrying tens of thousands of passengers on over 2,000 commercial flights the age of the rigid airship had come to a sudden and tragic end. The *Graf Zeppelin II (LZ130)* which flew for the first time on 14 September 1938 was never used for carrying passengers. Before being scrapped it was employed, 2–4 August 1939, on a reconnaissance mission over the east coast of Britain. The chief purpose was to discover whether Britain had a viable radio detection system, but despite recording mysterious antennae their instruments failed to confirm its existence.[17]

Acknowledgements

My thanks to Robin Diaper for access to the photographs, documentary material and artefacts in Hull Museums, and to Caroline Rhodes for images of the Zeppelin bomb and 'buzzer' in the museum store. To Paul Gibson for some outstanding images from his collection of local photographs and Robert Barnard for his ready help. A very special 'thank you' to Nigel Caley for use of his splendid airship library, containing rare and probably unique items relating to the Zeppelins. To David Baker for providing the illustration of the 'Paradox' specification sheet and bringing my attention to Gareth Jenkins' account of the raids on Bury St Edmunds. To Michael Pearson, archivist, Hull and East Yorkshire NHS Hospital Trust, Derek Grindell who lent me Count Zeppelin's book *Die Luftschiffahrt* and other airship publications, as well as sending many interesting nuggets of information regarding Zeppelin history. John Richards reminded me of the Zeppelin references in Stanley Duncan's diaries and Bill Harriman (BASC) kindly made them available to me.

Mike Boyd provided stimulating discussion and details of Special Constables' badges, Mike Thompson useful background reading on airships, while Tobias Flümann of the Zeppelin Museum in Friedrichshafen sought out wartime photographs of Zeppelins for me. Gareth Jenkins, formerly of the Moyses Hall Museum, his successor Chris Mycock, and Victoria Goodwin, Suffolk Record Office, at Bury St Edmunds, all responded enthusiastically to my enquiries. The staff of the Hull History Centre provided many vital documents and illustrations and Christine Brown, conservation officer brought my attention to the photographs of bomb damage, from the Hull City Engineers' department, which she discovered after the archives were transferred into the new History Centre. Simon Green and his colleagues at the Hull Central Library, with enthusiasm and efficiency tracked down source books essential to the writing of this study and the staff of the National Archives supplied copies of key documents.

I am further indebted to Dr David Neave, Dr Martin Evans, Dr Nick Evans and Capt. Coggin for commenting on various draughts of my manuscript.

Appendices

Appendix 1
List of Zeppelin Raids across Britain

(NB *the attacks by Gotha bombers, which entered service in 1917, and the later Giants, are not included.*[1])

The port of Dover close to the continent and both a naval and army base was raided over a hundred times; it received the first aerial bomb dropped on British soil 24 December 1914, though from an FF29 floatplane rather than a Zeppelin. Ramsgate, also on the Kent coast, experienced 119 raids. The first victim of the Zeppelins were Samuel Smith and Martha Taylor killed 19 January 1915 at Great Yarmouth bombed by *L3*. The first Zeppelin to be shot down by a British aircraft was the *LZ 37* brought down by Reginald Warneford VC, 7 June 1915, flying a Morane Saulnier, near Ostend.

Only two, *L14* and *L20*, out of eight airships, intending to attack Rosyth naval base and the Forth Bridge 2/3 May 1916 managed to reach Scotland. *L14* and *L22* attacked Edinburgh 2/3 April 1916; *L14* returned 2/3 May aiming for the Forth Bridge but his bombs landed in fields near Arbroath.

1915

- 19 January. Great Yarmouth and district [*L3* Kapitänleutnant Hans Fritz, and *L4*, Count Magnus von Platen-Hallermund; *L6* Oberleutnant zur Horst von Buttlar Brandenfels returned home with engine failure].
- 21 February. Colchester [*FF 29 Seaplane*].
- 14 April. Tyneside [*L 9 Wallsend*].
- 15 April. Lowestoft and East Coast [*L5* Lowestoft, *L6* Maldon].
- 16 April. Faversham.
- 29/30 April. Ipswich and Bury St Edmunds [*LZ 38*].
- 10 May. Southend-on-Sea [*LZ 38*].
- 16/17 May. Ramsgate, Margate [*LZ 38*].
- 26/27 May. Southend [*LZ 38*].

31 May. London; bombs dropped on Whitechapel, Stoke Newington; ninety-two bombs were located, thirty HE, but a good many failed to explode. There were three large bombs, one made a crater in Kingsland road, another buried itself in a garden to a depth of eight feet but did not explode, and another had gone through the roof and floor of a stable and was found seven feet deep. These were 150 lb and three feet in diameter. The Zeppelin had followed the tracks of: the Great Eastern Railway as far as Bishopsgate station where it dropped a bomb, and had then followed the branch line towards Waltham Abbey powder factory, but it dropped a bomb on the wrong side of the river and missed the factory altogether. From Waltham Abbey it turned east, and was not seen again.[2]

4 June. East and South East Coast [L10 Sittingbourne, Gravesend].

6/7 June. East Coast [L9 Hull].

16/17 June. Newcastle-upon-Tyne[L10].

3 July. Harwich.

9 August. East Coast [L9 Goole].

12 August. East Coast [L10 Woodbridge].

17/18 August. Eastern Counties [L11 Ashford].

7 September. Eastern Counties.

8 September. Eastern Counties and London [LZ74], Cheshunt, London; Skinningrove [L9]. A piece of crested china was recently sold: 'Model of first bomb dropped from Zeppelin on Skinningrove Ironworks Sept 8th 1915 at 9.30 p.m.'[3]; Dereham [L14].

11 September. East Coast.

12 September. East Coast.

13/14 September. East Coast.

24 September. L33 brought down by gunfire at Little Wigborough, Essex.

13 October. London Area and Eastern Counties [L16 Hertford].

1916

31 January. Norfolk, Suffolk, Lincolnshire, Leicestershire, Staffordshire and Derbyshire [L13] Scunthorpe; Stoke-on-Trent [L13]; Overseal, Swadlincote [L14]; Burton-on-Trent [L15, L19]; Tipton, Wednesbury and Walsall [L19 and L21]; Loughborough, Ilkeston, Burton-on-Trent [L20]; in the Midlands 67 people killed and 117 injured.

5/6 March. Yorkshire, Lincolnshire, Rutland, Huntingdon, Cambridgeshire, Norfolk, Essex, Kent; Hull, Killingholme [L11] and Beverley, Hull [L14].

31 March/1 April. East and North-East Counties [SL11 brought down] 31 March by Lt W. L. Robinson at Cuffley, Herts.; Sunderland [L11]; Stowmarket [L13]; Sudbury [L14]; L15 brought down near Margate; Bury St. Edmunds [L16]; Cleethorpes [L21]. In the collections of Hull Maritime Museum is a watercolour of the armed trawler *Olivine* (Hull fishing register H849), sending a boat to rescue the crew of the L15, Kapitänleutnant Joachim Breithaupt.[4] Returning from a raid on London she was damaged by the anti- aircraft batteries at Purfleet in the Thames estuary (31 March) and then attacked by Second Lieutenant Alfred de Bathe Brandon RFC flying a B.E.2c. Brandon dropped 1 lb explosive Ranken darts and small

incendiaries and the airship came down off Margate, near the Kentish Knock light vessel at 12.15 a.m., 1 April 1916. One of the crew drowned but the other sixteen were rescued. The painting, dated 1916, was made and signed by, J. S. Riches, probably one of the trawler crew.

2 April. South-East Counties of Scotland.
4 April. East Coast.
5/6 April. North-East Coast, Hull [*L11*]; Skinningrove [*L11*]; Evenwood [*L16*].
24/25 April. Norfolk and Suffolk, Dilham [*L11*]; Newmarket [*L16*].
25 April. Essex and Kent.
26 April. Kent.
2 May. North-East Coast and South-East Scotland, Carlin How [*L17*]; York [*L21*]; Skinningrove [*L23*].
17 June. South-East coast, Ramsgate [*L42*].
29 July. North-East and North Coast.
8/9 August. Whitley Bay [*L11*]; Hull [*L24*].
23/24 August. East (and South-East) coast, Scartho (Grimsby) [*L22*].
2 September. East and South-East Coast, Retford [*L13*].
2/3 September. East and South-East Coast, Essendon [*L16*]; Sandringham [*L21*]; Boston [*L23*]; Bungay [*L30*].
23/24 September. Essex and London, *L32* brought down at Great Burstead, Essex by 2Lt Frederick Sowrey, 24 September; *L33* brought down by artillery over London, 23 September.
24 September. Nottingham [*L17*].
25/26 September. South-East and North-East Coasts and North Midlands York [*L14*]; Rawtenstall [*L21*], Holcombe, Bolton, Astley Bridge, Bolton; Sheffield [*L22*].
1/2 October. East Coast etc. *L31* brought down by Lieutenant W. J. Tempest at Potters Bar, 1 October; Corby [*L34*].
27/28 November. Ten Zeppelins left Germany *L13*, *L14* (approached Hull no bombs dropped), *L16*, *L21*, *L22* (reached Selby, no bombs dropped), *L24*, *L35* and *L36* Yorkshire and Durham. York [*L13*]; *L34*, brought down at Hartlepool by 2Lt Ian Vernon Pyott. *L21*, initially attacked Leeds and then headed south-east and was brought down off Lowestoft by Sub Lt E. I. Pulling, Flt Lt E. Cadbury and Sub Lt. G. W. R. Fane.

1917

16 March. South-East Counties.
23 May. Eastern Counties.
16/17 June. Suffolk. *L48* came down at Leiston, 17 June, after an attack by the aircraft of Lt L. P. Watkins using Pomeroy bullets; the crew buried at Theberton, Suffolk, but later transferred to Cannock.[5]
21 August. Yorkshire Coast 2 September. East Coast.
24/5 September. North-East Coast. Hull [*L41*].
18 October. A Zeppelin bomb demolished the front of Swan and Edgar's, Piccadilly, at 11 p.m.[6]
19/20 October. Birmingham [*L41*]; Northampton [*L45*].

1918

12 March. Hull [*L63*].
12/13 March. North-East Coast. Hartlepool [*L42*].
12 April. South and Eastern Counties etc. Wigan [*L61*]; Birmingham *L62*].
20 May. Eastern Counties 5 August (Bank Holiday). Eastern and North-Eastern. Peter Strasser, Fregattenkapitan of the German naval Zeppelins, killed when *L70* was brought down in flames off the Norfolk coast.

National Statistics

A total of 554 aerial raids on Britain; 5,611 casualties, killed and injured.
Air ship raids 217: 557 killed, 1,358 injured (i.e. an average of eight casualties per raid).
The recorded number of deaths should no doubt be higher if we take into account those who were injured, but died some days, or even weeks, after a raid, but these figures are unknown.

Number that crossed the English coast: 202 airships; 452 aeroplanes.

Weight of bombs dropped 205 tons, airships; 75 tons, aeroplanes.
Aeroplane raids 282: 857 killed, 2,050 injured (an average of ten casualties per raid).

Naval raids 55: 157 killed and 634 injured

Enemy airships brought down, two by AA guns, eight by aeroplanes. Enemy aeroplanes brought down, thirteen by AA guns, nine by aeroplanes.

From the airship raids Hull suffered ten per cent of the total number of fatalities nation-wide.

Appendix IIa
The reports, correspondence and photographs submitted by T. C. Turner after the first raid on Hull, 6–7 June 1915 are now in the National Archives, Kew, Richmond, Surrey:

Report AIR1/619/16/15/355; Report and correspondence AIR1/564/16/15/79; Report and correspondence AIR1/569/16/15/142 Photographs AIR1/569/16/15/142/1-45; the places recorded are as follows and bombs are identified, I = incendiary and E = explosive. The river Hull flows north/south and enters the Humber dividing the city into two separate communities, to the west and east:

WEST HULL; Edwins Place, Porter Street E; Sarah Ann's Place, Porter Street I; St Thomas's Terrace, Campbell Street E; 102 Great Thornton Street I; Edwin Davis' store I; Fleece Inn, next door to Edwin Davis' store, destroyed I; 39 Blanket Row, Mullins grocer, bomb set fire to where three boys were sleeping I; Upper floor 18 Great Passage Street, A. T. Hiller's shop I; 11 Walker Street I; 154 Walker Street I; Upper floor of motor garage and lower floor with two burnt out motors,109½ Constable Street I; High Street, hole six feet across created by explosive bomb breaking a one-inch-thick hydraulic pressure pipe[1] E; High Street, Grimsby Lane E; 50 South Parade, Porter Street I; the Rabbit market, Feller Lane off Queen Street. Bomb fell through corrugated roof and burnt out the market stalls I; Skyton Gate (Myton Gate is no doubt intended), an unoccupied house I; 153 Coltman Street, empty house I; Humber dock, cargo lighter Crocus E.

EAST HULL Walters Terrace, Waller Street, looking towards Southcoates station, and other views E; 3 Ellas Terrace, looks onto Walters Terrace I; 30 Bright Street, Palmer's grocer's, destroyed I; St. Pauls Terrace, Clarence Street E; 11–12 East Street, Clarence Street E; Clarence Street, on wooden blocks of roadway I; yard of St Mary's Roman Catholic school, Wilton Street, hole twelve inches across and ten inches deep, through asphalt into clay below I; Victoria dock, Wades timber yard, Tower Street, dropped on railway line E; Wades timber yard, through roof of shed I; Victoria dock basin, fell on concrete of the composition deck making a two inch dent, SS *Igos*, Capt. Chris Johnson Helsingburg I; Alexandra dock, fell 250 yards north of coal conveyor among pile of pit props which were scattered E; Hewetson's saw mill and timber yard, Dansom Lane, various views I and E; Lears Stables, Dansom Lane I; Craven Street football ground, 200 yards from centre of east stands, fell on the grass, no damage, but burned out leaving a crater twelve inches across and ten inches deep I.

Turner photographs in the Hull Maritime Museum; in shallow green cardboard box with printed inscription 'TURNER AND DRINKWATER Photographer to the Royal Family Established 1859, Regent House Hull':

Mounted on card; photograph 8 x 5½ inches and 11 x 8 inches overall:
Zeppelin bomb, mounted and with two inscribed brass plaques; probably 50 kg 2. An array of deactivated HE bombs W 3. 'Golden Lion' public house, Queen Street; 4. Rabbit market; 5–6. Thomas's Place, Campbell Street; and St Thomas's Church; 7. Collier Street; 7. Edwins Terrace, Porter Street; 9. Turners Place, Campbell Street E; 10–11. Waller Street: 11. Sawmill, Dansom Lane.

Unmounted 8 x 5½ in:

WEST HULL 1 & 2. Edwin Davis' drapery store; 3. 154 Walker Street; 4–5. Mr and Mrs Scott, 154 Walker Street; 6–7. Thomas Place, Campbell Street; 8–13. Porter Street, including Edwin's Terrace and 2 Sarah Ann's Place; 14. 102 Great Thornton Street; 15. Premises at rear of Market Hall (rabbit market); 16–18. High Street.

Appendices

EAST HULL 19–20. Church Street (in background, the 'Ship Inn', Prospect Place and sign of Alfred Harrison, builder, Beeton Street); 21–24. Waller Street; 25–26. Explosive bomb: Wade's timber yard on Tower Street; bomb dropped on railway line which bent it to an angle of forty degrees and made a hole ten feet deep, 2-5 inch indents in the bricks of John A. Scott warehouse; 27. Incendiary bomb; Victoria dock, Citadel estate, timber stacks; 28. Citadel estate; timber on railway wagons, large crater in foreground; 29-31. Sawmills, Dansom Lane; 32. Vessel in Victoria Dock; 33. Allotments, Marfleet; 34. Bright Street; 35-44 not identified.

Photographs by Turner and others of the effects of the Zeppelin attacks were reproduced in the newspapers immediately post war; a selection can be seen in one of the cuttings books compiled by George Thorp.[2]

The Turner photographs as well as capturing the physical effects of the bombing are social documents illustrating the interiors of dwellings in some of the most deprived areas of the city.[3] The bedrooms of some of these rented properties captured by the camera are starkly bare and empty with little sign of furniture (except for what might be packing cases) other than a bed. Other pictures show bedsteads, charred bedding and burnt walls.

See also National Archives 'Zeppelin raid-night of 5/6 August 1918, aeroplanes (including pilot's reports) 5/8/18–1/10/18' AIR 1/619/16/15/355. This gives details of the aircraft sent up to intercept the airships in what would prove to be the final raid of the war.

Appendix IIb
T. C. Turner's Report, transcribed from the Hull Times.

Part One
The Zeppelin Raid on Hull, June 6-7, 1915
11.45 a.m. to 12.15 a.m.

At the close of a perfect summer day, the sirens had sounded a Zeppelin warning, and curiosity and a lovely night caused the streets to be unusually full of people, even for a Sunday.

The wind blew softly and steadily from the north-west. Over the city the sky was clear, but in the fields and on the Humber flats patches of fog were rising.

At Immingham on the Lincolnshire side, a considerable amount of this ground fog had accumulated, and may have explained the absence of aeroplanes when the attack was on. An airship had been seen at Flamborough Head at 10.20 p.m., also away in Holderness lying low at 10.30; at Hornsea at 10.40, and off Withernsea as well.

At Hornsea she is said to have dropped a green flare, which may have been a signal to another airship, which many people persist in saying accompanied her to East Yorkshire as an observation vessel.

I saw only ONE airship, and am quite sure only one airship raided Hull on this occasion. Just after 11 p.m. the Zeppelin moved from Westella (on the west of Hull) towards the city, following the railway line as far as Dairycoates, at which point she veered out over the Humber.

A remarkable story was narrated to me by a lady client (living at New Holland, on the Lincolnshire side) on the morning after the raid. Her husband, abed at the time, heard the sound of motors in the air, and looking out of the window saw on the road the light of a motorist flashed several times towards the vessel, and then the man, quickly replacing his lamp, rapidly vanished down the Barton Road. The Zeppelin proceeded down the Humber. Steering eastward, and while still over the Humber, the airship dropped two white or yellow flares, which the wife of a dock gateman, living at the side of the Albert Dock lock-pit, saw fall, into the Humber from a considerable height.

When opposite or a little beyond Marfleet (on the Yorkshire side), she turned in towards the land and the raid commenced over the new King George Dock. The raid began at 11.45 p.m., June 6th and officers and men of the mercantile marine whom I interviewed assured me that two or three incendiary bombs fell in the water of the King George Dock, while they were on vessels in that dock. They also confirmed the statements that before the raid the Zeppelin came down the Humber from the west.

As the Zeppelin advanced towards Hull from the east a gunner on one of H. M. ships on the slipway at Earle's Yard (the Adventurer?) opened fire with shell and, as if taken by surprise, she shot out some distance over the Humber, but, quickly returning, she launched her first explosive bomb, which fell (not very far from the ship itself) within the Alexandra Dock Reservation. At the same moment an incendiary bomb was released, which reached the ground about 100 yards towards the south east of this spot, and within an area stocked with piles of pit props. The simultaneous arrival on the ground of explosive and incendiary bomb at one spot materially affects the chances of creating a great fire. (See Hewetson's big timber fire).

From the enemy point of view the chief factors counting towards a successful raid seem to be:

a. Absence of strong wind.

b. Low velocity of the airship when bombing.

c. Low elevation [ie. low altitude] when releasing bombs.

d. Sufficient daylight to distinguish areas marked on maps.

e. At night, when this is not possible, I fear there may be sudden outbreaks of fire, started within the city by enemy agents.[2]

Probably considerations of weight prevent the Germans from making explosive and some of the incendiary bombs of identical weight and size, so that when released together they shall fall together at one spot.

The course of the airship is clearly marked on the large map in red, and that portion, which is beyond all contention correct, is furnished by the bombs themselves (marked black for explosive and red for incendiary). The order in which the bombs fell is given by the numbering on this map, and on the photographs. The first part of the raid up to the east bank of the River Hull was an attempt to fire all Drypool by a huge conflagration of timber yards and saw mills which extend around and northwards from, the Victoria Dock.

Probably bomb 15 was intended for Rank's immense flour mill, and it is significant that, after leaving the district of circle B (Holy Trinity Church and the Old Town Area.) she went back to Rank's Mill. I cannot help thinking some undiscovered bombs lie in that direction or else this retour becomes meaningless. (Many months afterwards one was found in Scott's warehouse). The Zeppelin could have gone right on due west from the church, destroying valuable dock and railway property, without making the long course of apparent uselessness before commencing to bomb again at No. 27.

This long course of quiet progression (about 10 minutes) might have been necessary to get fresh bombs into position for release, or to make fresh calculations as to wind pressure or height. At all events when she recommenced at Bomb 27, she was much lower, and her object from. No. 27 to No, 40 seems plain.

She must have been seeking to destroy the great goods sheds, railway sidings, and dock warehouses of the North Eastern Railway Co. (which practically stands for Hull). Bomb No. 40 was possibly aimed at the headquarters of the Wilson Line, or at the Kingston-street Goods Depots. How they came to miss the marks is difficult to account for, unless they hoped to lay waste the whole dense neighbourhood of small houses by fire, and trust to its overwhelming the riverside, fanned by the north-westerly breeze. It will be noticed that the red bombs in nearly every case fall away towards the S. E. of the line in which the vessel is travelling, as marked by the heavier explosive bombs. I suggest that this was due to the prevailing N. W. wind carrying the lighter, more slowly descending incendiary bombs (with their larger area of wind surface) too far away from the zone of the explosives.

To this accident may have been due the comparative immunity from wide- spread havoc. For in Hull we had no defence. Aeroplanes were ineffective through the ground fog, and, after the first momentary surprise shown at the fire of the gun at Earle's, the airship commander showed his contempt for common shell by descending to a low elevation when, on this return trip from west to east, he tried to fire the Hessle road area.

The Zeppelin was impressive. I had never seen a Zepp. before, but I have known Germans at, Hamburg, who have often described them to me. The vessel seemed to be under complete control ascending and descending easily, and with remarkably free turning movements. I should think she must have been 600 foot long.

There were three cars under the balloon and they appeared to be worked by a system of loud sounding gongs, such as one hears in a ship's engine room. When over the West Park the ringing of these signals could be distinctly hoard as the vessel made the big turn round. When standing in front of the Royal Station Hotel, Paragon Square, I first heard the distant booms, and at last saw the Zeppelin come up into view. She was very high. She appeared as a black bar against a clear, cloudless, greenish sky such as one sees in the North of Scotland or at Bergen in the summer. In fact, I do not remember an England so light at mid-night as on this occasion.

I tore pieces of paper out of my time-table and found that a strip one inch long by ¼ in. wide hold at arm's length represented her size against the sky, and I imagined her to be about 14,000 ft, high. (Have seen scores of balloons ascend from the Crystal and Alexandra Palaces in my younger days).

The appearance just before she finished her raid was vastly different; she had, from bomb 27 to bomb 45, descended so low that, in the words of the fisher people and workers living in the Hessle-road district she had become as 'large as a big trawler,' 'as large as a whole terrace of houses,' and that when she slowly floated over the terraces she 'looked like a great black cloud shutting out all the view of the sky over head for a moment.' It was very low, probable less than a thousand feet.

As the Zeppelin was again nearing my house and passing between the Humber and Anlaby Road going eastwards, a great explosion (Porter-street) made the basement floor quake, and a cloud of very black smoke drifted along above the housetops.

One more explosion over the Humber Dock, and the raid on Hull was over at 12.15 a.m., June 7th.

From this point, the Zeppelin did not follow a direct course down the Humber and out to sea, but rapidly ascending she steered over the town in a north-easterly direction towards Wyton (where an incendiary bomb was afterwards found).

One may speculate as to motive. Was it to have another view of the big fires then raging at Davis's drapery store, next to Holy Trinity Church, and at Hewetson's timber yard in Dansom-lane.

Was it, to have another shot, at Rank's Mill, which was not on fire? Or was it to take no risks from the gunner at Earle's shipyard?

At all events, the Zeppelin followed the line of the Holderness-road, as far as Wyton before turning south over Preston and Hedon, and then, avoiding Immingham, made for Grimsby.

Arrived there at 12.30 or 12.40 she dropped six more incendiary bombs, which appear to have done very small damage. The distance from Hull to Ghent is 212 miles (Hull Navigation School calculation), and allowing her speed to be 60 miles an hour, travelling light, and perhaps something extra with a north-west wind on her beam, she might well be the Zeppelin Lieut. Warneford met coming in from the coast and destroyed at 3.30 a.m.[3]

End of Part 1, which gives all the essential particulars of the raid itself. In the next few sheets these details are elaborated, and the question of defence in case of future visits touched upon with apologies, as they are the views of a civilian, with no military knowledge, and may, therefore, be of no value.

(Note.—This first part was written in June, 1915. It is our duty never to forget these things. For if we forget it will be a sign, not that we have grown more Christian, but that we have become more callous. T. C. T.)

The second half of the report concerns the tactical and strategic considerations raised by the Zeppelin raids and elements, like the case for a military road along the coast, and despite what the author says, are suggestive of the author having consulted an officer or officers in the military establishment at Hull, possibly with General Ferrier himself, who was soon to be replaced by Von Donop (AGC).

Part II
(This second part was completed at the request of the Intelligence Department)

Watching the Zeppelin at work from a distance of half to three-quarters of a mile, one could distinguish when explosive and when incendiary bombs fell. On reaching the earth the ex- plosive bomb caused an extremely instantaneous wink of light over the vault of the sky.

And so brief in duration that the nearest description is the breaking of an electric contact, such as a trolley pole on a tram overhead wire, viewed from a neighbouring street to that in which it occurs. A dull, heavy, bursting boom followed some two or three seconds afterwards.

The incendiary bomb gives a peculiar metallic ping—perhaps the sound of crashing slates at a distance—and a rich amber colour glows on the underneath side of the Zeppelin, probably due to the flare up of the thermite (?), petrol, and tar, when the flame first rushes up after striking (this flame is about 12ft. high). The amber light on the airship lasts about four seconds, then fades away, leaving the skin once again black against the greenish background of the night. Later in the autumn while living at Bridlington (just below Flamborough Head) I saw on more than one occasion distant glare on the clouds, which came and lasted for just such a brief period, and lighting small areas on the screen of clouds vividly suggested incendiary bombs. The raid on Lowestoft, I believe it was on the 8th Sept., showed quite clearly in this way, and an hour or two later (about 1a.m.) and in direction due south of Bridlington I detected these spots of light in the clouds, very faintly, but unmistakably again. I surmised they might be over London, and wiring to my relatives there, found Walthamstow had been also attacked.

The shape and construction of the incendiary bombs are now too universally known to need description, but several photographs have been taken to give an idea of their striking force at high and low elevation, and on variously resisting surfaces eg.

Bomb 4 – on a football ground

Bomb 6 – falling through a house, when airship at its highest

Bomb 10 – on an asphalted school yard, showing height of flame [4](12 ft.)

Bomb 12 – on wooden street blocks

Bomb 16 – on a ship's deck

Bomb 17 – on closely stacked deals

Bomb 20 – piercing and breaking down a corrugated iron roof

Bomb 24 – cutting very clean hole in ceiling and stopping on first floor and others.

Illustrations are given to show how important it is to know what may happen and guard against panic. Bomb 32 hit a house in South-parade and fell through the ceiling into a bedroom in which the wife of a soldier in France slept with her two children. She rushed screaming out of the room and the children were burnt to death.

But when bomb 37 fell on 154 Walker-street, Mrs Scott retained sufficient presence of mind to fling the bedroom utensils[5] at the flames, and to shout for her husband to bring pails of water. The photograph shows these people, and the success with which they attacked the fire, even though the roof was in chaos through the bomb hitting the wall and disturbing the rafters [see illustrations].

Human courage under the stress of such emergency must operate unequally, but a higher general level of bravery would be shown if the public could be educated to the real character of incendiary bombs, and the possibilities of averting tragedies and serious loss of property. The Press could surely be used to spread a great deal of useful information, so that people would not be so inclined to leave their homes to the Fire Brigade, instead of attacking the fire bomb promptly themselves.

In the war of incendiarism by Zeppelin it is surely of the greatest importance that the whole community should learn its duty as fire-fighters if the nation is to be spared irreparable loss.

It is conceivable that Germany will, in the absence of great military or naval success against the British, supplement her submarine policy on the sea with the ruthless destruction of property on land, by conflagrations. It may be that in the European race to bankruptcy she is determined to destroy as much of her enemy's capital as she can and the fact that the policy carries with it the chance of ruthless murder, may weigh as little on land as at sea.

Yet it is hard to believe she does not by this time realise the futility of breaking a nation's spirit by threats of 'frightfulness' nor that she wishes deliberately to pile up undying odium through inhuman crimes such as follow the use of high explosive bombs on non-military places. Rather one must consider the use of the high explosive bomb less as a means of terrorism than as a factor in producing great fires [This was written, of course, before the second raid, March 6th 1916]. In the Hull raid the destruction of human life by high explosive was extremely small (about 24 died through both kinds of bombs and this loss of life in a population of over a quarter of a million is too negligible to have a terroristic 'Bernhardian'[6] effect).

But if a great city like Hull is successfully set on fire and burned to the water's edge the economic effect of such a catastrophe would be immediate and of national importance.[7] And looking at this map and carefully considering the line of attack this seems to have been the real object.

At first I thought it was a military raid intended to destroy the junction of railways and docks and to render the city still more defenceless against a sudden raid on the Holderness coast, and the bombing of Driffield junction a night or two before gave colour to this assumption.

When the war broke out, such a sudden descent might have been momentarily successful and the effect of a raid across the heart of manufacturing England to which Hull opens from the North Sea, would have been tremendous. Hull people have an implicit and affectionate faith in the British Navy, and although they know or think they know, two danger spots on the Holderness coast it has not greatly affected the 'residential trains'[8] leaving for the Coast each night.

Yet fogs often enshroud our coast. The navy has had serious losses by mine and submarine. The Germans locked up in Kiel have had few. No one knows how strenuously naval construction has gone on in Germany the last 17 months, or what surprise venture may be undertaken by a nation that reckons not the cost of human lives.

Therefore it may be wise to regard Zeppelin visits of military importance as well as economic, and to endeavour to compass their destruction with as much vigour as the Navy showed against submarines.

There are few things more distressing than to see a Zeppelin hover, with an undisturbed deliberation, near one's home and to know that neither guns nor aeroplanes are opposed to it.

And however stringent lighting regulations are applied, it is against British traditions to trust to darkness for safety, and to make the population cower under what is, after all, an uncertain defence.

What could be easier in a port like this than for alien enemies to start guiding fires when the siren alarms have given warnings.

The provision of guns would go far to calm popular anxiety and to prevent what may be one, if a minor aim of a Zeppelin policy, the terrorism of the very poor and miserable, whom the war may have rendered extra discontented, and perhaps, wavering in their patriotism.

These poorer classes deserve special consideration, for they live in dangerous localities, near the docks, and in such ramshackle houses that if an explosive bomb hits, it is pretty sure to kill.

Then the natural position to fight Zeppelins seemed to be at the coast, and not to wait for them to attack inland cities, where the damage from our anti-aircraft guns might equal or exceed the damage done by the enemy.

Hull and the Holderness coast have many advantages for the purpose, but we want a new military road making close to the sea to avoid serious detours. I have sent three maps of the Holderness district, which shows the need of something better than a mere galloping track over the grass.

This is of especial importance between Bridlington and Barmston, further south, for the old coach road has long since disappeared into the sea. With such a new road from Bridlington to Spurn and from Spurn to Hull, patrolled by an adequate motor service with gun, dynamo, and searchlight, and made to run on road or railway, great things might be done.

Aeroplanes are so handicapped by 'sea-rokes'[9] on this coast and the Zeppelins can keep still and listen for their whereabouts and then retreat into a cloud or go up to an unapproachable height. With mobile gunnery they could be better caught 'on the hop' and in unexpected places.

The progress of the ordinary sea artillery defences of the Humber which appear to be under some extremely live gunnery officer, or officers, is continually referred to in Hull with admiration.

Many people regarded the port as practically undefended when the war broke out, and what has been done since is said to be remarkable, for the time which has been available.

Cannot something be done to provide a real anti-aircraft defence by these or equally energetic officers?

In any case Zeppelins lose half of their potential dangers if they are hustled, while if they are hit on the coast, the interior towns will be calmed, and cease making such a fearful outcry. Shall we in this district be too late, or an example of an intelligent anticipation of events? For Zeppelins will assuredly come this summer, if they stay till then [They did come a few weeks after writing this, on 6 March 1916: A. G. C.] Directly the Baltic is free of ice and timber begins to crowd our wharves and yards the Germans will seize the opportunity to burn, if they do not come to slay.

Hull is the gateway to Industrial England, and perhaps even London itself is of no greater importance than this crowded belt of manufacturing cities and towns which when Hull is endangered are seriously menaced as well.

T. C. TURNER

Appendix III
Photographs of the Hull Raids

The Turner photographs have already been discussed and those from the Hull City Engineers Department. A large selection of images, many of them by Turner, were published in the two memorial editions of the *Hull and Lincolnshire Times*, 25 January and 1 February 1919.

In the Nigel Caley collection there is an example of a tiny picture album 'reproduced from views from the Hull Daily News and Hull Weekly News'. Entitled *A pictorial record. Hull and the Zeppelins. Scenes of damage sustained in Hull 1915–1918 Price 6d.*

Inside the front cover there is a list of raids on Hull, the Humber and East Yorkshire region:

4 June 1915 Driffield—no casualties; 6 June 1915 Hull—25 dead, injured c. 100; 9 August 1915 Goole—16 dead; 31 January 1916 Scunthorpe—4 dead; 5 March 1916 Hull—17 dead c. 60 injured; 5 April Hull 1916—Zepps driven off; 9 August 1916 Hull— 9 deaths, several injured; 3 September 1916 Hull—Zepps driven off; 21 August 1917 mouth of the Humber—2 dead from shock [presumably casualties were in Lincolnshire]; 24 August 1917 Hedon—no casualties; 24 September 1917 Hull—no casualties; and 12 March 1918 Hull—no casualties.

There are ten images, printed five on either side of a concertina pull out. Most do not give name of the photographer and were presumably taken by newspaper staff, while those with name credits were clearly taken by freelances:

Roof of St. Thomas' church, Clarence Street (Watson, Hull); House in Campbell Street, Anlaby Road (Watson, Hull); Campbell Street, Anlaby Road, Queen Street (Barnard, Hull); Holy Trinity church and Market Place (Barnard, Hull), Bright Street, Holderness Road; High Street, Hull's oldest property; Clarence Street[1]; Church Street, Drypool; Terrace in Waller Street, Holderness Road.

Marcus Barnard, a deaf mute, was first in partnership, c. 1901–1906, as a photographer with Mr Gledstone; both men were originally artists. He advertises himself as a 'marine photographer' and most of his postcard pictures were of ships frequenting the port. Both the shops he occupied were ideally placed for passing seamen and members of the public in the old town area, including the pier and the town docks. Continuing at the same address, 23 Humber Street, the heart of the Hull fruit market, he continued alone, though briefly in partnership, c. 1911–1914, with Thomas H. Straker (on the staff of the *Hull Daily Mail*). Thereafter he had his premises at 30 Queen Street, near the pier, c. 1915–1927 when he gave up the business having apparently inherited some money. The other freelance photographer was Robert Thomas Watson of 70 Anlaby Road, Hull, about whom nothing is known.

Appendix IV

See maps of the city, A and B, revised by Fryer, discovered during the transfer of the Hull Archives into the new History Centre among material which came from the City Engineers Department. In association was a folder containing a series of twenty-six photographs, apparently contact prints from quarter plate negatives, illustrating the bomb damage caused by the first raid.[1] There are eight sheets of foolscap cartridge paper each with three or four prints pasted on each. The sheets are numbered 14, 18, 19, 24, 25, 27, 28 which coincide roughly with the numbers on the first map and thereby suggesting that originally there were batches of photographs covering the bomb sites 1 to 30.

The grey blue folder stamped B6/17 on the outside is not the original container for the sheets, for inside the front flap is written, 'C. T. M. Begg Hull Corporation 1930' which suggests that they were discovered while tidying up old files, some dozen years after the end of the war.

These images were probably taken by someone in the engineers department and the viewpoints are not the same as in the Turner pictures; the picture most closely resembling a Turner photograph is that of Bright Street.

Each sheet is punched for insertion in a ring binder.

No. 14/1. Davis's from Market Place 2. Davis's from Vicar Lane 3. Davis's from east end of church, see windows in wall.

No.14/4. Davis's from east side of Market Place 5. Davis's from South Church Side 6. Davis's and Holy Trinity church from Market Place.

No.18/7. East side of High Street 8. 50 feet west of High Street 9. 100 feet west of High Street 10. West side of High Street.

No.18/11. East side of High Street 12. East side of High Street 13. High Street showing hydraulic power main and water main broken by bomb.

No.18/14. East side of High Street 15. West side of High Street. 16. Damaged chimneys and roofs 100 feet to west of High Street.

No.18/17. Wall at end of Grimsby Lane, near High Street.

No. 19/18. Wall of building 45 feet from where bomb fell. 19. Hole in building opposite where bomb dropped.

No. 24/20. St Pauls Avenue from Prospect Place [visible are the sign boards of 'C. Harrison, joiner and undertaker, builder, jobbing bricklayer and plasterer, estimates free']. 21. St Pauls

Avenue from destroyed houses 22. East Street from Clarence Street. 23. St Pauls Avenue looking towards destroyed houses.

No. 28/24. Dansom Lane front [entrance to J. A. Hewetson & Co. Saw Mills]. 25. Bright Street front. 26. From Bright Street & showing site of no. 27 shop and house corner of Braidwood Place.

Appendix V
Memories of an Old Town 'Special'[1]

Was sworn in December, 1914, and posted for air raid duty in the Old Town, two miles away from home, with one valiant special to assist. Then followed a hunt for recruits. After many nights' search, collected 20 good and suitable men, had them sworn in, divided up into sections, and duties detailed for execution when 'Mournful Mary' sounded. The next call upon one's time was the inspection of motor halts. This entailed one night per week, walking to the control hut, one mile from the tram terminus, at 6 p.m., 10 p.m., and 2 a.m., signing the men on and off duty, taking reports, etc. A nice job in the early hours of the morning on a wet or snowy night. This went on for over two years.

Then started the street patrol. At this period the fatherly Watch Committee kindly provided us with a suitable uniform, consisting of a cap—a splendid protection against inclement weather! The duties of an inspector consisted in visiting the Concentration Point at 3 p.m., 6 p.m., 9 p.m., and midnight, signing the men on and off duty, and going round the beats during one of the periods. This took another day each week out of one's wet and wicked life, and has continued for over two years. 'The powers that be,' not being satisfied that one had enough to do for the large remuneration that they paid for those valuable services [nothing per week and no bonus], started the Dock Guard at the Railway Dock. This meant visiting [one day per week] the Guard Hut at 2 p.m., 6 p.m., and 10 p.m., with a surprise visit in between, seeing the men on and off duty, taking reports, etc. This has lasted about a year.

Turning out at once on the air raid alarm being sounded was a small addition to the above pastimes—on some occasions four times in a week, lasting four or five hours at a time. This kept one from not feeling absolutely tired of life. In connection with all the above duties one had to undertake the necessary correspondence, interviews, etc., appertaining to each branch of the work, including the continuous reorganization of the arrangements necessitated by so many of the men joining the Navy or Army, and finding suitable men to fill the positions. Frequent attendance at the Police Court in the morning was another form of amusement that entailed several hours out of the few left to give evidence of offences against the laws and D.O.R.A. On the whole, a fairly strenuous time of it, the duties taking on an average about 17 hours per week, excluding the air raid alarm periods.

Now for some idea how Specials carried out their duties on a 'Buzzer' night. The district in question is divided up into sections, each in charge of a section leader who has a certain number of men allocated to him. On the alarm sounding, each man proceeds to his station, seeing that all lights are out on his way, and reports to his section leader. Then, if any case of lights being visible, and no reply received to his warning, the section leader, with some of the men, proceeds to force an entrance, either through the door or window, sometimes with the assistance of the fire escape. As soon as the streets of each section are covered, the leader reports same, and the number of men on duty, to the officer in charge at the Concentration Point. Some of the men are detailed for the purpose of directing and assisting people, into the various shelters provided for them, a description of which will be given later. Next comes the dreary period of waiting. Each section has to be continuously patrolled, the men (usually in pairs) keeping observation that no lights have been put on (which usually happens about supper time), and also to prevent groups of people collecting in the street, or at terrace ends, the rest of the men standing handy in case they are required. If no raid occurred and the 'relief' was sounded, the men were dismissed by the section leaders at the various points, who then report at the main Concentration Point.[2] In the case of an actual raid the special is a kind of general handy man, comforter, and consoler to all and sundry, and on occasion has had to act as fireman. Altogether, a giddy life!

A word must be said here for the valuable services rendered by the boy scouts attached to this division, who acted as despatch riders. One Scout was detailed off to each section leader, and the duties given them were many and various, especially acting as guides to old people, in the dark and devious streets and passages that have to be traversed. As a rule they seemed to take a delight in their duties, and the only regret one has, who had a deal of experience with them, is, that as soon as they got to be a real value, they were taken away into His Majesty's Forces. The discipline that was taught them at their Scouts parades etc., made them fit in at once with the routine required, and accustomed them to carry out their duties expeditiously and efficiently, under very trying and at times hazardous conditions.

May they long continue, and others like them! This is from 'one who knows.'

Another piece of work was the organization of a body of men to undertake the control of a number of large warehouses in the centre of the city. It was apparent that if one of these buildings was struck by an incendiary bomb, it was hardly possible for 'specials' or others to get about efficiently, owing to the fact that sometimes they would be full up with goods, hence the proper men to look after them were those who worked in the buildings and knew their way about. So the firm was approached, and the managing director giving his hearty co-operation to the proposed plan, ten of the foremen were sworn in as 'specials' for warehouse duty only, and about 40 men who were on staff of the firm were enrolled for the duty of guarding the warehouses on alarm nights. These men wore a distinctive armlet, and on an alarm being sounded each proceeded to his allotted place under the charge of the foreman, and remained on duty until the 'release' went. The managing director and his deputy took charge of the proceedings alternately. The arrangement proved most valuable, and relieved the leader in charge of this district of a lot of detailed responsibility. When this arrangement had been in vogue for a few nights the idea was formed that provision could be made for receiving and looking after a number of people living near, who were wandering about the streets looking for a place of safety, after their late experiences of an actual raid. So when the men were filling up the warehouses with foods, etc., spaces were left and provided with benches and lights, and the word passed round for them to come along. This accommodation was immediately taken advantage of with feelings of gratitude by many who previously had a harrowing experience. The relief from nerve strain was exhibited very plainly in the faces and cheery attitude of those who took advantage of the firm's consideration for their welfare. In one cellar, under five floors filled with grain, which made the shelter practically bomb proof, one could see three or four hundred women, children, and men, closely packed, perfectly comfortable, and as contented as could be expected under such trying conditions. The luxury of 'reserved seats' was afforded to the families of employees of the firm, and fully taken advantage of. Those shelters were inspected at regular intervals during the alarm period, and it was a pleasure to see the helpful and considerate attention of the men in charge to the people under their care.

In addition to these warehouses, provision was made in several of the Bank cellars for a number of people, living in the immediate vicinity, who eagerly took advantage of this accommodation.

In one cellar, under the kindly supervision of Mr. Metcalfe, 100-150 people, and on some occasions a greater number, were extremely comfortable. This was a 'shelter de luxe'.[3] Notwithstanding the number of people who used these shelters on so many occasions, there was never any cause for complaint or of damage being done, which clearly shows their appreciation of the arrangements made for their welfare.

Many and varied were the incidents that occurred. On one occasion lights were reported from a Government building, and on visiting the place, found six electric lights blazing, and no blinds drawn. As the caretaker with the key could not be found, a ladder was obtained, the window smashed, an entrance effected and the lights switched off. Summons and fine followed.

Another incident was the continuous blowing of a steamer's whistle. This was located in the darkness and found to be caused by the tide dropping and tightening a mooring rope across the whistle lanyard of a tug, lying in the Old Harbour. As it was dead low tide, pitch dark, and three other vessels between the quay and the tug, it was not a picnic to get this matter put in order—but it was done without delay.

On another occasion a light was reported shining on a whitewashed wall from a house where no reply could be got. As the constables had been instructed not to break into any premises unless told to do so by a senior officer, the 'special' went there and found a small boy, who answered to a gentle tap on the door. Asked if his father or mother were in, he replied 'No, only my grandmother.' 'Tell her I want, to speak to her.' 'You can't; she's dead,' was his reply.

So the constable went upstairs, put the light out in the room where the old lady was laid at rest, beyond the cares and terrors of the enemy up aloft, took the lad away, and looked after him until the relief sounded, and his parents could return.

Once in a narrow street an old man, about 80, stood on his doorstep shaking a stick up at the Zepp visible overhead, was heard to say, 'You -----, if I could reach you I'd break your ---- neck!' A good old sport!

Sometimes the ferry boat service was suspended.[4] Then we would have to deal with the passengers, who had nowhere to go, and no place or shelter provided for them. Some took the position philosophically; others insinuated that the 'specials' were the cause of their discomforture [sic].

One old gentleman, very irate after two hours walking up and down the Pier, having refused to go into a bank cellar, said (and really meant it),'I believe you've arranged this on purpose'. Having been instructed to be always polite and truthful, replied, 'Certainly! Will you please advise us when you are coming to Hull again, so that we can have arrangements made for a similar performance'. That 'put the-lid on it', so; we left him to blow off his superfluous steam in the early morning's river air.

Another time a light was shining over an archway, and as no distinguishing feature in the architecture could be used as a guide to which house the room in question belonged, after much difficulty an entrance was effected, and we found at once, with usual luck, that we were in the wrong place. This is the way it always happens! So we entered next door, and put the light out. Result: A summons and fine for one, and a most irate and ungrateful letter from the infuriated owner to the 'powers that be" from the other, whose dignity seemed more damaged than his door was in getting into the place. However, later on, after pointing out that what we had done was for his benefit, and on his realising that while we were shivering with cold and tiring ourselves out looking after his interests, when he was at home surrounded with every luxury, the matter was amicably arranged.

A rather amusing thing happened to a certain well-known hotel proprietor in the district, whose premises had twice been visited by 'dud' incendiaries, in addition to the halo of bombs that usually dropped in the immediate vicinity. Suffering from 'nerves,' he declared that he 'would never stop in the house again when 'Lizzie'[5] went, but go down to a friend's house on the Holderness-road, although his family took advantage of the shelters provided near to. This he did several times; then came a raid night, and an explosive bomb dropped at the back of the house he was in. Then he said that the Zepp. commander must have known his movements, and was after him personally, because no bombs were dropped in that part of the town he had left.

These are just a few of the many incidents that occurred, but the details of what happened when a raid took place and bombs dropped in this district are well known to the men who had to carry on, and better left to the imagination of those who were lucky enough to be away from the scenes.[6]

One cannot help remarking upon the devotion to duty, adaptability and resource in helping all who required assistance of the 'Specials' whose duty lay in this part of the town, which has earned them on several occasion the compliments and approval of the Chiefs.—R.

NOTE—Out of a total of 22 men originally sworn in as special constables in the Old Town, 13 have continued their duties to date.

Fifty-three men have been attached to this district during the last four years and four months, and out of this number the following numbers have left for the reasons below:—15 joined Navy or Army, three gone on munitions, three invalided out (following air raids) and eight removed or transferred.

Average attendance of men throughout 53 alarm nights 86 per cent. Average of hours on air raid duty at each alarm, 4 hours 33 minutes.—R.

Another piece appears in the second Zeppelin memorial edition of the *Hull Times*:

Another Town 'Special'

June 6th, 1915 Called out at about 10 p.m., on duty 10.15, and soon busy getting the people to put out their lights. Many laughed at us, said we were getting panicky, and gave it as 'their' opinion the 'Zepps' would never reach Hull. About 11.45 went to quell a disturbance in a court[7] in Blanket Row. Found a robust Amazon, whose chief hobby seemed to be 'punching' her 'better half': spoke in quite a policeman's tone of voice to her, and ordered her into her house; received the kind intelligence (garnished plentifully with swear words)that neither 'Chief Constable' nor police constable would get 'her' into the house, much less a —— special constable. Was just deliberating with my worthy colleague as to the best means of transporting the 'kind lady' to the 'Central Police Station' when in the distance was heard the noise of aircraft engines, and the report of explosions. This apparently had more effect on the 'lady' than all the majesty of the law, for she immediately whispered, really and truly whispered, 'What's that; by G—, it's a—Zeppelin' and vanished into her house. We then set off for the Market Place, and 'Great Scott, how we ran', and reached Grimsby –lane just as the brutes dropped their souvenir on High street. This had the effect somehow of blowing us back into the open, and our friend the policeman was down. Immediately a bomb was dropped on the Chicken Market, which burst into flames; another found its billet on the roadway opposite Bristow's shop,[8] which sent up a flame as high as the buildings on either side. By that time we had got a view of the Zepp, and saw the direction it appeared to be taking. In order to get a better view of proceedings we moved towards the open Market- Square when there was a sharp flash and a thud, followed by a short, sharp detonation, which spun me round and threw me to the ground. This was an incendiary bomb which had fallen into the premises of Messrs Edwin Davis and Co., not 20 yards from where I had stood. Quickly jumping up I saw the whole end of the premises were blazing furiously, and I met the caretaker and his wife coming out of their doorway. After ascertaining from them there was no human being left on the premises, we turned our attention to getting pipes and hose fixed from the fire box. The heat was terrific, indeed, it was impossible to approach nearer than 20 yards, and how the firemen bore it passes my comprehension. In a remarkably short space of time they were on the scene, and then followed a fight with fire which looked like getting the upper hand of them, and enveloping the whole block of buildings up to Mytongate end. They however succeeded in confining the flames to that block, and when it is remembered that there was also a large conflagration at a timber yard in Dansom-lane, and another in the Chicken Market, it will be admitted by all their task was herculean, in view of the shortness of their number.

By this time the town presented the appearance of a fair, crowds flocking in from all parts. It might have been 12 o'clock at noon instead of just after midnight. It was necessary to draw cordons across the roads to prevent the crowds getting to near the place. The heat was growing in intensity, and the windows all round were breaking in a most alarming manner with a sound like an explosion. In Blanket Row there was quite a panic, and when I and my colleagues went there we were met by a screaming crowd of men and women, all of whom were more or less hysterical, and it was impossible to ascertain with any degree of certainty what had actually happened. This was a pity, as perhaps if the specials had got the truth of the matter at the first they might have helped the two poor little chaps who were involved. I do not know for certain: I only say they might. However nothing seemed necessary but to try to calm down the people, and after having done our best in that direction, we returned to the Market-place, and were posted for various duties from which we were not relieved until after 6 a.m., when our places were taken by a number of H. M. Forces who were brought on the scene. We observed a 'lady' wreaking her vengeance with a boot,[9] but as she took to her heels and ran like a 'hare' we did not succeed in getting an interview with her. Before leaving this date. I would like to mention one humorous incident which occurred. On the Friday night previous we had been beguiling the time on duty by looking in the windows of Davis' shops, with the aid of our lamps, and choosing articles we would like to secure in the unlikely event of anything happening to those premises (little dreaming the Zepps had been as near as Driffield that night) I had chosen a big piece of linoleum. (I was contemplating marriage at the time, and was, in fact, married soon after.) Now about 1a.m. on the Monday morning, while temporarily holding a hose for the firemen, I was amused to hear a colleague shout: 'Aye! Look at your bally lino. Get it now, it's yours, if you dare.'

March 5, 1916   We were called out practically just after people had left church. It had been snowing the greater part of the afternoon and night. Soon after 11 p.m., whilst I was on duty with a P. C. at the fire-box in the Marker-place, we heard the sound of a Zeppelin west of the city. We were congratulating ourselves that it had gone away, when before we could reach cover it was practically over us. The only thing was to throw ourselves upon the ground. This I did whilst bombs were dropping. I was laid on my stomach a minute or two, but it seemed like an hour. Bombs were falling around, and I crawled on my hands and knees to the corner of Lowgate and Silver Street. By the time I got there the German had dropped all the bombs he intended to drop.

There was a great pandemonium in the neighbourhood—women screaming, men shouting, dogs barking and cats spitting. We heard a woman screaming loudly, but though we tried to trace her we failed. Traversing the Market–place towards the Pier, we found the enormous damage at the corner of Blackfriargate and Blanket-row. In the darkness we nearly fell into the big hole on the roadway in Queen Street. One man was killed in a shop at the corner of Blackfriargate, and we could just see one of his hands protruding through the debris, but it was impossible to get to him. As a result of laying and crawling through the snow during the actual falling of the bombs I was incapacitated from work and duty for some time through an attack of rheumatism.

August 8th, 1916   On the night of another raid I was at Beverley road motor halt. It was pitiable to see the hundreds of old people seeking shelter in the open country. Old men and women, infirm and children. There was some panic, but we subdued it by forcing some of the noisy elements to lie down, and this calmed the rest.

During one of the raids I was told that a bright light was showing in High street, so I sent a man to investigate. He returned and reported that no light was visible. Later on another messenger came and insisted that the light was still visible. I therefore went personally and discovered that someone had brilliantly whitewashed a passage wall during the day, and the reflection of the whitewash had caused it be mistaken for the reflection of a light.

On another occasion I came across a very old man who was sitting on the coping of the King William Statue. In reply to my inquiry why he was there he replied, 'I've come here for shelter.'

'What from? 'I asked. 'From Zepps' he answered. He proceeded to point out that the bombs had never been dropped in the precise place where he was, and he believed they never would be. After hearing such a view, I concluded, 'Great is thy faith', and I left him undisturbed.

It was remarkable how many people who had gone to bed were unaware of the happenings. It sounds like a fairy tale, but it is perfectly true that on the morning following one raid, in which the damage was done in the Old Town, we were on duty in Mytongate corner, when the men were going to work. When they saw us and the damage, several of them asked 'What's up. Has there been a fire?' When we told them what had happened they actually stared at us with open mouths.

On one occasion I was accosted by a man, apparently a commercial traveller. C.T.; Hello, constable, do you think the Zepps will come tonight?

Special: I don't know, sir. Hope not.

C.T.: Do you know, constable, I rather hope so. I should like to see one whilst I'm here. I'm staying three days. I came from Liverrpool, and I think Hull folk make a big scream about very little.

Later on he got his wish. Result. Next morning I found my friend had had enough, packed his bag and shaken the dust of Hull from his feet as early as possible.

A very deaf old lady came to the door of her house in which doorway I was sheltering during a terrific bombardment by our anti-aircraft guns. 'Aye, what a grand night, mister. I shouldn't be surprised if buzzers was to blow'. I didn't make her any wiser.

Scene.—Motor Halt: Old gent., in trap from the country.

Old Gent.: What's gates shut for mister?

Special Constable: Buzzers have blown and Zepps are about.

Old Gent.: Why, you don't expect them things 'll hinder them getting in, do you?

Firebox. Market-place night pitch dark. A knock at the door. Charming young lady: I say, Constable. I've lost my bonny little kitten. It's got out somehow while our door has been open. Have you seen anything of it?

Constable: No, what colour is it? Lady: Black. Collapse of S.Con., who recovers in the open air.—T.

Appendix VI
Dressing Stations with Doctors in Attendance

As listed in the *Hull Times*:

East Hull
    Pearson Institute, Cleveland Street—Dr Walton
    Reckitt's Tin Works, Stoneferry—Dr Holt
    The Hall, Garden Village—Drs Kaye and Townend

Escourt Street School—Drs Hollingworth and Eddie
Marfleet School, Delhi Street—[no name]
Drill Hall, Holderness Road—Drs Divine and Baine
Ripon Hall, Holderness Road—Drs Lilley, Walker and Weatherall
Raikes Street, Mission Room—Dr Savage
Crowle Street School—[no name]
St. Mary's Parish Hall, Sculcoates Lane—Dr Cummings
Higher Grade School, Brunswick Avenue—Drs Dowsing and Florence Stacy
West Hull: Fire Station, Worship Street—Dr Harrison
Queens Hall, Alfred Gelder Street—Dr J. Verdun

Royal Infirmary
Spring bank Orphanage—Drs Briggs and McNidder
Technical Schools, Park Street—Dr Davy
St. Augustine's School—Drs Ponsonby and Evans
Sidmouth Street School—Dr Jacobs
Perth Street, P. M. Church—Dr Fraser
Wheeler Street Schools – Drs E. Barker and E. B. Laslett
Carnegie Library, West Park—Drs Mc Gibbon and Webster
Tram Sheds, Liverpool Street—Drs Fawley and Moir
Fishermen's School, Boulevard—Drs Crawford and R. Rodger
Madely Street Baths—Drs Croke and Grieves
Thornton Hall, Great Thornton Street—Drs Wilson and Wales
Naval Hospital, Argyle Street [no name].

These are presumably the doctors in charge at the end of hostilities. For the situation in 1915, and list of personnel see *Special Constables' Gazette* nos. 2 and 3, 2 July and 9 July 1915.

Appendix VII
'Buzzer Nights'

List taken from *Hull Times* 25 January 1919:

1915. 12 April, 15 April, 11 May, 12 May, 4 June, 6 June, 8 June, 15 June, 21 June, 3 July, 13 July, 9 August, 11 August, 12 August, 15 August, 17 August, 8 September, 11 September, 13 September, 13 October, 27 October, 27 November.

1916. 31 January, 10 February, 13 February, 5 March, 19 March, 31 March, 1 April, 3 April, 4 April, 5 April, 24 April, 2 May, 28 July, 31 July, 4 August, 8 August, 2 September, 23 September, 25 September, 1 October, 27 November.

1917. 21 August, 2 September, 24 September, 19 October.

1918. 11 March, 12 March, 12 April, 20 May, 5 August.

The alarm was sounded fifty-three times in total and 206 hours were spent waiting for the release. The buzzers blew seven times on a Sunday night, fourteen times on a Monday, ten times on a Tuesday, six times on a Wednesday, four times on a Thursday, six times on a Friday, and six times on a Saturday: twenty-two in 1915, twenty-two in 1916, four in 1917 and five in 1918 [the total for 1917 has been adjusted, because the warning on 2 September has been omitted from the press report. Similarly the total for 1916 should be twenty-two not twenty-one, if fifty-three is the accurate total].

From 31 March to 5 April, 1916, the buzzers blew five times in one week (seven days), a slightly greater average than 9–17 August 1917, when the alarm sounded five times in eight days.[1]

Appendix VIII
Artefacts in Hull Museums:

A. Zeppelin bomb

Body and tail painted green and bears a brass plaque fixed with two screws and inscribed:

50 KILO H.E.BOMB/DROPPED FROM A ZEPPELIN ON HULL/DURING THE NIGHT OF SEP 24-25 1917/RECOVERED & EMPTIED BY CAPT. W. R. S. LADELL A. O. D. 1.0.0 N.C.[1]

Recorded dimensions: height 1040 mm (41 inches).
It is the typical pear-shaped bomb as described below. According to the confidential publication *German Rigid Airships*, February 1917:

> German naval airships of the new series, commencing with the L30, have carried larger types of bombs than those used by the older airships. There had, it is true, been several instances in which bombs of 220lbs. in weight had been employed previously, and in one case a bomb weighing 650lbs. was used, but they do not seem to have formed part of the standard armament of an airship

until the raid of the 24-25 August 1916. Both these types of bombs are similar as regards shape and construction to that shown in Fig.11 [a line drawing of a pear- shaped bomb], with the exception that they are considerably larger and of heavier construction throughout. For example, the walls of the 650lb. bomb are ½ inch thick, instead of 3/16 inch the base plug is 8½ inches in diameter and weighs 27lbs. In the 220lb. Bomb the base plug is 7 inches in diameter and weighs 17lbs., as against a base plug of 4 inches and 6½ lbs. weight in the smaller bomb.

A low standard of armament of the new series of German naval airships may be said to consist of the following:- 2 – 300 Kilogram [660lb.] bombs. 10 – 100 Kilogram [220 lb.] bombs.15 or 16 – 50 Kilogram [110 lb.] bombs. 20 incendiary bombs. Flares.

This would bring the weight of the total armament up to 5,780lbs., or about 2 ½ tons but – it is possible to carry a much greater load.

A percussion fuse was screwed into the tail and the spinning of a propeller disengaged a needle weight which was held off the percussion cap by a light spring. When the bomb made impact the inertia of the weight overcame the spring and the needle fired the detonator. As well as the usual safety pin another device prevented the propeller revolving until the bomb has fallen some distance. This was an inverted brass saucer which when lifted by air pressure on the falling bomb by about half an inch, causing 'two pins which, when the saucer is down, prevent the propeller from revolving, disengage and permit it to rotate.'[2]

Thomson refers to a little propeller: which turned during the ascent and unscrewed the fuse. Fastened to each bomb was a piece of stuff like the leg of a stocking.[3]

Those bombs dropped for example by *L3* and *L4* on Great Yarmouth 19 January 1915 were pear-shaped, 24 to 36 inches long and 12 to 18 inches in diameter.

The High Explosive bombs carried by the army airships were spherical, like large cannonballs. Painted black they varied in size from 50 to 230 lbs. and 8½ to 14 inches diameter. The projecting fuses were clockwork with a delay of 0.5 seconds and the oil-hardened steel of the bomb casing fractured 'into knife-edged pieces with the line of fracture at about 45 degrees to the surface. This type of bomb is intended solely for the destruction of property and life.'[4]

Buttlar-Brandenfels tells us:

Very often I have heard it stated that the dropping of a bomb must give the ship a sudden impulse upwards. This is not the case, for one cannot detect on board the moment when a bomb is released, only the helmsman notices, by the action of the horizontal rudders, or elevators, that the ship has quickly become lighter by the discharge.

Numerous incendiary bombs are dropped between the explosive ones, so that the English gentry get something from all of them, and what is destroyed by the explosive bombs is afterwards properly burned. I generally end up discharging one especially heavy bomb, so that my crew may notice its detonation, by the vibration of the ship, for the various bombs can be easily recognised by the degree of the explosion.[5]

B. Incendiary bombs

There are no incendiary bombs surviving from the Hull raids and the Turner photograph features mainly the explosive type, but does include a partially burnt incendiary minus its case. A complete example in the Moyses Hall Museum, Bury St Edmunds resembles a bucket or hanging lamp:

Iron (painted black, possibly later), with a convex, lead-weighted base, its height is 13in. plus a carrying handle [when released a three foot calico streamer was attached to the handle]its maximum diameter 9in. A priming device on top is operated by releasing a sprung pin. The lead was probably to assist roof penetration'. Another in the museum of the Suffolk Regiment is slightly larger, 15¾ in. high and 9½ in. maximum diameter. It is unpainted, the fuse is missing, and the upper canister was clearly wired to the base. Probably the wires made the whistling sound so commonly reported.[6]

A contemporary photograph shows at least forty-one incendiaries collected by police after the first raid on Bury, 30 April 1915.

In many cases the metal casing is wholly or partly missing and the coil of tarred rope is clearly visible. There was a central perforated brass tube enclosing a detonating mixture, and surrounding this an incendiary mixture of benzol, tar and thermite. Tarred rope was wound around all of this and the whole enclosed within the metal casing. Probably the most complete incendiary, though minus its metal casing is the one in the Whitaker Park Museum, Rawtenstall, Lancs. It has its white fabric streamer which was intended to prevent the bomb tippling and keep it descending nose downwards. Two instruction labels are attached to the tarred rope body and the fuse mechanism remains in position.[7]

There are examples of Goss china souvenirs, approximately 3½ inches by 2½ inches, in the form of an incendiary, decorated with the Bury coat of arms and inscribed 'Model of German bomb dropped on Bury St. Edmunds from a Zeppelin 30 April 1915.' There are similar pieces by the Shelley pottery too. A miscellany of crested china souvenirs of airships, and Zeppelins bombs, is illustrated in the catalogue of The David Kirch collection of Zeppelin and other memorabilia Pt. 1, lots 176–185, illustrated pl. 8, Wallis and Wallis, Lewes, Sussex 21 March 2012.

Buttlar-Brandenfels informs us that:

…the [early] incendiary bombs had to be thrown by hand. A pin had to be taken out of them to make then 'live', after which they were flung in a gentle curve overboard, to crash and burst below a moment later and burn merrily.[8] These bombs were filled with a composition that burnt so furiously that it was absolutely impossible to extinguish the flames, however much water was poured over them.[9]

Judging by the numbers recovered from those dropped on Bury many were either extinguished on landing or failed to ignite.

Special Constables were advised that 'water be promptly applied in fair bulk' at the seat of an incendiary blaze, or sand or soil in the absence of water. Any bomb that failed to burst was to be thoroughly drenched in water and removed to the nearest police station. According to the writer, in the Special Constables' Gazette, some melted white phosphorus was present in the bottom of the cap which produced nauseous fumes and sometimes celluloid chippings were added, and occasionally a small quantity of petrol.

An incendiary bomb, dropped by *L21* at Height Side House in the Rossendale valley, now in the Rossendale Museum, Rawtenstall, Lancs. is complete except for outer metal casing. The fabric streamer to control descent is still present.

Any unexploded HE bombs were reported to the military and cordoned off from the public.[10]

C. Constantinesco Interrupter Gear

Manufactured by the Rose, Downs and Thompsons foundry, Hull, it hydraulically synchronised the firing of fixed machine guns so that the bullets did not hit the blades of the spinning propeller. Previous to this the crude solution had been to fix metal plates to the blades so as to deflect the bullets. The earliest aerial gunnery consisted of pilots and observers shooting hand held pistols, rifles or shotguns from the cockpit! In 1915 double-barrelled shotguns (supplied by Holland and Holland, the eminent London gun makers), one barrel with chain shot and the other with an incendiary bullet were in use.[11]

After the war an example of the interrupter gear, partially sectioned, was placed in a case in the managing director's office but this was wrecked by enemy action in 1939-45, hence its current condition.[12]

Gogu Constantinesco (George Constantinescu is the usual form of his name now encountered), a Romanian, along with Walter Haddon of Haddon Engineering works, Middlesex, patented his invention 4 July 1916 Controlling gun-fire, 129,299, Classes 9(ii), 69 (ii) and 92(i). Thomson refers to his work being tested by the Royal Navy, including:

> ...the most marvellous things in connection with electrical wave transmission. Boats and aeroplanes can be sent off without crews and controlled from the ground, and listening apparatus can be constructed by which submarines may be located and attacked by wave- controlled torpedoes.[13]

Ernest Shackleton, the polar explorer, was in touch with the inventor in 1918, interested in investing in his ideas on hydraulics.[14]

Rose, Downs and Thompson's main production was of machinery for the processing of oil seed but the company received a number of commissions for high specification work outside this field. They made the jigs for setting up the joints of the air frame of the R100 airship designed by Barnes Wallis for the Airship Guarantee Company Ltd. at Howden. Though test flights were a success it was scrapped in 1929 after the loss of the *R101*. They also made cartridge presses (Ian Tyler, *The Gunpowder Mills of Cumbria Blue Rock Publications* 2002, p. 24, illustration).

D. The Steam Whistle from Messrs. Blundell & Spence

Its history is neatly engraved on the brass cylinder:

This buzzer erected by the Hull corporation at Messrs Blundell & Co. Works was used for the purpose of warning the inhabitants of the city of impending raids by enemy air craft during the period of the great war 1914-18 and was presented to the municipal museum by the Water and Gas Committee P. Gaskell Lord Mayor Chairman C. B. Newton M.I.C.E. Engineer. In 1939 this buzzer was brought from the municipal museum and erected at the Kingston upon Hull corporation power station and fulfilled the same function 823 times throughout the Second Great War Sept 1939—May 1945. Also sounded the last all clear on 8th May 1945.

Appendix IX

A vivid eyewitness account of the shelling of Scarborough comes from the pen of Winifred Holtby, later to achieve fame as an author (*South Riding*, etc.) and political and social campaigner, but who tragically died at the age of thirty-seven. The following is from a letter she wrote to the head girl of Queen Margaret's School, Scarborough (moved to Escrick, York, in 1949), and first published by Vera Brittain in *Testament of Friendship* 1940, pp. 39-44.

When I got up on Wednesday morning, if somebody had told me it was going to be the most exciting day I ever had, I should have laughed and said 'Rats'. I went down to breakfast in high spirits. There was an end-of-termy feeling in the air, and breakfast was at 8 A.M. I was sitting next to Miss Crichton, and I distinctly remember she had just passed me the milk, and I was raising my first spoonful of porridge to my mouth.

I never tasted that porridge! Crash! Thu-u-d! I sat up, my spoon in the air, all the nerves in my system suddenly strung taut, for the noise was like nothing I had heard before—deafening, clear-cut, not rumbly—as though a heavy piece of furniture had crashed in the room overhead. I looked at Miss Crichton, saying with a laugh, 'Hello! who's fallen?' when the look on her face arrested me. She was deathly white, and with fixed eyes was looking towards Miss Bubb. Suddenly I felt a tightness across my chest and an icy hand laid on my spine. I could see the hand that held my spoon trembling, and yet I had not realised what was happening, only something caught at my heart and for an instant it stopped beating.

I was about to speak, when Cr-r-ash—a sound more terrific than the first—and then all the windows danced in their frames. Each report was doubled—first a roar, and then an ear-splitting crash as the shell exploded. Then someone whispered 'guns'. The word, like magic, passed from mouth to mouth as we sat white-faced but undismayed, with the uneaten food before us. Another crash, and two mistresses rose and spoke together a moment and went out. Still not a girl moved or spoke all sat as under a spell. Another crash, and another then one by one the girls rose to their feet that was the moment—the only moment—when panic could have occurred.

We did not know, we could only guess what was happening, but a steady voice brought us to our senses.

'Lead out to the cloak-room and wait there.'

We led out yes, but not as sedately as usual quite slowly and quietly, and then we stood awaiting orders. If anybody felt fear, and I know that some did, no one showed it save by a white face or an excited laugh. We talked quietly in awed tones. Each time a shot was fired some started and flinched, others stood calm and motionless. Then Miss Bubb appeared on the stairs, with her dear, familiar smile and her steadying voice, and we seemed to have caught in a bad dream on to something that was safe, and real, and solid. She was our saviour. And yet the words she said were so absurdly familiar and commonplace: 'Put on your long coats, tammies and thick boots we are going for a walk into the country till it is over.'

We dressed and started, Nellie calm and placid as ever, waiting till we were all in line. Just as we got through the gate another shell burst quite near, and 'Run!' came the order—and we ran. Ran, under the early morning sky, on the muddy, uneven road, with that deafening noise in our ears, the echo ringing even when the actual firing stopped for a moment—it never stopped for more, ran, though our hastily clad feet slipped on the muddy road.

Over the town hung a mantle of heavy smoke, yellow, unreal, which made the place look like a dream city, far, far away. Only the road was real, and the tight pain that caught us across our breast—it was not fear, but something inexplicable that hurt, and yet in some strange way was not wholly unpleasant. Round the corner leading down to the Mere we ran—now all puffing. Someone was down with a bang they fell full length on the road and lay winded then somebody picked her up and they ran together.

In an instant's pause I looked round. I heard the roar of a gun, and the next instant there was a crash, and a thick cloud of black smoke enveloped one of the houses in Seamer Road, a tiny spurt of red flame shot out. Then I was swept on down the hill to where the Mere lay grey and placid in the cold morning light. Where the road joins at the foot of the hill we hesitated a second we were moving to the level crossing, when a shell struck the ground some 50 yards away, throwing up earth and mud in all directions. 'Back, back!' came the cry, and we turned and ran with dragging feet along the Mere path. It was all so like a bad dream. I wondered if I should wake and find myself in my dormy! Well, we just had to jog on, and we tried to keep our spirits up by singing 'Tipperary,' but it took too much breath.

We left the Mere path where it turns, and went along 'No Man's Land' strewn with old tins and broken crockery and we tripped on the pottery and slipped on decaying refuse and staggered along through the mud. Miss Trethowan still ran behind, helping stragglers, encouraging, laughing, and being just the brick she is. It was an awful responsibility but she bore it capitally.

We crossed the [railway] line into the Seamer Valley. Along the road was a stream of refugees; here was every kind of vehicle, filled to overflowing with women and children yes, and men too. I saw one great brute, young and strong, mounted on a cart horse, striking it with a heavy whip, tearing at full gallop down the road, caring nothing for the women and children who scrambled piteously out of his path, with the fear of death on his craven face. I could have killed him with pleasure.

Oh! those poor things on the road. There was a young mother with a tiny baby clutched in her arms, an old woman, only partly dressed, with her pitiful little bundle of worldly goods on a rickety perambulator. There were mothers with tiny children clinging to their skirts, crying for fear of this unknown horror. There was one particularly touching old couple, tottering along side by side, perhaps the last time they would ever walk together. I think I shall never forget them—those people of the Dream that was Real. With white faces they passed on. Whither? Where to go? Only an instinct urged on their weary feet, and fear lent wings to the old and tired.

We paused at the foot of the hill that leads to Seamer to rest for a moment, for shells had been bursting not far from the top, and we knew that when we were half-way up we must run for our lives, all our strength was needed for that, so we stood for a moment and watched the living stream sweep past. I saw a rulley laden with children pulled at an unsteady amble by an old, old horse, driven by a young girl, then a motor built for two with at least five in it, then a country cart with old women and children driven at full gallop then with a warning honk! Honk! a splendid car swept by at a terrific speed with one occupant—a woman wrapped in costly furs, alone in that great car, yet she would not stop to take up one of the poor old women who staggered on weary to death, yet fleeing for their lives.

Here, also, some of the girls found four tiny mites, half-dressed and almost mad with fear, yet not understanding in the least why. They had lost their mother, so we took them with us, some put coats round them and carried them. At the top of the hill we found their mother. The poor thing was almost wild with joy when she saw her 'bairns' safe and sound.

Just outside Seamer we sat down, tired out. As we sat, new comers came with dreadful tales. 'The School was shattered'—(two mistresses had stayed in!)—'The Grand Hotel was in flames'—'The South Cliff lay in ruins'—'The Germans had landed.' All this we took with salt, and waited for the mistresses to come—they had carried on their hands a mistress who was ill. Some of the servants came up and told us Miss Fowler was on the road with our breakfast. Our breakfast! At this awful moment they had stopped to get chocolate, dates, and biscuits, parcels of which they had ready in case of emergency. How good those biscuits were, eaten as we sat by the side of the road and shared them with other refugees.

While we sat there a nice looking officer, who seemed to be directing the traffic, came up and said he was the Vicar's son, and we were to go to the Vicarage. Miss Fowler demurred, how could she land fifty dirty, tired schoolgirls and maids on the Vicar's wife? But he waved away her hesitation with a kindly gesture, saying, 'Tell them I sent you.' Bless him! we went, and the kindness of the Vicar of Seamer and Mrs. Stapleton will never be forgotten by any of us. They set us to make tea and cut bread and butter, knowing that occupation was the best thing for our overstrained nerves.

Then Miss Fowler appeared, armed with a time table, and read out the names of the London girls who had to be put on the train just due. The Leeds girls had to wait some time, so the Vicar had a fire put in the parish room and turned us in there to give vent to our high spirits in songs and games and some of us he took to see the quaint old church.

How strange it all seemed! Only an hour or two ago we were sitting calmly at breakfast. Another few minutes—seven, to be correct—we were running for our lives in the chill morning twilight, and here we were in the peaceful village street, which seemed miles and miles away from guns. Finally we returned to school by train to find a meal ready for us. I just can't describe the cool way everything was arranged. Poor Miss Miller had been brought back by car and put to bed again. We set to work to pack, and then walked round the town to see the havoc.

In the letter to Mrs. Lucas, that havoc was further described:

The South Cliff looks pretty bad. The poor old Prince of Wales [Hotel] has a good many shells through it, and the darling Hall has had its hat knocked off by a German shell... Don't you wish', she added—doubtless to the exasperation of her correspondent—'you'd stayed at school?' She had already concluded her letter to the head girl with a characteristic aspiration: 'I can only finish with an earnest hope that never again will England suffer as she did on that awful December 16th, 1914—but if she does, may I be there to see.'

Appendix X: Aerial Bombardment

This was a major subject of debate between the First and Second World Wars and its opponents sponsored a memorial, albeit a rather ambiguous one, which became familiar to me while living in London in the 1970s. In the form of a stone plinth surmounted by the sculpted form of a bomb, it is situated alongside the public footpath in front of 587 High Road, Woodford Green, Essex.

It was erected in 1936 as an 'Anti-War Memorial', on land then belonging to Sylvia Pankhurst, suffragette and social reformer, who was living in a cottage nearby. Despite its aim of being a declaration against the horrors of aerial bombing, it is curious that the image of the bomb stands alone, not opposed by a dove, an enfolding hand or other symbol of peace. Ambiguity is further increased by the nature of the inscriptions on the plinth. The text on the south face taken by itself reads like an endorsement for the use of bombing, 'To those who in 1932 upheld the right to use bombing aeroplanes', unless one follows this by reading the text on the east face: 'This monument is raised as a protest against war in the air'. The first is apparently a deliberate irony, and a reference to the statement from politicians at the 1932 Geneva disarmament conference who argued against a ban. A further inscription, on the north face reads 'Originally unveiled by R. Zaphiro Secretary of the Imperial Ethiopian Legation supported by James Ranger E. L. A. Webster, J. Davey, Sylvia Pankhurst October 20th 1935', and on the west face 'The site of this monument is the property of Sylvia Pankhurst Design and work by Eric Benfield'.

Sylvia Pankhurst had witnessed the Zeppelin and Gotha raids on London in the Great War and was appalled by the invasion of Ethiopia by Mussolini's troops and the use of indiscriminate bombing against defenceless tribesmen. This was followed by tear gas and mustard gas, and, on New Year's Day 1936, by the bombing of the Swedish Red Cross resulting in eighty-five casualties. It was indeed the Italians who in 1911 had dropped a bomb for the first time ever from an aeroplane, outside Tripoli, during another colonial excursion.

Woodford Green was Winston Churchill's constituency for some forty years and a full length standing figure, a bronze statue erected in 1959, is a rather more prominent feature of this London suburb.

Endnotes

Prelude to War

1. Steinhauer was also a bodyguard to Kaiser Wilhelm II.
2. S. T. Felstead (ed.), *Steinhauer, The Kaiser's Master Spy; the story as told by himself*, London 1930, pp. 16–17. The British security service lost track of Steinhauer, a master of disguise, who after visiting his agents was able to reach Orkney and investigate Scapa Flow, ostensibly on a fishing trip. He was back in Germany eight days before the start of the Great War. As soon as war began all of his agents, [except one who escaped] ,were arrested.
3. William Le Queux (1864–1927), born in London of a French father and an English mother. He was among the highest paid fiction writers of the period, receiving the same rate of twelve guineas per thousand words as H. G. Wells and Thomas Hardy.
4. *Op. cit.*, Steinhauer, p. 62.
5. The red cloth cover of the book is stamped in gold with the German imperial eagle. Along with G. T. Chesney's *Battle of Dorking* (1871), it is probably one of the most famous pieces of future-war fiction. An earlier book, *The Great War in England* (1894) is the story of a surprise invasion of Britain by the French, published at a time when many were still suspicious of France and her world-wide ambitions.
6. Similarly, in 1930, Admiral Sir William R. 'Blinker' Hall (1870–1943), retired director of Naval Intelligence, took the opportunity of voicing his condemnation of recent decisions regarding the Navy in an introduction to the English translation of the memoirs of Gustav Steinhauer, the 'Kaiser's master spy'. He berated the government for concluding a naval treaty with the USA and Japan, but not signed by either France or Italy, thereby condemning the ships of the Royal Navy to obsolescence in the face of our rivals and 'in effect reduced us to a second-class Power'.
7. Frederick Sleigh Roberts (1832–1914) VC GCB, had an impressive career in India (where he won the VC during the Mutiny), Afghanistan and South Africa before being appointed Commander-in-Chief of the British Army in 1900. The post was abolished in 1904 but he was appointed to the new Imperial Defence Committee in the following year. He died of pneumonia in November 1914 while visiting Indian troops fighting in France. A few days before he had been appointed honorary colonel of the East Yorkshire Regiment.
8. Though its role is uncertain in a post-imperial world!
9. The Queen's dock was filled in during 1930 and the Wilberforce monument, a full length statue on a tall column, of the emancipator William Wilberforce, was moved to a new location, beyond what had been the eastern end of the dock.
10. This is where passengers boarded the ferries plying across the Humber between Hull and New Holland in Lincolnshire. It was also a favourite place to watch the water traffic pass up and down river, either from ground level in Nelson Street, or from the upper deck of

the splendid cast iron structure (now dismantled) which provided idlers with a wonderful vantage point.
11. *i.e.*, Hedon Road.
12. Built in 1871, it ceased to be the Dock Offices in the 1960s and since 1975 has housed the Hull Maritime Museum, where the author worked for some 35 years. A distinctive triangular building with a dome at each of the three corners.
13. The Legion of Frontiersmen; see above.
14. Arthur Conan Doyle, *His Last Bow, 1917.*

Terror from the Skies

1. See Thomas Geraghty, *A North East Coast town* Hull 1951 (reprinted 1978); Philip Chignell *From Our Home Correspondent – Letters From Hessle In The Second World War*, 1989; Mike Ulyatt *Hull at War: A Photographic Recollection, 1939–45* 1988; Denis Upton 'The Second World War—Enemy air activity over Hull and East Riding of Yorkshire, 1939–45' *East Yorkshire Local History Society Bulletin* 45, Winter 1991-2, pp. 5–14; Philip Graystone *The Blitz on Hull* 1991; Derry W. Jones Hull 'Blitz, scientific surveys and city bombing campaigns: 1941-2 surveys of morale in much bombed Hull' *East Yorkshire Historian*, vol. 9, 208, pp. 27–36; Sean Mullen 'How successful was the evacuation of Hull in reducing casualties during the Blitz of World War II?' *East Yorkshire Historian*, vol. 10, 2010, pp. 95–107; Malcolm Shields 'Evacuees—a reminiscence' *East Yorkshire Historian*, vol. 11, 2011, pp. 65–69 and in the same volume, Derry W. Jones 'Evacuation from Hull to Pocklington: a schoolboy's story', pp. 71–73.
2. Probably the earliest prediction of a 'lighter than air' craft delivering artificial fire, bullets, and bombs from the skies is in *Prodromo overo saggio di alcune invenzione nuove permesso all'arte maestra*, by Francesco Lana de Terzi, published at Brescia in 1670.
3. Ballooning was an event at the Paris Olympics of 1900. There was a lone female competitor Madame Maison who took fourth place in the endurance and distance discipline.
4. Ferdinand Adolf Heinrich, Graf von Zeppelin (1838–1917) applied for a patent in 1895 for a large manned airship, which he considered would be useful for reconnaissance, survey work, exploration, meteorological research and developing a world-wide postal service. The maiden voyage of *LZ1*, from Friedrichshafen, took place in 1900 but lack of government support resulted in bankruptcy. Remarkably he raised enough money from a public appeal to re-establish his company and in 1905 *LZ2* took to the air. After further problems, over 6 million reichsmarks were collected from a public lottery which enabled the construction of *LZ4* which took off in June 1908. In 1909, *LZ3* was handed over to the German army for trials and at the outbreak of war the army had twenty-five Zeppelin airships. The navy initially had just one but they soon realised their value in reconnaissance for the fleet and the Kaiserliche Marine were to play the lead role in attacks over Britain. The ZF (Zahnradfabrik, *i.e.* gear factory) company Graf Zeppelin founded in 1915 to make gears for airships and aircraft later diversified into gears for motor vehicles. The current ZF company, is the Zeppelin Foundation, almost wholly owned by the city of Friedrichshafen. It has recently acquired Hansen Transmissions, a Belgian Company and the world's largest wind turbine gearbox maker, to become a major player in the technology of renewable energy (*The Times* 26 July 2011).
5. *LZ1* (LZ = Luft Schiff Zeppelin) was 420 feet long, 38 feet in diameter, and had a capacity of nearly 400,000 cubic feet; driven by two 16 hp petrol engines, attaining a speed of 20 mph.
6. Apparently twenty to thirty maximum in these early stages of development. In 1909, the tenth Zeppelin, named *Schwaben*, inaugurated a regular passenger service between

major German cities by the world's first passenger airline Deutsche Luftschiffahrts Aktien Gessellschaft (DELAG).
7. Graf Ferdinand v. Zeppelin, et. al. *Die Luftschiffahrt ; Dem heutigen Stande der Wissenschaft entsprechend dargestellt* Stuttgart 1909; a paperback book priced at 1 mark 60 pfennigs. It begins with an historical account of the evolution of the balloon and includes chapters by Count Zeppelin on the developments at Friedrichshafen, with illustrations of the Zeppelin airships Model 1907 and 1908. There are contributions from other specialists including a description by D. Stelling of the Parseval balloon.
8. Freiherr Treusch von Buttlar-Brandenfels *Airship Attacks on England* London 1919, p. 31. From a lecture made by this experienced Zeppelin pilot in January 1918.
9. H. G. Wells had envisaged that most of these would have been of glass, presumably to reduce weight; see *The War in the Air*, ch. IV, section 9.
10. Freiherr Treusch von Buttlar-Brandenfels, *Zeppelins over England* London, 1931, p. 41.
11. Freiherr Treusch von Buttlar-Brandenfels, *Airship Attacks on England* London 1919, p. 33. A translation of a talk given to the Marine Institute, Berlin University.
12. 1881, 1884 and 1885; but there were also bombings in Chester, 1881, and Glasgow, 1885. After the Great War, there were various Bolshevik and Anarchist bombings and shootings across Europe including England, and in the USA.
13. A memorable description is given by a sixteen-year-old Winifred Holtby (1898–1935); for which see Appendix IX. The Hartlepool bombardment lasted over an hour; that on Scarborough, some 45 minutes, leaving 18 dead ranging from a 14 month old baby to a man of 65. The *Derflinger* and *Von der Tann* attacked both Scarborough and Whitby, where three died in a ten-minute assault. A number of the buildings in the Crescent, Scarborough, still exhibit scars on their stonework caused by German shell splinters. One military building was destroyed, the fine eighteenth century barrack block in the confines of the mediaeval castle!
14. The Kaiser and King George V were cousins, and both grandsons of Queen Victoria.
15. The Hague Declaration of 1908 forbade the launching of projectiles and explosives from balloons or other aircraft, but Germany was not a signatory, though Britain and the USA were. See H. A. Jones *The war in the air* 1935, vol. 3, pp. 69–70.
16. By Rudolf Martin. The Germans had established a rail route from Berlin to Baghdad, begun in 1888 it was extended in 1914 to Basra, giving access to the Indian Ocean.
17. Originally serialised in the *Pall Mall Magazine*, it was published in book form later in 1908. Martin's book is referred to in chapter IV, section 1, 'Rudolf Martin, the author not merely of a brilliant book of anticipations, but a proverb "The future of Germany lies in the air"'.
18. The 1939–4 war, in which had taken place the most intensive bombing perpetrated up till that time, resulted neither in a wholesale collapse of civilian morale nor the destruction of the industrial means of producing more weapons of defence and offence. See note 1 above, Jones 2008, for the situation in Hull during the Second World War. During continuing aerial bombardment the 'engine of war' continued to drive innovation in both Britain and Germany resulting in the development of jet aircraft by both sides, as well as Germany's V weapons, the world's first guided and intercontinental ballistic missiles. Eventually the power of nuclear fission was harnessed in the atomic bomb which was to bring the war with Japan to a rapid conclusion; Nagasaki and Hiroshima were each destroyed by a single bomb.
19. H. G. Wells, *First and Last Things: a Confession of Faith and a Rule of Life* 1908, p. 224.
20. Sven Lindqvist, *A History of Bombing* London 2001; four 2-kilo Danish hand grenades were dropped (see section 4).
21. The first sustained, controlled and powered flight by a heavier-than-air machine was achieved in 1903 by Orville and Wilbur Wright at Kittyhawk, North Carolina, USA.

22. H. G. Wells, (1866–1946).
23. The Gotha was a twin-engined heavier-than-air bomber with a crew of three and a wingspan of some 77 feet; 28 of them were shot down. The Zeppelin-Staaken 'Giants', four engined biplanes introduced after the Gotha, had a massive wingspan of 138 feet.
24. Interviews by students of the Humberside College of Higher Education, guided by their tutor Peter Adamson, as part of the Diploma of Higher Education course, 1980-3 ; and also a programme of interviews sponsored jointly by the college and the Manpower Services Commission, 1984–5. A selection appears in John Markham *Keep the home fires burning—the Hull area in the First World War* 1988, pp. 53–94.
25. Steven C. Suddaby, 'Buzzer nights: Zeppelin raids on Hull' *Over the Front* vol. 12, no. 2, Summer 1997, pp. 100–130. Suddaby, an American with English antecedents, was greatly helped by Chris Ketchell of the Local History Unit, and Jill Crowther, then librarian of the Hull Local Studies Library.

No Defence

1. Barry D. Powers, *Strategy Without Slide Rule* London 1978, p. 12.
2. *Hull and Lincolnshire Times*, 25 January 1919 (Zeppelin memorial number); 'The German naval airship attacks. How they were defeated. The climax of Teutonic 'Frightfulness', p. 3 and 7 and photos on p. 6; second memorial issue 1 February, with an account of the ant-aircraft volunteers p3, and more photos, p. 6, brief accounts of Grimsby, Brigg, Sheffield, Mexborough, Goole, York and Barton; third issue, 8 February, pp. 2, 3 and 7, photos p. 6. Anti-aircraft volunteers and further details of Hull, also Coventry and Wigan. Final issue, 15 February; more on Hull and brief account of Driffield and Selby. Most of the photographs of the effects of the raids reproduced within these newspapers were provided by T. C. Turner.
3. Each with a thermite core wrapped in tarred rope.
4. The German's had hitherto been enabled to discover their navigational errors and the locations they had *actually* reached by picking up British reports published in continental newspapers, often those printed in the neighbouring Netherlands, a neutral country. Censorship and the control of information was governed by the Defence of the Realm Act (DORA) 1914 (with subsequent amendments), and the Official Secrets Act 1911.
5. Steel darts some five inches long and five sixteenths of an inch diameter were released from boxes, slung under the aircraft in boxes and released in batches of as many as 200 at a time. The twin Blackburn seaplane with twin floats, and fuselages, and biplane wings, was built to Admiralty requirements with provision for dropping these anti- personnel darts (*The Blackburn story 1909–1959* Brough 1960; an anonymous company history).

Warnings: The 'Buzzers'

1. *L6*; Freiherr Treusch von Buttlar-Brandenfels was commander, but Peter Strasser, chief of the German Naval Airship Division was on board.
2. Commemorated by a plaque installed by the Sheringham Preservation Society. My thanks to Joe Ingleby for bringing this to my attention.
3. In the main text this is referred to henceforward simply as the *Hull Times*.
4. Hull Maritime Museum; boxes marked 'Flying'.
5. Its history is neatly engraved on the brass; see Appendix VIIId. Measurements are slightly different from those recorded *i.e.* the cylinder is 1,400 mm (55.1 inches) long and 310 mm (12.2 inches) diameter.

6. Presumably the steam engine had been put on standby at the end of the normal working day so this occurrence would have been a warning to keep pressure up around the clock.
7. Steven Suddaby, notes compiled for 'Buzzer nights'; see note 25, Terror from the skies.
8. Hull Corporation Minutes, 9 December 1918. The Water and Gas Committee were responsible for supplying the 'buzzers'.
9. *Hull and Lincolnshire Times*, 25 January 1919.
10. *Eastern Morning News*, 6 April 1916.
11. *Hull Daily Mail*, 5 April 1916.
12. Hull History Centre, CTED/2/109; hours were to be 9–11.45 a. m. and 1.15–3.30 p.m.
13. The 3rd was a Training Battalion. Hull History Centre CDMX/319/1 and 2.
14. *Special Constables' Gazette*, no. 103, 22 June 1917.
15. A complete set, the pages numbered continuously 1–748, bound in two volumes is in the Hull History Centre, shelf mark L352. 3; of 187 issues (18 June 1915–31 January 1919), the second appeared 2 July 1915, a fortnight after the first, but thereafter on a weekly basis. It was printed by the well-known Hull printers and booksellers A. Brown & Sons who stood the early losses but increased advertising revenue from local retailers which recovered more of the costs. A special thank you appears in the last issue to Mr Drysdale, manager of Messrs Browns., who was himself a Special, probably involved in protecting the company premises. In issue no. 18, 29 October, 1915, p. 70, there is a cartoon 'Hints for Specials' by Ern Shaw the well-known local cartoonist (Olwyn Cossins 'The story of the Hull cartoonist Ern Shaw, 1891–1986' *East Yorkshire Historian* (Journal of the East Yorkshire Local History Society) vol. 12, 2011, pp. 9–19. The *Gazette* also includes a brief history of the Hull City Police, in issues no. 97, 11 May, to no. 100, 1 June 1917.
16. Born in Bethnal Green, London, Francis Askew was apprenticed in the printing trade and settled in Hull 1876. Entered Hull City Council in 1897, elected Alderman 1908 and succeeded Hargreaves as Lord Mayor in 1916. Chairman and Deputy Chairman of the Health Committee for 24 years, Chairman of Education Committee from its formation in 1903, and Chairman of Hull and Goole Port Sanitary Committee for more than 25 years.
17. *Special Constables' Gazette*, no. 2, 2 July and no. 3, 9 July 1915. Districts and their commanders, and locations of first aid stations (dressing stations) : Dr Milburn was in charge of ambulance arrangements Central District *Mr James Downs* Out Patients Dept., Brook Street, Royal Infirmary; Picture Palace, Market Place; Newland Church Schools, Clough road; St Mary's Parish Hall, Sculcoates lane; Higher Grade School, Brunswick Avenue; Worship Street Fire Station North West District *Maj. A. H. Rishworth* Spring Bank Orphanage, Technical School, Park Avenue; St Augustine's School; Sidmouth Street School; Temporary church, corner of Perth Street and Chanterlands Avenue West District *Mr John Watson* Wheeler Street, Carnegie Library, West Park; Liverpool Street Tram Sheds; Gordon Street School ; Madeley Street baths; Thornton Hall, Gt. Thornton Street East District *Capt. W. S. Walker* Ripon Hall; Drypool Schools, Prospect Place; Crowle Street school; Marfleet Schools North East District *Mr C. Raine* Pearson Institute, Cleveland Street; Reckitts' Tin Works, Stoneferry; The Hall, Garden Village; Estcourt Street School; Holderness road tram sheds. River District personnel were to respond to an imminent, or actually occurring, hostile landing (see *Special Constables' Gazette* 14 January 1916); they were not called out for threatened air raids. The Special Constable Commander was Major Arthur J. Atkinson JP (later Sir Arthur Atkinson, owner of Brown Atkinson, ship owners and agents), Deputy Commander, Commander H. L. Walton RNR, with headquarters at Wilson's Marine Department (Thomas Wilson & Sons were Hull's biggest steamship Company, purchased by Sir John Ellerman in 1916);the Group Leaders of Tugs and Lighters were R. W. Wheeldon (principal of a major towing company and councillor for Coltman ward), office at the headquarters of the Aire and Calder Navigation Co. and

G. W. Heseltine, headquarters at J. A. Scott Ltd.; the Secretary to the Committee was A. W. Franklin, Humber Conservancy. Like all the districts (except the River District) the West District was divided into three groups each with two Group Leaders: TRANSPORT Walter Johnson, J. C. Forty TOOLS and WORKMEN Peter Gaskell, John Work JP TRAFFIC (*i.e.* motor halts) Haggitt Colbeck, R. C Follett. Headquarters, Gordon Street Police Station. The Chief Police Officer for the district was Superintendent Machin. The Specials reported to Concentration Points to be given their orders: TRANSPORT Anlaby Road, Carnegie Library; Hessle road, Madely Street Baths TOOLS and WORKMEN Anlaby road, Wheeler Street tram sheds, Hessle road, Liverpool Street tram sheds TRAFFIC Gordon Street Police Station. The men in the Tools and Workmen section were largely recruited from Amos and Smith, and C. D. Holmes, the city's premier engineering firms; they were not sworn as Specials but were available to clear obstructions, rubble of bombed buildings and expedite rescue of anyone who might be trapped. Overall there had been about 600 T and W men during the war. Haggitt Colbeck (1865–1934) was the eldest son of Ann Martha Haggitt and Christopher Colbeck. A solicitor with Walker and Colbeck, 9 Parliament Street, he was founder and first captain of the Hull Golf Club; pictured in the *Hull Daily Mail* 23 October 2008. Haggitt was also a member of the Royal Yorkshire Yacht Club and named his YOD (Yorkshire One Design) 2, the *Southern Cross*. He was the elder brother of William Colbeck (1871–1930), a master with the Wilson Line, who was magnetic observer with the Southern Cross Expedition (1898–1900) to Antarctica and selected by Clements Markham to command the SY *Morning* in which he sailed in 1902 to the relief of the *Discovery* expedition of Captain Scott.

18. This is specifically stated, so maybe all the other Specials wore it on the left arm. Nowhere is the colour of the brassard given or the wording on it or the various badges worn by the different grades. A report of a despatch riders gauntlet found on the roadside states that it was marked no. 69; *Special Constables' Gazette* 12 October 1917, p. 474.
19. Downs, born in Glasgow 1856, educated at the High School, Glasgow, in Hull and Elloughton; his father was appointed manager of the 'Old Foundry' in Hull. In 1916 James became chairman of the company, Rose, Downs and Thompson, manufacturers of oil seed-crushing machinery etc. Their factory was the site of the notorious dummy gun! The Downs brothers and employees of the firm made up battery, no. 11, of the East Yorkshire Artillery Volunteers.
20. Sir George Morley (1873–1942; see *The Times*, 14 October). A graduate of Oxford University; intended being a barrister but joined the Royal Irish Constabulary as cadet becoming District Inspector at Kenmore. He was 37 when he came to Hull in 1910 after eleven years previous experience of police service. In 1915 he received a salary of £700 per annum and an allowance of £50 in lieu of cab fares, horse hire and local travelling expenses. The next year his salary was raised to £800 plus the £50 allowance. He left to become Chief Constable of County Durham, appointed CBE in 1920, and was knighted in 1937 (see A. A. Clarke, *The Policemen of Hull* Hutton Press, Hull 192, p. 27; and Durham county archives).
21. See note 17. During the course of the war a total of 26 stations had been set up; see final *Special Constables' Gazette*, 31 January 1919.

22. The first motor car was acquired by the Hull police force in 1914; see A. A. Clarke *The Policemen of Hull*, Hutton Press, 1992, pp. 94–5.
23. One of these was C. E. Exley, later partner in Exley and Son, estate, insurance agents and valuers; a councillor for Coltman ward. Born in 1900 he was a despatch rider until 1918 and then served in the Royal Navy as a Senior Sick Berth Attendant, 1918–19. See Francis G. Tadman, *Hull's Whos's Who* Hull, 1933.
24. *Special Constables' Gazette*, no. 17, 22 October 1915.

25. The Specials worked on four-hour shifts throughout the 24 hours.
26. As part of the effort to prevent anyone signalling or communicating with the enemy all keepers of homing or carrier pigeons were required to hold a 'buff coloured permit' and no pigeon was allowed to be liberated or flown in any circumstances, except those employed by the Admiralty (see *Special Constables' Gazette* no. 11, 3 September 1915).
27. *Special Constable' Gazette*, no. 1, 18 June 1915.
28. Hull Corporation Minutes, 6 October 1915.
29. A post card from 5 Parliament Street, 29 May, 1917, signed Arthur Lockey, Acting Adjutant, was sent to C. H. Ross (ex-Hohenrein) apprising him of the first drill, 'Thursday next 31 inst' at the Wenlock Barracks, Anlaby road, from 7.30–8.30 p.m. Participants were instructed to bring an orderly who would also attend drill and be enrolled. Wenlock barracks established 1910 remain in use by local Territorial Army volunteers.
30. No women seem to have been recruited locally as 'specials', but Hull had Volunteer Patrollers and women police. The *Special Constables' Gazette* no. 97, 11 May, 1917, p. 386, records the first female special in Britain was sworn in to serve on the Great Western Railway. For the annals of women's emancipation it is interesting to note that in 1914 Elfriede Riotte piloted a *Parseval* P IV dirigible airship. My thanks to Tobias Flümann (Zeppelin Museum) for this information.
31. *Special Constables' Gazette*, no. 187, 31 January 1919.
32. *Special Constables' Gazette*, no. 86, 23 February 1917.
33. Details of the beats are in *Special Constables' Gazette* no. 82, 26 January 1917, p. 326.
34. These were spherical glass containers filled with a fire suppressant, usually carbon tetrachloride, thrown at the seat of a blaze.
35. *Special Constables' Gazette*, no. 18, 29 October 1915.
36. Distributed by the Fire Commander, Humber Defences.
37. *Op. cit.*, Buttlar-Brandenfels, 1919, p. 29.
38. Patrick Beesly, *Room 40, British Naval Intelligence 1914–18* London, pp. 141–5.
39. This seems to be the battery nearest Hull, some six miles east of the city centre; Spurn is some 25 miles away.
40. Major Robert Hall, Fire Commander, Humber Defences; National Archives AIR 1/569/16/15/142.

The First Hull Raid, 6 June 1915

1. Thorp Diaries, vol. 6, 1914, p. 36v, L9. 7083, Hull History Centre.
2. This was the beginning of the British policy of strategic bombing as a defensive deterrent, firmly established by Sir Hugh Trenchard as Chief of the Air Staff, 1919–29. Aerial bombardment would be used to strike at the main elements of the enemy's capacity for making war. Attacks on industrial centres and adjoining urban areas, the homes of the workers, it was believed would both directly damage the 'war machine' and undermine civilian morale.
3. Thomas Charles Turner came to Hull in the 1880s (apparently from London; he had relations in Walthamstow, east London) and established himself as a photographer, advertising portrait, technical and commercial photography. In publicity and letter headings 1859 is claimed as the foundation date which implies that he had acquired a pre-existing business, presumably that of Mr Drinkwater who is otherwise unknown. Turner and Drinkwater are first recorded in trade directories in 1882; at 1 Elm Terrace and Park Street, 1879–91; 8 Regents Terrace 1895; 226 Anlaby road 1899–1900; 26-28 Anlaby road 1901–4; Regent House, Anlaby road 1905 etc. Charles Turner was living

at 36 Coltman Street at the beginning of the twentieth century. Turner photographed Edward VII, King George V and other members of the royal family as well as members of parliament and numerous notable citizens of Hull. A past president of the Professional Photographers' Association his death, aged 63 on 30 June, is announced 7 July 1928, *Hull News* (p. 6). His son Neville had predeceased him a month earlier, 30 May, and his eldest son Eric continued the business. Funeral arrangements were made by H. Moses and Son and after a service in Holy Trinity church he was buried in the Northern cemetery. The address of the shop post Second World War is given as Regent House, Paragon Square, and the firm ceased trading sometime in the 1960s. Regent House is at the corner of Anlaby road (north side) and what used to be Brook Street, a few doors from Paragon Square. The terminology of this section of the Anlaby road is confused and strictly speaking it should be named Carr Lane. Ferensway replaced Brook Street in the 1930s, though the northern end of the latter still remains. The Regent House premises currently comprise a café, and office accommodation. Whether or not it is still accessible the shelter created by Turner probably still exists, and one assumes it was also used as a refuge during the blitz in the 1939–45 war.

4. The information he provided, along with 45 photographs, are preserved in the National Archives AIR 1/569/16/15/142. See Appendix II.
5. Suddaby, *op. cit.*
6. Hull Maritime Museum; boxes marked 'Flying'; lists of casualties 6 June 1815, 5–6 March 1916 and 8–9 August 1916.
7. J. Wright Mason MB, CM, DPH, MRCSE was appointed as MOH at Hull in 1881 and wrote his last report for the year 1924(published February 1925) after which he was replaced by Dr W. Allen Daley. His appointment is incorrectly given as 1886 by the Bickfords, who also tell us that he was convinced that glandular and bone tuberculosis in humans was due to tubercular cattle and supported the testing of dairy herds. See J. A. R. Bickford and M. E. Bickford *The Medical Profession in Hull 1400–1900—a Biographical Dictionary* Hull, 1983. Mason like the Chief Constable of Hull received a horse and carriage allowance and he is known to have had a brougham.
8. Annual reports of the Medical Officer of Health, of the Hull Corporation, are preserved in the Hull History Centre.
9. Heinrich Mathy (1883–1916). On 1 October 1916 attacked by Lieutenant Wulfstan Joseph Tempest over Potters Bar, *L31* was set on fire with incendiary bullets, and Mathy was killed jumping from the burning airship.
10. At Nordholz there was a revolving double shed for the airships which could be rotated to any point of t he compass depending on which way the wind was blowing. Manoeuvring these large and unwieldy machines in and out of their hangars was a tricky operation, accidents and severe damage were not infrequent. Nordholz also had a direction finding station, part of a system to provide navigational fixes for the airships, and also to plot movements of allied shipping in the North Sea.
11. *Op. cit.*, Buttlar-Brandenfels, p. 3. He was awarded Germany's highest decoration, the *Ordre pour le mérite* a decoration instituted by Frederick II of Prussia in 1740 and which ceased with the abdication of the Kaiser at the end of the Great War. Popularly known as the 'Blue Max', probably after Max Immelmann, the German fighter ace who was the first pilot to receive the order. Peter Strasser and Joachim Breithaupt also received the award.
12. The supply of gas to the street lights was cut off.
13. *Ibid.*, The translation of Buttlar-Brandenfels memoirs refers to these as 'light mines' (pp. 152-4), which had a dual function. If adjusted to ignite just above the earth a parachute deployed and the mine would float, illuminating the ground with a dazzling magnesium light. On the other hand if the parachute came into play soon after release the light would dazzle the eyes of the men serving the search-light and anti-aircraft batteries below.

14. A bomb fell on the bulwarks of the cargo lighter *Crocus* and the side of the vessel was shattered; see photograph(one of those provided by Turner) in National Archives AIR1/569/16/15/142/45.
15. Most likely the Royal Station Hotel, adjacent to Paragon station, the principal rail passenger terminus; or maybe the Grosvenor Hotel, Carr Lane, not far from Regent House, which itself was roughly halfway between Paragon station and the Grosvenor.
16. Report by Major General Ferrier, Commander Humber Defences; National Archives, AIR 1/569/16/15/142.
17. A battery, and base for Royal Engineers.
18. Starting with the first report at 7.25 a.m. the initial indications were that two Zeppelins were in the vicinity, though only one pressed home the attack.
19. National Archive, AIR 1/569/16/15/142.
20. Edwin Davis' new store in Bond Street was destroyed in the 1939–45 war, but was again rebuilt in 1952; the firm ceased trading in the 1970s.
21. John Markham, *Keep the Home Fires Burning* Beverley, 1988, pp. 68–9.
22. AIR1/569/16/15/142/25; taken from a note by Turner on the back of photograph in the collection at Kew. Described in 1923 as a former Hull rugby footballer, Franks was then licensee of the South Myton Arms, St Luke's Street (*Hull Daily Mail* 22 June 1923, p. 5).
23. AIR1/569/16/15/142/26; note by Turner.
24. The garage was gutted and two motors destroyed; see photograph in National Archives AIR1/ 569 / 16/15 / 142 /29.
25. National Archives, AIR 1/569/16/15/142/5.
26. Typescript notes accompanying Turner photographs.
27. The diary of George Thorp includes some details of the raid but these are mostly second hand, since he was living well away from the old town area. He gives us a more personal response to the later raids and extracts are quoted below.
28. Hull History Centre, CD/JR/1A/C No. 10/04. Punctuation has been added and contractions expanded.
29. She may have seen a parachute flare, or maybe an incendiary taking light.
30. *Special Constables Gazette*, no. 3, 9 July 1915, p. 11.
31. The figures of bombs and casualties are clearly her own estimates from information immediately available after the raid.
32. She was a Scot and tenement housing was the norm in Edinburgh and Glasgow and other large cities in Scotland. In Hull the overcrowding was mainly in court housing (referred to locally as 'terraces'), comprising an enclosure with a yard, around which dwellings were closely packed, with a single exit/entrance. This was a feature of 'old Hull' where a particularly dense concentration of dwellings, as well as commercial activity including slaughterhouses and tanning and other activities resulting in noisome effluent, was crammed into the area originally defined by the mediaeval walls and later by the encircling group of 'town docks'.
33. Hope Malleson, *A Woman Doctor; Mary Murdoch of Hull* London 1919.
34. Born in Elgin 26 September 1864, youngest of seven children, her father was a solicitor. Attended the London School of Medicine from 1888, taking her examinations in Edinburgh, her finals in 1892. She gained a Licentiate of the Royal College of Physicians and of the Royal College of Physicians (Edinburgh) and a midwifery qualification at the Brighton Maternity Hospital. Her first post was as House Surgeon to the Victoria Hospital for Children in Hull, replacing Dr Annette Benson, then moved to the Tottenham Fever Hospital in 1895, returning to Hull as a GP in 1896.
35. In a number of cases she undertook to remove women and children into the country to recuperate.
36. *Hull and Lincolnshire Times*, 25 January, p. 3.

37. Described in the *Hull Daily Mail*, 5 April 1916, p. 4. Sunderland is referred to as an 'East coast town'.
38. Anlaby Road; Albert Smith proprietor. The cinema is listed in the trade directories for the first time in 1916.
39. Hull History Centre, Steven Suddaby Collection, L9. 7083. Copies and transcripts of material collected for 'Buzzer nights' (see note 25, *Terror from the Skies*). He had placed an appeal in the local press for survivors of the Great War to write to him and other contributions were collected by Chris Ketchell and his colleagues at the Hull Local History Centre and Jill Crowther at the Hull Local Studies library).

The First Women Police and Self Help by the Citizenry

1. Margaret Damer Dawson, (1873–1920). Not active in women's suffrage but took an interest in the attempts to suppress the trafficking of women and children. She was a member of the Criminal Law Amendment Committee in 1914.
2. Former inspector of special schools for the London County Council.
3. By the end of the war WPS personnel were on duty in Edinburgh, Birmingham, Glasgow, Bristol, Belfast, Portsmouth, Plymouth, Brighton, Nottingham, Southampton, Folkestone, Oxford, Cambridge, and Reading as well as London, Grantham and Hull. See David Mitchell *Women on the Warpath—The Story of the Women of the First World War* London 1966, p. 217. This was first published in the USA in 1965 as *The Monstrous Regiment of Women— The Story of the Women of the First World War*. It is interesting to note that Hull was the first provincial town to ask, *c.* 1830, for two of Sir Robert Peel's trained police officers.
4. Mary Sophia Allen (1878–1964); a prominent campaigner for women's suffrage.
5. Mary Sophia Allen, *The Pioneer Policewoman* London 1925, p. 43. At the death of Margaret Damer Dawson in 1920 she succeeded as commandant. Mary Murdoch was only present at two raids before her death but was called out to the dressing station whenever the alarm sounded. She would also be answering calls from her regular patients day and night.
6. Corporation of Hull, Minutes of the Court of Common Council, volume 28(1), 19 October 1914, p. 21.
7. Corporation of Hull, Minutes of the Watch Committee, vol. 28(3), p. 62.
8. Presumably the WPV, later the WPS. No reference appears in the minutes to the presence in Hull of Miss Dawson and Miss Harburn.
9. The name of the other woman is not recorded, possibly this was Miss Harburn.
10. Corporation of Hull, Minutes of Watch Committee, 12 July 1916, vol. 29 (3), p. 103.
11. Corporation of Hull, Minutes of Watch Committee, 8 May 1918, vol. 31(3), p. 100.
12. Corporation of Hull, Minutes of Watch Committee, vol. 31(3).
13. Suffragan bishop of Hull from 1913 to 1929; only the fourth person to hold this office.
14. *Ibid.*, pp. 45–6.
15. *Ibid.*, p. 141.
16. Mary Sophia Allen, *The Pioneer Police Woman* 1925.
17. A. A. Clarke, *The Policemen of Hull* Hutton Press, 1992, p. 95. Mary Allen, *The Pioneer Police Woman* London 1925, p. 46
18. This was a term that had already been in use for many years in the police and prison service for women employed to deal with female prisoners.
19. Allen *op. cit.*, p. 46.
20. The members of the Women Police Service were employed at munitions factories, including shell-filling and arms factories (Enfield Lock and the Royal Gunpowder factory, Waltham

Abbey), across the country. Two constables were attached to the Royal Irish Constabulary in Dublin. A presence was maintained in the Royal Parks too.
21. Corporation of Hull, Minutes of Watch Committee, vol. 32 (3); but see preceding note. See also Corporation of Hull, Minutes of Watch Committee, vol. 32(3)1918–19, p. 106 ; on 14 May 1919 it was resolved that three pairs of breeches and three waterproofs be provided for Women Police Inspector Malpas, and Constables Atkin and Baldwin also two summer coats for the constables and a peaked cap for the Inspector.
22. Contrary to popular belief the VAD recruited men as well as women.
23. Where Hewetson's timber yard and saw mill was situated; set on fire by incendiaries.
24. Became Reckitt and Colman and is now Reckitt Benckiser, a multinational corporation, manufacturer of household and health products, including *Dettol, Harpic, Gaviscon* and *Strepsils*.
25. Grate polish used to burnish iron kitchen ranges, fire dogs etc.
26. Added to the wash to whiten the linens.

Counting the Losses, and Those Seeking Advantage from the Raid

1. See House Committee Minute Book, Hull Royal Infirmary, 9 June 1915, pages 144–5; archives of Hull and East Yorkshire NHS Hospital Trust, Hull Royal Infirmary. The new building was opened 1967 on the Anlaby road, the site of the Naval Hospital, a former workhouse; the original Infirmary building in Prospect Street, was demolished.
2. Based in the museum room of the Royal United Services Institute, Whitehall.
3. A house called 'Beechcroft'. See W. H. Willatt, vol. 25. *This Incarnation* Malet Lambert Local History Originals, Hull, 1985, p. 58. Newland Park, off Cottingham road, was some way north of the city centre. Though if we accept Buttlar-Brandenfels description of the impossibility of putting out the incendiaries it may be that this particular bomb never ignited (see appendix VIII, item b.) Willatt was second-in-command of a training camp for Royal Engineers at Silkstone near Barnsley; before his leave he had apparently been inspecting the Sunk Island battery (near the mouth of the Humber estuary) where a generating plant and search lights had been installed. An attack occurred at Silkstone too : 'Not far from our camp was a steel works' slag heap, a huge mound, with some of the slag shewing a glowing light on the burning heaps; the Zeppelin emptied its cargo of bombs thereon, under the impression that they were bombing some Sheffield steel works!' (p. 58).
4. *Eastern Morning News*, 19 June 1915.
5. The manufacturer was based in Eastbourne.
6. Grenades containing a variety of powders and liquid fire suppressants had been available since the previous century.
7. *Eastern Morning, News* 9 June 1915.
8. *Eastern Morning, News* 8 June 1915.
9. Lot 178, 'The David Kirch collection of Zeppelin and other airship memorabilia' 25 July 2012, *Wallis and Wallis*, Lewes, Sussex.
10. See J. C. Smith, *Zeppelins over Lancashire* Neil Richardson 1991, p. 31.
11. *Hull Daily Mail*, 7 March 1916, the day after a raid which cost many lives.
12. Barry D. Powers, *Strategy without Slide Rule—British Air Strategy, 1914–1939* London 1976.
13. Hull History Centre, LRH/2/612, 'Midnight raid by Zepp, Market Place Hull, June 6. 15'; see also post card from the aftermath of the second raid 'Zepp damage in Queen Street, Hull, 6. 3.16.' LRH/2/611. Also LRH/31/315; a card depicting a Zeppelin over a cityscape with flashes of explosions indicated, entitled 'The midnight assassin' and a cartouche

'Press Bureau, Official Message. "A Zeppelin visited the North East Coast on Tuesday night (15 June 1915) and dropped bombs. Killed 16; injured 40". This was a raid on Newcastle-upon-Tyne. Images exist of the flaming wrecks of the Hartlepool and Cuffley Zeppelins falling through the night sky, though how much this is retouch in the dark room is impossible to say.

14. W. H. Willatt, 1985 op. cit., p. 59.
15. Archives of the Hull and East Yorkshire NHS Hospital Trust, at the Hull Royal Infirmary, Anlaby road.
16. Douglas H. Robinson, *The Zeppelin in Combat; a History of the German Naval Airship Division, 1912–18* London, rev. edition 1966, p. 96.

Public Reaction to the Bombing

1. Derry W. Jones, 'Hull blitz, scientific surveys and city bombing campaigns' *East Yorkshire Historian*, vol. 9, 2008, pp. 37–54. Sean Mullen 'How successful was the evacuation of Hull in reducing civilian casualties during the blitz in World War II' *East Yorkshire Historian*, vol. 10, 2009, pp. 109–128.
2. John Henry Hargreaves JP, b. 23 April 1856–d. 19 November 1934. He was brought to Hull as a two year old, from Barton in Lincolnshire, and became a councillor in 1901. Mayor 1878–9 and the city's first Lord Mayor, 1913–16. Elected an Alderman in 1916 and made a CBE. in the same year and an honorary Freeman in 1918. He finally retired from the council in 1928. Hull was designated a city in 1897, the year of Queen Victoria's Diamond Jubilee, and the office of Mayor elevated to Lord Mayor, 26 June 1914, by King George V ; on the same day he opened the new dock named after him. Founder of J. H. Hargreaves and Son in 1875, Coal Merchants and Colliery Agents, Jameson Chambers, Jameson Street, also founder and secretary of Hull Coal Supply Association. His home was at 108 Westbourne avenue but retired to Bridlington where he died at 'Ferrymoor' Kingsgate. See John O'Hara *Men of the city* Hull, 1914, and obituary *Hull Daily Mail* 20 November 1934, p. 7, repeated in *Hull and Lincolnshire Times* 24 November, 1934, p. 15. A portrait was painted of him by Sir William Llewellyn for the City Art Gallery, at a cost of £500 (Ferens Art Gallery). Two photographic albums recording places and events associated with his mayoralty, including the funeral of the crew of the submarine *E13*, arrival of the first German prisoners, damage inflicted by the bombardment of Scarborough (but surprisingly no pictures of the Zeppelin damage in Hull), the City Hall with banners proclaiming it as a recruiting centre, collecting for the ambulance fund and the washing of the Lancashire Fusiliers strung across Baker Street etc. (Hull History Centre CDMX/319/1 and 2).
3. *Hull and Lincolnshire Times*, 25 January, p. 3.
4. Mary Allen, 1925, pp. 4–5.
5. Does he mean he was to stake a claim to a park bench, or did his family and others carry chairs with them to the park, maybe put on top of a perambulator, which was always a readily accessible means of transport?
6. Suddaby Collection, ref. 'Buzzer nights'; Hull History Centre: Mrs McIntyre, aged 88.
7. Mary S. Allen, *The Pioneer Policewoman* London 1925 p. 44.
8. *Ibid.*, p. 45.
9. Suddaby collection, ref. 'Buzzer nights'; Hull History Centre,
10. *Ibid.*
11. See Appendix V.
12. Hull History Centre, CTED /2 /15. Predating the decision to close schools after a raid, announced in the press in 1916.

Endnotes

13. Hull History Centre, Suddaby collection, ref. 'Buzzer nights'.
14. Stepney Primary School, Hull; *Centenary Souvenir 1886–1986*; copy in Hull History Centre.
15. From 1900 pictures had been displayed on the upper floor of the Royal Institution, Albion Street, the home of the Municipal Museum and Hull Subscription Library. The purpose-built Ferens Art Gallery was opened in 1927, named after its principal benefactor T. R. Ferens. A. H. Procter, (the spelling in the Council Year book, but sometimes rendered Proctor) in 1915 received a salary of £200, raised to £210 the following year.
16. Hull Corporation Minutes, Property Committee, 24 June 1915 and 10 September 1917.
17. Sadly the museum was completely gutted by incendiaries, dropped on the 24 June 1943, with the destruction of important natural history collections, coins and medals, militaria and the museum accession records. The shell of the building, the design of Cuthbert Brodrick (1821–1905), a native of Hull and best known as architect of Leeds Town Hall, was subsequently demolished and the site still remains empty, used as a municipal car park. Sheppard received a salary of £250 in 1915 raised to £265 the following year.
18. See *Eastern Morning News*, 9 June 1915, p. 2.
19. Thomas Robinson Ferens (1847–1930). Born at East Thickley, Co. Durham, son of a flour miller he became a clerk with the Stockton-Darlington Railway. Moved to Hull 1868 as personal assistant to James Reckitt, head of the well-known manufacturers of household wares. He became a director and eventually joint chairman. Member of Parliament for Hull East, High Steward of Hull and Privy Councillor. A great benefactor of the city he donated £35,000 in 1917 for a new art gallery named after him, which opened in 1927, and in 1925 £250,000 and 60 acres of land to build the University College, now Hull University.

Attacks on the German Community

1. Thorp Diaries, vol. 6, 1914, p. 19v, Hull History Centre.
2. See reprint of William Le Queux, *Spies of the Kaiser—Plotting the Downfall of England* London, 1996; introduction by Nicholas Hiley.
3. John Buchan, *Mr Standfast* 1918.
4. Friedrich Wilhelm Nietzsche (1844–1900); *Also Sprach Zarathustra* 1883. Nietzsche's philosophy embracing the 'death of god', the 'will to power' and the idea of the 'Übermensche' (Superman) has been embraced by those seeking power at any cost. He was opposed to nationalism and also the antisemitism which was interpolated by his sister, who oversaw the posthumous edition of his works. German militarism and ultimately the Nazism which claimed his influence would have been anathema to him.
5. *Eastern Morning News*, 10 May 1915, p. 2.
6. Barbara M. Robinson, *The Hull German Lutheran church 1848–1998*, Beverley, 2000.
7. D. G. Woodhouse, *Anti-German Sentiment in Kingston-upon-Hull: The German Community and the First World War* Hull City Record Office, 1990.
8. William Le Queux, *Spies of the Kaiser—Plotting the Downfall of England* London 1909. See chapter 13, 'Our wireless secrets'. Le Queux had an interest in wireless and in 1924 was involved in some experiments with radio in Switzerland. The same year he was elected first president of the Hastings, St Leonards and District Radio Society, for which John Logie Baird gave the inaugural lecture.
9. Christopher Andrew, *The Defence of the Realm; The Authorized History of MI5* London 2009, chapter 1, 'Spies of the Kaiser: counter-espionage before the First World War'.
10. *Ibid*.
11. *Ibid*.

12. Basil Thomson, *The Scene Changes* Doubleday, New York, 1937, p. 246.
13. S. T. Felstead (ed.), *Steinhauer, the Kaiser's Master Spy. The Story as Told by Himself* London, 1930, p. 42. Karl Hans Lody (1877–1914) arrived 25 August and was executed in the Tower of London, 6 November 1914.
14. Basil Thomson, *The Scene Changes* Doubleday, New York, 1937, p. 335.
15. At the outbreak of war the Secret Service Bureau actively sought and pursued those thought to endanger national security, but had no mechanism for their arrest. This function was therefore taken on by the CID at New Scotland Yard and the key figure in these counter-espionage operations was Sir Basil H. Thomson, sometime colonial officer and prison governor, who was appointed Assistant Commissioner of the Metropolitan Police in 1913, and head of the Special Branch which had been founded in 1883 in response to the Fenian outrages.
16. Leonard Sellers, *Shot in the Tower—The Story of the Spies Executed in the Tower of London During the First World War* Barnsley 1997 and 2009.
17. *Ibid.*, See also John Markham *Keep the Home Fires Burning* Highgate publications, Beverley 1988 esp. 18–23.
18. *Eastern Morning News*, 22 June 1915.
19. D. G. Woodhouse, *op. cit.*
20. *Ibid.*, At the beginning of the war there were some 60, 000 Germans in Britain, and following progressive internment a total of about 32,000 were incarcerated. Many male immigrants retaining their German nationality were interned while wives and families took over the running of their businesses.
21. The businesses of Ross and Kress and Wagner were to survive a Second World War and they only ceased trading in the late 1960s or early 1970s.
22. John Markham, *Keep the Home Fires Burning* Beverley, 1988, pp. 31–52.
23. The gold medals for Paris and Vienna and Grand Prix medal for Vienna, 1909, as well as for Brussels, 1910. are in the Hull History Centre LDBHR/1/5/21. Proudly shown in the shop window display, 7 Waterworks Street. From 1912 the shop address was 34 Waterworks Street.
24. The allied internees, totalling about 4,500, were concentrated at Ruhleben. A considerable number of merchant seamen were interned here, their ships having been detained in German ports at the outbreak of war. These included a contingent from various Hull ships of the Wilson Line; see Arthur G. Credland *The Wilson Line* Tempus books, 2000, esp. pp. 67–8. A total of 78 men signed a testimonial sent to Lady Nunburnholme (Mrs. Wilson) in appreciation of her efforts to supply comforts throughout their imprisonment.
25. Barbara M. Robinson, *The Hull German Lutheran Church*, Highgate Press, Highgate Press, Beverley, 2000, p. 44.
26. As in 1939–45 the greatest number of internees were kept on the Isle of Man, most in the large camp at Knockaloe Farm, near Peel, on the west coast, and also in a small one, Cunningham Camp, at Douglas. Others were held on the mainland, at Wakefield, Lofthouse (Leeds), Ripon, Handforth (Manchester), Spalding, Stobs Camp, (near Hawick), and in London at Hackney Wick, and Islington Workhouse. By the end of the war almost 23,000 men were held at Knockaloe. Those who died in captivity were buried locally but in 1966 exhumed and transferred to the German war cemetery at Cannock Chase. See John Walling, *The Internment and Treatment of German Nationals During the First World War* Riparian Publishing, Grimsby, 2005.
27. Hull History Centre, LDBHR/2/1/10
28. John Markham, 1988, p. 46.
29. At 7 Waterworks Street; founded 1850. Received Grand Prix and Gold Medal for their home-cured Yorkshire hams, and bacon and sausages at Brussels in 1910. .
30. See D. G. Woodhouse, *op. cit.*

Endnotes

31. Hull History Centre, LDBHR/1/1/14. Stamped and, and, and in this case, addressed to one of the shop staff rather than Hohenrein himself: 'THE SHOPMAN 'George' THE GERMAN PORKSHOP WATERWORKS ST.'
32. Hull History Centre, LDBHR/1/1/13. Addressed to Mr Hohenrigne [*sic*], Pork Butcher, Waterworks Street, Hull'.
33. While Lord Wenlock was in command; and was member of rifle team which won the regimental cup outright. A well-known game shot, keen deep sea angler and an enthusiastic horse rider since being a boy. His elder brother had been in the Yeomanry too, before departure for Germany. Charles Ross (ex-Hohenrein) died 23 August, 1974, aged 91. A photograph, with annotations, (*c.* 1906) of the children attending the Misses Weatherell's Preparatory School, 32 Park Street, Hull, includes a Fritz Hohenrein with a note '*German Artillery 1915*'. Also in the picture is a young Hohenrein girl, presumably his sister, as well Edna Leighton, Ken Gilyott, Vera Teesdale, three Heeney girls, Maurice Spikins '*killed 1915*', Stanley Simpson, Jack Grainger '*killed 1916*', Frankie Robson, Abie Rosenberg, Georgie Vice, Ken Harris '*Wing Commander RAF*', Jack Harris, Shultz (*sic,* perhaps one of the children of Max Schultz), Dolly Taylor '*Mrs Matthews, who sang under the name Dorothy Yorke*' and Allanson Hick (architect and artist). The four Misses Weatherell are all present, Ella, Annie, Lucy and Alice and several schoolmistresses, Miss Soulsby, Miss Runton, and Miss Clarke. The photo came from the possessions of Sadie Hick, widow of Allanson Hick (1898–1975); my thanks to Alan Bray for this item.
34. Ross was a keen motorist himself and his pork butcher's business used delivery vans too.
35. John Markham, *Keep the Home Fires Burning* Highgate Publications, Beverley, 1988, p. 46. Like most excavations in Hull, (a city built on alluvial mud) it tended to fill with water which regularly had to be extracted from a sump with a hand pump.
36. Max Wilhelm Emil Hugo Schultz (1875–1924); his early death was largely the result of his privations in captivity, especially the poor diet towards the end of the war when Germany as a whole was suffering severe food shortages. (Not to be confused with Dr Max Schultz, a German national arrested in England for spying—see above).
37. See pp. 217–220 and 425–6, Alan Judd *In Search of C* London, 1999; along with Vernon Kell founder, in 1909, of the Secret Service Bureau which evolved into MI5 (internal security), and MI6 (SIS) of which Cumming became first director.
38. In Landsberg; then in Prussia, now in Poland.
39. Ian Sumner, '*Despise it not*', a Hull Man Spies on the Kaiser's Germany Beverley, 2002. His story was highlighted in a remarkable way when a model of the Hamburg-Amerika liner *Imperator* was discovered in a Hamburg antique market in 1999. During restoration a note was found underneath one of the funnels indicating that it had been made by Schultz in 1913 while in Fuhlsbüttel prison (there was also a Zeppelin base at Fühlsbuttel). It is extraordinary that it should have survived both the chaos that reigned in Germany after the end of the Great War and the devastating bombing of the city in the 1939–45 war. Judd (1999, p. 451) when referring to establishing a post-war network of agents in Germany, says 'Sent Commander Goff over and sent for Hilton and ordered him to leave for Tiaria [Germany] tonight'; presumably this was Schultz, by then using his wife's maiden name?

An Organised Defence

1. Born 22 February, 1860, the younger son of Vice Admiral Edward Pelham Brenton von Donop (1811–90). On the staff of the Royal Military Academy till 1900 when appointed staff captain to Lord Roberts headquarters in South Africa and selected for 'special service' to organise and command an irregular mounted cavalry corps against the Boers. In 1903

Assistant Superintendent of Experiments at the School of Gunnery; and in 1908 Chief Instructor at Shoeburyness. In 1908 appointed Chief Instructor of School of Gunnery, in 1911 Director of Artillery, and Master General of Ordnance in 1913, with a seat on the Army Council. Promoted Major-General, October 1914. He retired 1 February 1920 and from 1925 was Colonel Commandant Royal Artillery. Made a CB in 1913, KCB in 1914, KCMG 1916. Also Commander of the Legion of Honour in 1917, Commander of the Order of Leopold (Belgium) and Order of the Rising Sun (Japan). He died at Bath 17 October 1941 and after a funeral service at St Andrews church was buried in Locksbrook cemetery *(See The Times*, 18 October, p. 6, obituary; and account of funeral, 21 October, p. 7). There is no detailed account of his career known to the present writer but his private papers are held in the Imperial War Museum: Cat. no. Documents 1417/ Archive Reference 69/74/1 Summary; also National Archives WO79/78. His elder brother, Lieutenant Colonel Edward Pelham Brenton von Donop, a Royal Engineer, was godfather of P. G. Wodehouse to whom he gave his name of Pelham, the P in P. G., and this was transformed into 'Plum', the nickname used by the friends of the creator of the immortal Jeeves and Wooster. A keen sportsman, playing cricket he represented the Royal Military Academy, Woolwich, at Lords in 1870–71, and was in the Royal Engineers team for the FA Cup finals of 1874 and 1875.

2. D F stations were set up at Lowestoft, Lerwick, Aberdeen, York, Flamborough Head, and Birchington. Some of these were also Y stations intercepting German wireless traffic. See Patrick Beesly *Room 40, British Naval Intelligence 1914–18* London, pp. 69–70.
3. The College of Heralds were charged by Queen Victoria with deciding her late husband Albert's true surname. They concluded it was Wettin but this was never used, and the dynastic name of Saxe Coburg Gotha was retained until the change to Windsor.
4. *Op. cit.*, Jones, 1935, vol. 3, p. 171.
5. H. A. Jones, *The War in the Air* 1935, vol. 3, pp. 180–1. In six volumes, 1922–37, part of the *History of the Great War Based on Official Documents*; vol. 1 was written by Walter A. Raleigh and the remainder by Jones.
6. See Appendix V.
7. B. H. Liddell Hart, *The Memoirs of Captain Liddell Hart*, vol. 1, London, pp. 17–18. Sir Basil Liddel Hart (1895–1970); from the 1920s he was an important war theorist.
8. Her partner from 1901–1906. Louisa Martindale (1872–1966), was also a campaigner for women's suffrage, and the two of them in 1909 had attended the International Council of women] in Toronto. Martindale became a distinguished gynaecologist and was a pioneer in the use of radium therapy for the treatment of uterine and ovarian cancer (*see Dictionary of National Biography* and Louisa Martindale *A Woman Surgeon* London 1951).
9. Florence Stacey, her partner in medical practice from 1906.
10. She started her practice in 1896 at 61 Spring Bank and in 1901 engaged Dr Louisa Martindale as a partner. She had moved to Beverley Road in about 1900 and also opened a surgery in Grimsby, Lincs. On her return to Hull Murdoch was made Honorary Assistant Physician to the Victoria Children's Hospital and Honorary Senior Physician in 1910. Elected Vice President of the East Yorkshire branch of the British Medical Association.
11. All Saints was later demolished. The first cremation in Britain took place at Woking, Surrey, in 1878, but the first municipal crematorium was opened at the Hedon road cemetery, Hull, in 1901. It still stands, but is no longer in use, and the city crematorium is now at Chanterlands avenue.
12. One of the aeroplane hangars, used now for agricultural purposes, can still be seen, from the A64, on the east side of the A1 intersection, see J. Smith *Zeppelins over Lancashire* Neil Richardson 1991, p. 10.
13. *Ibid.*, pp. 101–3. The Anti-Airship Light Cruiser Squadron was renamed the 6th Light Cruiser Squadron in June 1915.

Endnotes

14. *Ibid.*, p. 119.
15. Basil Thomson, *The Scene Changes* Doubleday, New York, p. 342.
16. The type used by the German army; a rigid airship but with a wooden frame not the aluminium construction of the Zeppelins.
17. The promontory of Flamborough Head, with its white cliffs, was always a useful visual mark and German bombers heading inland to industrial targets frequently oriented themselves by it. It was a guide also for the return journey across the North Sea. In 1939–45 any aircraft which had failed to reach its target would tend to release its bombs over nearby Bridlington. Thomas Hopper Alderson (1903–65), an ARP warden of that town, was the first person to receive the George Medal, for his courageous rescue of bomb victims, including eleven people trapped in a basement shelter. For a photograph of Alderson and further details see Paul Bright Air *War over East Yorkshire in World War II* Flight Recorder Publications, 2005, pp. 59, 67–71. The George Medal was instituted 1940 and those already holding the Albert Medal were invited to swap it for the new award.
18. Kapitänleutnant Boemack.
19. *Op. cit.*, Jones, 1935, vol. 3, pp. 101–2. The bombs presumably landed in the East Yorkshire countryside.

Raids in 1916

1. *Op. cit.*, Buttlar-Brandenfels, 1919, p. 18.
2. *Ibid.*, p. 28.
3. *Op. cit.*, Robinson, 1966, pp .131–2. Joseph Harrison *The German Air Raids on Great Britain 1914–1918* London 1925.
4. The 'Golden Lion'. Compensation of £100 was paid to the brewery (Moors and Robson); the pub was put on the 'redundancy list' in 1917 and further compensation of £3, 137 was paid in 1919 (my thanks to Rob Barnard for these details).
5. The 'Mikado cafe'. A postcard in the History Centre, Hull, inscribed ZEPP DAMAGE IN QUEEN STREET, HULL, 6. 3.16, shows a roofless, windowless, three storey, building with a name in faded paint 'The White cafe'. It is boarded up on the ground floor level; to the left is a gap in the street where a building has been completely destroyed and fixed above the boarding is a 'For sale' sign (LRH/2/611).
6. See *Eastern Morning News*, 29 March 1916. Sir William Alfred Gelder (1855–1941), son of William Gelder of North Cave, East Yorkshire, and Elizabeth Parker. Mayor of Hull 1899–1903; architect by profession and responsible for major improvements to the city of Hull during his 43 years active on the city council. Received Freedom of the City in 1930. MP for Brigg in Lincolnshire 1910–18 and a member of the Government Munitions Works Board during the war.
7. Brother of James Downs.
8. Hull History Centre, CDBHM 17/1/17 (*Hull Daily Mail* archive). An eleven-page handwritten account of the wooden gun by Arthur Tidman, who wrote for the *Hull Daily Mail* under the bye line Artid.
9. *Ibid.*
10. *Ibid.*
11. From the type-written notes accompanying the Turner photographs.
12. *Hull Daily Mail*, 8 March 1916, p. 5.
13. George Thorp (1847–1939), 91 Ella Street and 1 St Mary's Chambers, Lowgate. Sixty volumes of his diaries are preserved in the Local Studies Collections, Hull History Centre; L97. A devout Christian he was a member of the congregation at Newland Methodist

church. As a surveyor he was involved in the assessment of damage to property by the raiders for compensation claims to the government.
14. George Thorp, cuttings book, 'Cartoons etc', p. 128 newspaper photograph of the damage done to the railings and coping ; Box 2, L9. 7083, Hull History Centre.
15. Thorp Diaries, vol. 9, January–June 1916p. 28v.
16. George Thorp, cuttings book, 'Cartoons etc', p. 137, Box 2, L9. 7083, Hull History Centre.
17. House Committee Minutes, 8 March 1916, pp. 187–8; archives of the Hull and East Yorkshire NHS Hospital Trust.
18. This was a naval airship similar to the Zeppelin in the first raid. First flew 7 June 1915 and was lost 25 April 1917.
19. Op. cit., Jones, 1935, vol. 3, pp. 185–6; taken from O. Groos *Der Krieg in der Nordsee* 1922–37, vol. 5, pp. 63–4.
20. *Eastern Morning News*, 6 March 1916.
21. *Eastern Morning News*, 7 March 1916.
22. *Eastern Morning News*, 9 March 1916.
23. Wife of John Large, English master at Kingston High School until the late 1960s. Two of his students and protégés, John Alderton and Tom Courtney, became well known actors on stage and screen.
24. Hull History Centre, Steven Suddaby collection, ref. 'Buzzer nights'.
25. *Hull and Lincolnshire Times*, 25 January, p. 7.
26. Apart from the summary record of where bombs landed, and quick on the spot assessments immediately after a raid, there is no evidence of a considered and detailed account being made of the impact of bombing on strategic targets, though an accurate picture might be discovered if the various insurance claims records could be found. See Robinson, Morris, Jones and Hook.
27. Sir Mark Sykes Bt (1879–1919), a Lieutenant Colonel of the Green Howards. Elected as a Conservative MP for Hull Central in 1912 and succeeded as 6th baronet in 1913. He had served in the Second Boer War, became a specialist in Middle Eastern affairs and spent 1914–18 in the War Office working for Lord Kitchener. Died in the great influenza pandemic ('Spanish flu') while at the Paris Peace Conference in 1919. He has left his mark on international politics as co-deviser, with François Georges Picot of the Sykes-Picot agreement which set out the French and English spheres of influence within the Middle East to be assigned after the defeat of the Ottoman Turks.
28. Letter sent from 61 Murchison Street, Scarborough, 15 March, 1916; DDSY2/1/30/191.
29. Hull History Centre, DDSY2/1/30/168.
30. Anthony Fokker, a Dutch aircraft designer who made aircraft for Germany but had also offered designs to the British military.
31. *Op. cit.*, Suddaby, 'Buzzer nights'.
32. *Op. cit.*, Jones 1935, vol. 3, p. 188.
33. Charles Wilson (1874–1924), son of the late Charles Henry Wilson, first Baron Nunburnholme, whose father Thomas had founded the Wilson shipping line. Served like his father as Liberal MP for Hull West and was Lord Lieutenant from 1908 till his death.
34. Norman Flower ed., *The Journals of Arnold Bennett*, 3 vols., 1932; vol. 2, p. 180. Mobile units initially consisted of machine guns, 1 pounder pom-poms and searchlights on trucks. There are a number of references in the journals to raids on London and other locations including Epping Forest and Sittingbourne. He also records a Zeppelin downed at Peldon, between Colchester and West Mersey in Essex (p. 174).
35. The Hull Golf course was then situated on what was then the western edge of Hull on the east side of the northern stretch of Pickering road and was subsequently covered by

Endnotes

a housing development. The course was north of the Roman Catholic church and the Fiveways roundabout and extended as far east as what is now North road and occupied roughly the space between Crossfield and Sunbeam roads. A gun placed here would have been roughly halfway along a north/south line between where emplacements were later established near Priory sidings, Hessle road, and that north of the factory of the Radiator Co. (later Ideal Boilers, and Ideal Standard).

36. *Op. cit.*, Buttlar-Brandenfels 1919, p. 21.
37. Note that it was *not* Von Donop, GOC of the Humber Garrison.
38. *Op. cit.*, Jones, 1935, vol. 3, pp. 188–9.
39. Barry D. Powers, *Strategy Without Slide Rule* London 1976, pp. 18–19.
40. Sibree was gazetted 2nd Lieutenant 12 December 1915. He was the great grandson of the Revd James Sibree (1805–1891), Congregational minister, and author of *Fifty Years Recollections of Hull*, Hull, 1884.
41. Hull History Centre, CDMX 84/1 and 2. Two note books with marbled boards, a paper label on each inscribed 'Bennett-Pleydell Height Finder Notes' and inside 'J. Oswald Sibree RE (T)[Territorial] Headquarters AA, Humber Garrison, 2 West Parade, Anlaby Rd. HULL'. The sites are at Hull (Harpins, just north of the Radiator Works and the Hull and Barnsley railway line), Hessle Priory, Marfleet, Kilnsea, Spurn, Easington, Sutton, Selby, Howden, and on the Lincolnshire side of the Humber, Scunthorpe, High Santon, New Holland, Killingholme, Scartho Top, and Grimsby.
42. These sites were on the edge of the city rather than in the centre.
43. Hull History Centre, C DBHM 17/1/17.
44. P. C. Sands, C. M. Haworth and J. H. Eggleshaw, *A History of Pocklington School, East Yorkshire, 1514–1980* Highgate Publications(Beverley) 1988.
45. *Hull and Lincolnshire Times*, 25 January, p. 3.
46. *Ibid.*
47. *Ibid.*
48. See above and note 51.
49. *Hull Daily Mail*, 5 April 1916.
50. Hull History Centre, Steven Suddaby collection, box of copies of letters and transcripts of material collected for 'Buzzer nights'(see note 25 *Terror from the skies*).
51. One of Peter Strasser's two deputies, Korvettenkapitan Schütze accompanied Kapitanleutnant Eichler in *L48*, one of a group of 'Height climbers' intending to attack London during the lighter nights of early summer, 16/17 June 1917. After engine trouble and a frozen compass the Zeppelin lost height over the east coast and crashed to the ground at Theberton (Suffolk) following an attack with incendiary bullets from the aircraft of Lt. L. P. Watkins, from 37 Home Defence Squadron, Goldhanger, Essex. Only three of the crew survived, Schütze was not one of them; Peter J. C. Smith 'Nemesis of the bombing Zeppelins' *The Armourer* Beaumont Publishing, issue 85, Jan/Feb 2008, pp. 52–3. My thanks to Michael J. Boyd for bringing this to my attention.
52. *Op. cit.*, Jones, 1935, vol. 3, p. 201.
53. By 1917 Schütze was Commodore of the North Sea Airship Division and received a silver plaque (23 x 16 cm) with the imperial cipher and facsimile of the Kaiser's signature inscribed *Willelm II Deutsche Kaiser und Konig von Preuss Begluckwungschung fur eine beforderung Victor Schutze Kommodore Nordsee Luftschiffe Div 1917*. Lot 368, pl. 23 'The David Kirch collection of Zeppelin and other airship memorabilia' pt. 1, 21 March, 2012, Wallis and Wallis, Lewes, Sussex.
54. *i.e.* comparing it to a glowing gas mantle, so familiar in every home before the installation of electric light.
55. *Hull Daily Mail*, 6 April 1916, p. 2.
56. Respectively north, west and east Hull.

57. Thorp Diaries, vol. 9, January–June 1916, 37v.
58. *Hull Daily Mail*, 6 April 1916.
59. In the Great War anti-aircraft guns and their shell fire were referred to as *archies*; apparently derived from a contemporary music hall song, 'Archibald, certainly not', alluding to serious doubts about its effectiveness! In the 1939–45 war *ack-ack* was the usual expression, from the old telegrapher's alphabet, *ack* = a, as in *ack emma* for a.m. (morning) but as the war progressed the German word *flak* was adopted, certainly among military personnel, to refer to anti-aircraft fire. Flak is an acronym derived from *fliegerabwehrkanone*, 'aircraft defence cannon'.
60. *Special Constables' Gazette*, no. 102, 15 July 1917, p. 406.
61. L24 broke its back on the door of the airship shed 28 December 1916.
62. In London St James Park lake was drained to prevent the reflection from the water surface providing a guide to Buckingham palace and neighbouring Whitehall.
63. *Op. cit.*, Buttlar-Brandenfels 1919, p. 20–1.
64. Typewritten notes accompanying the Turner photographs.
65. Typewritten notes accompanying Turner photographs.
66. *Hull and Lincolnshire Times*, 25 January 1919, p. 7.
67. A baby walker.
68. *Eastern Morning News*, 10 August 1916.
69. *i.e.* Ella Street.
70. Thorp Diaries, vol. 10, July–December 1916, p. 33.
71. *Op. cit.*, Jones, 1935, vol. 3, p. 218.
72. House Committee Minutes, Hull Royal Infirmary, 9 August 1916, p. 216; archives of the Hull and East Yorkshire NHS Hospital Trust.
73. Which they did, under military supervision.
74. *Eastern Morning News*, 11 and 14 August 1916.
75. 3-inch Quick-Firing AA 20-cwt; 4-inch Q-F AA; 3-inch Q-F 5-cwt AA; 12-pounder, 12-cwt QF AA; 13-pounde 9-cwt AA; 13-pounder 6-cwt Q-F AA; 6-pounder Q-F AA; 75 mm; 4.7 inch Q-F.
76. *Anti-aircraft attack of airships Home Defence (Provisional)* issued by the General Staff 1916; A 1949 40/WO/3255. There are 67 pages, including four plates of target and fuze curves, two plates ref. flank observation, and five abridged attack tables for 3 inch, 30-cwt, 13 pr. 6-cwt, 13 pr. 9-cwt, 12 pr. 12-cwt, and 4.7 inch guns which presumably indicates that these were the pieces of artillery which were in widest use. The example examined in the Nigel Caley collection had been issued to an anti-aircraft company in London.
77. Hull History Centre, L9. 7083.
78. Kenneth Hubert, *A Passion for Souls; the Story of Charles H. Hulbert, Methodist Missioner* London 1959, pp.30–31.My thanks to Sylvia Usher, great niece of Charles Hulbert, for bringing this to my attention.

Success in the South

1. Incendiary ammunition. The original design by Commander Frederick Arthur Brock, Air Intelligence Section of the Air Dept. of the Royal Navy was demonstrated in trials in 1915. He belonged to the family famous for making fireworks, 'a Brock's benefit' has become proverbial for any event involving big bangs and incendiary displays. Other types by Pomeroy and Buckingham were also employed and such bullets were found to be deadly when used in a variety of combinations along with tracer ammunition. The former was tested as far back as 1908, submitted to War Office in 1914 and entered service in 1916. An incendiary device designed to be dropped on a Zeppelin was lot 28 in 'The David Kirch

collection of Zeppelin and other airship memorabilia' pt. 2 *Wallis and Wallis* 25 July 2012; illustrated pl. 2. 'with guide fins and three wire feet which open out to ensure the device does not pass straight through the fabric and allows the igniter time to work'.
2. The forthcoming sale of his VC at *Christies*, 22 November 1988, was announced in the *Daily Telegraph* 19 September 1988.
3. Written (to his wife) from 9 Buckingham Gate, SW, 3 August 1916. The letter includes sketches of the way the airship was attacked and how it fell to earth (Hull History Centre UDDSY2/1/2f/59).
4. *Op. cit.*, Buttlar-Brandenfels, 1919, preface.
5. Another Zeppelin card sanctioned by the Press Bureau gives the copyright to H. Scott Orr. This one gives the impression it may be derived, albeit with some enhancement, from an actual photograph, unlike all the others seen by the author which are clearly made up images.
6. Admiralty War Staff, Intelligence Division *German Rigid Airships February*1917 CB. 1265, a detailed examination of *L33* brought down at Little Wigborough. This was a confidential document subject to the Official Secrets Act. Example examined in the Nigel Caley collection. There is also a copy in the library of the Royal Armouries, Leeds, reprinted in facsimile by the Naval and Military Press, 2007.
7. T. W. Jamison, *Icarus over the Humber–The Last Flight of the Airship R. 38/ZR–2* 1994 Lampada Press, 1994, p. 15.
8. *Special Constables' Gazette*, no. 9, 20 August 1915, p. 36.
9. *Special Constables' Gazette*, 22 October 1915.

Further Raids in 1917 and a Royal Visit

1. *Hull and Lincolnshire Times*, 23 June 1917, pp. 2, 3, 4 and 6. The previous royal visit to Hull had been 26 June 1914, shortly before the outbreak of war, when the King, accompanied by Queen Mary, opened and gave his name to the King George dock.
2. Sir Stanley's father, Edward Pelham Brenton von Donop, as Captain von Donop, had commanded the *Dauntless*, a guardship on the Humber station, 1864–68. He had been active on the committee which brought HMS *Southampton* to Hull as a training ship under the management of the Ragged and Industrial Schools (*Hull Daily Mail* 14 February, 5, 12 June, 3 July, 27 November etc 1868, and preceding years), and welcomed boys from it as visitors aboard the *Dauntless* (*Hull Daily Mail* 8 November 1867); the two vessels were moored quite close together at the mouth of the river Hull. The *Southampton* was finally towed away for breaking in 1912. Captain von Donop was present at the banquet to celebrate the opening of the new Exchange and replied on behalf of the Royal Navy to the toasts (*Hull Daily Mail* 6 April 1866). He was also present at the unveiling of the memorial statue to Prince Albert in Pearson Park (*Hull Daily Mail* 16 October 1868).The son of George Baron von Donop of Wöbell, Westphalia, he had entered the navy in 1827, promoted captain in 1855.
3. Hull City AFC occupied the former North Eastern Railway clerks cricket ground, which they leased from the Hull Cricket Club who used the adjacent Circle. They moved to Boothferry Park in 1946 but now occupy the KC Stadium (Anlaby road, adjacent to West Park) which is built on the site of their old ground and the Anlaby road Circle, the former cricket ground. An investiture conducted by von Donop in Lincolnshire when medals were presented to men of the Manchester and Lincolnshire regiments is recorded in *Hull News* (24 August 1917, p. 4). In his address to the troops he told them it was a hard road ahead, their commitment was essential, and conscientious objection to military service was not acceptable.

4. George Thorp, cuttings book, 'Cartoons etc', Box 2, p. 130, a newspaper photograph of the Primitive Methodist Chapel; L9. 7083, Hull History Centre.
5. *Op. cit.*, Jones, 1935, vol. 5, p. 55.
6. Morris, 1925, *op. cit.*, Rimell op. cit .p. 197.
7. Situated in the High Street, a meeting place for the business leaders of Hull.
. Hull History Centre, C DBHM 17/1/17.
9. There were no missiles carried by the Zeppelins other than incendiary and high explosive bombs. These lacked truly aerodynamic flights that would have resulted in a well-controlled descent and the angle at which they reached the ground was variable. Maybe the bomb had been released into exceptionally turbulent air currents, or possibly its path had been distorted by another explosion.
10. The tail fins.
11. *Hull and Lincolnshire Times*, 25 January 1919, p. 3.
12. George Thorp, volume of cuttings 'Cartoons etc. referring to the 1914–18 war; Box 2 L9. 7083, p. 134 a newspaper cutting showing Mrs Drewitt with the roller.
13. Thorp Diaries, vol. 12, June–November 1917, pp. 82–4.
14. George Thorp, cuttings book, 'Cartoons etc ', p. 137, a newspaper photograph.
15. Basil Thomson, *The Scene Changes* Doubleday, New York, p. 261.
16. *Op. cit.*, Jones 1935, vol. 5, p. 80
17. *Ibid.*
18. *Ibid.*, p. 80, note 1.
19. *Op. cit.*, Morris
20. *Hull Daily Mail*, 25 and 26 September.
21. Thorp Diaries, vol. 12, June–November 1917, p. 84.
22. Manfred Griehl and Joachim Dressel, *Zeppelin–The German Airship Story* London, 1990.
23. Freiherr Treusch von Buttlar-Brandenfels, *Airships Attacks on England* J. Selwyn & Co. London, 1919, pp. 14–15. A translation of the lecture published after the war.
24. A brass bodied compass, diameter 23 cm and height 21 cm, the ring marked 'W. Ludolph GMBH Bremerhaven'; attached to it a copper plate with a French inscription indicating that it came from a downed airship, 'Zeppelin descend a Banowvilliers 28 Août 1914'; see pl. 11 'The David Kirch collection of Zeppelin and other airship memorabilia', pt. 1, lot 260, Wallis and Wallis, Lewes, Sussex, 21 March 2012.
25. *Op. cit.*, Buttlar-Brandenfels, p. 59. A piece of crested china commemorates this event; see lot 178 'The David Kirch collection of Zeppelin and other airship memorabilia', pt. 1, 21 March, 2012, Wallis and Wallis, Lewes, Sussex, 'Model of an incendiary bomb dropped at Maldon 16 April 1915'.

1918: The Last Raids

1. *Op. cit.*, Jones, 1935, vol. 5, p. 122.
2. Man involved in the preparation of moulds in a foundry, prior to pouring the metal.
3. *Hull Daily Mail*, 14 March 1918, p. 4.
4. Thorp Diaries, vol. 12, June–November 1917, p. 91.
5. L61(LZ106), made nine reconnaissance flights and two raids on England, dropping 4,500 kg of bombs.
6. L62 (LZ107), made two reconnaissance flights and two raids on England, dropping 5,923 kg of bombs.
7. Morris, 1925, *op. cit.*, p. 191.
8. Sir Barnes Wallis (1887–1979); designer of the Wellington bomber and of the 'bouncing bomb' used against the Ruhr dams in Operation Chastise, May 1943.

Endnotes

9. N. S. Norway (1889–1960), wrote under the name Nevil Shute. His books include *Slide Rule, A Town like Alice* and *On the Beach,* the last two of which were also major successes on the big screen.

Measures and Countermeasures

1. Harry Woodman, *Early Aircraft Armament* London, 1989.
2. Hales incendiary bombs, 10 lb or 20 lb, were released, by a toggle, from racks fixed to the aircraft undercarriage. The Ranken dart, invented in 1915 was released in threes from a dropper box with 24 tubes, but like a match that is useless when wet the phosphorus needed to touch off the charge was often affected by damp. See R. L. Rimell *Zeppelins; a Battle for Air Supremacy in World War I* London 1984, especially pp. 81–2 and also Christopher Cole and E. F. Cheeseman *The Air Defence of Britain 1914–18* London, 1982, p. 103 for a diagram of the Ranken dart; pp. 102–109 for discussion of darts, fiery grapnel, Davis recoilless gun, Pomeroy explosive bullet, Brock incendiary bullet, Buckingham phosphorus incendiary bullet, and Le Prieur rockets. See also H. A. Jones *War in the Air* 1935, vol. 3, pp. 168, 170, 383–5. Two anti-Zeppelin darts, possibly prototypes and examples produced privately rather than officially approved varieties appear in the catalogue of 'The David Kirch collection of Zeppelin and other airship memorabilia' Pt. 1, Wallis and Wallis, Lewes, Sussex, see pl. 24: lot 416 dart with spring-loaded steel tip that activates a small explosive charge, fitted with alloy fins, 19 cm long, and lot 417 dart with hollow brass body and heavy cast metal pointed tip, furnished with a bundle of feathers as flights, overall length 38 cm. Lots 413 –15 are anti-personnel flechettes, three varieties, one marked Bristol Regd, in a presentation box, 'Souvenirs of the War Aeroplane darts. With the compliments if Henry Levin, Webb & Co.' [metal dealer, Stratford, East London], lot 414 illustrated, pl. 24 (see note1, *Success in the south*).
3. *Op. cit.*, Buttlar-Brandenfels, pp. 36–47.
4. Machine guns mounted in the gondola and platforms on top of the airship.
5. *Op. cit.*, Buttlar-Brandenfels, 1919, p. 11.
6. *Op. cit.*, Buttlar-Brandenfels, 1919, p. 32.
7. *Op. cit.*, Robinson, 1966, p. 204.

Götterdämmerung

1. 'A' Flight Leadenham (Lincolnshire), 'B' flight at Buckminster(Leicestershire). Headquarters Melton Mowbray, Leics.
2. Headquarters at Gainsborough.
3. Famous in the 1939–45 war as the home of the 'dam-buster' squadron.
4. 'A' Flight Mattishall (Norfolk), 'B' Flight Tydd St Mary (Lincs.) and 'C' Flight Marham (Norfolk). 75 Squadron, operating from Elmswell and Hadleigh, in Suffolk, also sent up aircraft.
5. Lincolnshire.
6. This account of the steps taken to intercept what proved to be the final Zeppelin attack is derived from the National Archives 'Zeppelin raids-night of 5/6 August 1918—Aeroplanes (including pilots reports) 5/8/18—1/10/18 AIR 1/619/16/15/355.
7. See additions to list of casualties and raids.
8. See National Archives, AIR1/619/16/15/355. The reference to the smoke bomb only occurs in the Zeppelin Memorial edition of the local newspaper, *Hull Times*.
9. *Eastern Morning News*, 7 August 1918, p. 1.

10. It seems that he means *out* in the same sense of the 'sun is out', rather than extinguished.
11. Thorp Diaries, vol. 14, 1918, p. 61.
12. Heir to the famous chocolate manufacturing family.
13. *Op. cit.*, Robinson 1966, p. 332. The German dead were initially buried close to where their craft had come down, but in 1966 the remains of the men from *SL11*, *L31*(Heinrich Mathy and 18 crew), *L32* and *L48* were reinterred at the German war cemetery Cannock Chase (Staffordshire), where also lie men from *L34* and *L70*. George Thorp writes that Captain Strasser: resided in Hull and sailed out of it before the war. He first lived in Linnaeus Street, then in Coltman Street and afterwards moved to Hessle, but he adds, German authorities contradict this; Thorp Diaries, vol. 14, 1918, p. 70.
14. *Op. cit.*, Buttlar-Brandenfels, p. 218.
15. *i.e.* the Schütte-Lanz airships used by the German army.
16. Its origins remain uncertain but the military clearing station at Étaples in France has been suggested as the epicentre. An excerpt from the Public Health (Influenza) Regulations, 1918, appears in the *Special Constables' Gazette* no. 177, 22 November, 1918, pp. 707-8.
17. Hull History Centre, CTED/2/13.

Reactions to the Raids

1. Many of the available 'fighters' were obsolete types, reconnaissance aircraft ('scouts'), or seaplanes, pressed into an interceptor role.
2. *Op. cit.*, Butlar-Brandenfels, 1919, p. 23.
3. Being so young some of the detail was probably absorbed from hearing the conversations of his parents but taking refuge under the metal table which was then moved by the explosion is surely an actual memory.
4. Suction effect when a vacuum is created by an explosion.
5. Correspondence of Dora Willatt (1894–1976), ed. Alan Wilkinson *Thank God I'm Not a Boy—The Letters of Dora Willatt, Daughter, Sweetheart and Nurse 1915–18* Lampada Press, Hull, 1997, p. 9. She was a young woman with lots of energy wanting to do her bit for the war and was instead exiled to Barnsley attending to her parents; though eventually she 'escaped' to continue working as a VAD nurse. Her father Captain William Henry Willat (1868–1942), in civilian life a director of Reckitt and Sons, Hull, and 46 at the outbreak of war, was second in command of the Royal Engineer's training station at Silkstone Common. Promoted to major he and the family moved back to Hull in 1917 where Willatt formed and commanded the East Yorkshire Royal Engineers (Volunteers) (see p. 168; and *op. cit.* Willatt 1985, pp. 53–9).
6. She looked after Mrs Willatt who was recovering from an operation; *ibid*, p. 24.
7. *Ibid.*, p. 27. She goes on to say 'Reggie is having a great time flying—he dropped a bomb on one of those German observation sausages not long ago and he saw it squash out flat and the old Hun would be under it'.
8. *Ibid.*, p. 65.
9. Captain Cecil M. Slack, MC and bar, (1893–1985) wrote a personal account of the trenches based on his letters home to Dora and his family, published as *Grandfather's Adventures in the Great War 1914–18* Ilfracombe, 1997. This and *Thank God I'm Not a Boy* together provide a marvellous record of one couple's experiences of war time at home and at the front.
10. *Ibid.*, p. 187. No doubt the shelter had been built under the supervision of her engineer father, though by this time he was probably too busy with the setting up his volunteer unit to ensure its maintenance. A premium apprentice at Earle's shipyard he became an electrical engineer and invented multiple-drilling rigs to prepare plates for riveting,

Endnotes 169

obviating the tedious hand drilling which had been the norm. He also designed dynamos and electric fans for use aboard warships. He was at the same time a volunteer in the Submarine Miners at Paull, on the Humber (David Smith 'Defending the realm: Paull's contribution to protecting the British coastline' *East Yorkshire Historian* vol. 7 2006, pp. 16–32). His technical and management skills were taken up by Reckitt & Sons where he eventually became a member of the board. See a memoir by W. H. Willatt *This Incarnation* (ed. A. G. Credland, Malet Lambert Originals, vol. 25, 1985).

11. Stanley Duncan (1878–1954), founder in 1908 of the Wildfowler's Association of Great Britain and Ireland, now the British Association for Shooting and Conservation. Author, with Guy Thorne, of *The Complete Wildfowler—Ashore and Afloat* London 1911; revised and reprinted 1950. He established a gun shop in Hull continued by his sons. It occupied various addresses and still survives, though no longer connected with the family.
12. Four diaries preserved at the BASC headquarters: book 2, 1911–16 and book 3, 1916–25 contain the Zeppelin references.
13. Eds. George J. Zytaruk and James T. Boulton, *The Letters of D. H. Lawrence* vol. 2, 1913–1916, Cambridge University Press, 8 vols. 1979–2000, pp. 389–390; he writes in similar vein, 9 September 1915, to Zoe Atkins, p. 396.

Aftermath

1. *Hull and Lincolnshire Times*, 25 January, p. 7.
2. Elsewhere pavement plaques were sometimes used to mark where a bomb had landed. I am not sure whether any remain in situ but an example was recently sold from 'The David Kirch collection of Zeppelin and other Zeppelin memorabilia' *Wallis and Wallis* 25 July 2012, lot 243 ; 'a heavy circular bronze pavement plaque. Neatly engraved in Roman capitals, AN INCENDIARY BOMB DROPPED FROM AN ENEMY AIRSHIP FELL ON THIS SPOT APRIL 25^{25} 1916' (26 cm diameter).
3. See lot 132, 'The David Kirch collection of Zeppelin and other memorabilia' Part 1. *Wallis and Wallis*, Lewes, 21 March 2012.
4. *Daily Telegraph*, 3 May 1997, p. 9.
5. The coloured glass in this window was preserved from the wreckage of those destroyed in the air raid over the city on the 6 March 1916; the plaque is on the inside of the west wall of the south transept, beneath the window, most of the which is made up of plain glass with the surviving portions of stained glass at the top of the arch.
6. V1, gyro-stabilised and carrying 1,870 lb of explosive, aimed and launched from a ramp; the target distance reached was determined by the location of the launch site and the amount of fuel available to the jet engine. Later some were air launched from bomber aircraft. The usual name given by the man-in-the-street was 'buzz-bomb' but the American influenced service slang 'doodle bug' seems to have been adopted by most writers and journalists in recent years. V2, mobile and usually taken by transporter to a chosen site; they rose some 60 miles into the atmosphere and made their descent at several times the speed of sound, carrying a ton of explosive.
7. My thanks to Nick Evans for this information.

A Consideration

1. The then Commander of the Humber Defences, General Ferrier, in his report seems happy with the response of his soldiers and the fire brigade to the fire at Edwin Davis' store, after the first raid, 6–7 June 1915 (see above).

2. Coal is a strategic commodity in both war and peace providing energy for heating and light, for driving machines by steam power, producing electricity or through the production of coal gas.
3. Francis Askew. See note 16 *Warnings ; the buzzers*.
4. The stress shows in the pictures of him undertaking his various duties around the town. He is unsmiling and looks increasingly care-worn (Photographic albums, Hull History Centre, CMX/319/1 and 2).
5. *Eastern Morning News*, 13 September 1918.
6. The fire brigade was part of the police force and remained so till the formation of the Auxiliary Fire Service in 1938. During the 1914–18 war two motor fire engines with wheeled escapes were purchased (see A A Clarke *The Policemen of Hull* Hutton Press, 1992).
7. As they did in 1939–45 too, often involved with the ARP teams in rescues from bombed buildings as well as the more routine jobs such as messenger boys.
8. Patrick Beesly, *Room 40, British Naval Intelligence* 1914–18 London 1982, pp. 216 etc.
9. Britain, France and Russia.
10. *Ibid.*, chapter 15, pp. 252–70.
11. A small printed notice, sent to registered retailers, is entitled 'Ministry of Food –Rationing order 1918 JAM RATIONING', Hull History Centre CDMX/271/5. It provides a correction for a misprint in the previous instructions. The lengthy serial number at the bottom terminating 10/18 indicating that it was printed October 1918, a month before the end of the war.
12. Hull History Centre, U DDSYX 2/1/35/77. Letter dated 11 June 1917.
13. Hull History Centre, Steven Suddaby collection, 'ref. 'Buzzer nights'.
14. Specials in some form can be traced back to the seventeenth century but their modern form took shape following the Act of 1831 'For amending the laws relating to the appointment of special constables, and for the better protection of the police'; and their role was further defined by the demands of the war in 1914–18.
15. Appendix IX.
16. Corporation of Hull, Minutes of Watch Committee, 1917–8, vol. 30(3), 1916–7, p. 164.
17. Corporation of Hull, Minutes of Watch Committee, vol. 30 (3), p. 49.
18. John Buchan, *Mr Standfast* London 1918, chapter 42. John Buchan (1875–1940), 1st Baron Tweedsmuir, was a diplomat, MP and writer; commissioned into Army Intelligence he was then appointed Director of Information in 1917, under Lord Beaverbrook, and in 1935 became Governor General of Canada.
19. Instituted by George V; a bronze medal with the sovereign's head on the obverse and on the reverse a partial laurel wreath and the wording FOR FAITHFUL SERVICE IN THE SPECIAL CONSTABULARY. A clasp inscribed THE GREAT WAR 1914–18 was awarded to those who qualified during that conflict. The medal is still current.
20. A medal was awarded by the civic authority in Hartlepool. On the obverse, the arms of the borough and on the reverse several legends: 'Borough of Hartlepool', 'Special Constabulary', 'Bombardment 1914', 'Air raids 1915–18', and 'Zeppelin destroyed 1916', encompassing the German naval bombardment and the Zeppelin attacks. Second Lieutenant Ian Pyott, shot down Zeppelin *L34*, in a B.E.2c over Hartlepool, 28 November 1916 and was awarded the DSO. He was so close to the airship his face was scorched. About 116 of these Special Constabulary medals were issued. An example was sold as lot 608 from 'The David Birch collection of Zeppelin and other memorabilia' pt. 1, 21 March 2012, Wallis and Wallis, Lewes, Sussex.
21. The war of attrition with its elaboration of defensive trenches was made inevitable by the firepower that was now possible, and victory ultimately went to the side with the economic resources to support huge armies in the field over a prolonged period. Though his conclusions were universally rejected by contemporary military thinkers Jean de Bloch had outlined just such a scenario in *La Guerre* (6 vols.)1898.

Endnotes

Anti-War Propaganda and the Bolshevik Scare

1. The 25 October according to the Julian calendar then used by Russia but equivalent to 7 November in the Gregorian calendar used elsewhere.

Lessons Learned

1. Giulio Douhet, *Il dominio dell'aria* (The Command of the air) 1921.
2. Major General James Archibald Ferrier (RE) CB DSO (1854–1934). He saw service in India and Afghanistan, Sudan, Natal and Sierra Leone and commanded the Humber Garrison from 1915 till his retirement in 1917.
3. *Hull and Lincolnshire Times* 25 January 1919, p. 7.
4. Barry D. Powers, *Strategy Without Slide Rule* London, 1976, p. 58. The people of central London became accustomed to using the underground railway tunnels as shelters as they also did in the 1939–45 war.
5. For an account of the Gotha and Staaken attacks on London see Andrew Hyde *The First Blitz—The German Bomber Campaign against Britain in the First World War* Barnsley 2002.
6. Giulio Douhet, 1921 *op. cit*. One or even two million casualties were suggested with a need for more than a million hospital beds, though this was reduced to an attainable number of 300,000. The planning and coordination nationwide and the attempt to upgrade standards of care, wheresoever they were deemed inadequate, was eventually to provide a framework for the post war hospital system in the new National Health Service. See A. S. Mc Nalty and William Mellor *Medical Services in War* 1968, and B. Abel-Smith *The Hospitals 1800–1948* 1964. An account of the Beverley hospital is a good case study, see John D. Goode 'Beverley Westwood Hospital; 1929–48' *Historian* 2012, vol. 13.
7. The Civil Defence service was established in 1935 and in 1941 embraced the ARP, wardens and firemen. Members of the ARP were given a small silver badge consisting of a crown over the letters ARP, in a pleasing design by the sculptor and typographer Eric Gill (1882–1940); issued up till 1940.
8. David and Susan Neave, *Hull* (Pevsner Architectural Guides) 2010, and also Geraghty; see note 1, *Terror from the skies*. As many as 3,500 houses and 25 schools were destroyed, and 85,000 houses and 85 schools seriously damaged. To try and lessen the degree of destruction a number of decoy schemes were developed with a fair degree of success. A series of ponds and arrays of lights around Paull, east of the city, created shapes resembling the outline of towns and docks; see also David A. Smith *Paull–An Illustrated History* Stenlake Publishing, 2011 pp. 34–5. The last civilian deaths from bombing by a piloted aircraft in Britain were in Hull, 17 March 1945, when a Junkers Ju 88 dropped two containers of anti-personnel fragmentation bombs at 21.50, killing thirteen people (including four children) close to the Savoy cinema. The last flight over Hull and East Yorkshire by the Luftwaffe was made by an Arado jet aircraft on a high altitude reconnaissance mission, 4 April 1945. See Paul Bright *Air War over East Yorkshire in World War II* Flight Recorder Publications 2005, pp. 158–163.

Summary of the Hull raids 1915–1918 and Lists of Casualties

1. Geoffrey Simmons, *East Riding Airfields 1915–1920* Manchester. See Appendix 2, pp. 94–7.
2. Raymond Laurence Rimell, *Zeppelin! A Battle for Air Supremacy in World War 1* London, 1984.
3. *Op. cit*., Morris, 1925.

4. See John Hook, extracts from *This Dear, Dear Land: The Zeppelin Raids on Hull and District 1915-18*, 1995; copy in Hull History Centre.
5. L9 (LZ36) a naval Zeppelin 161. 4 m (528 feet) with three engines. Made 74 reconnaissance flights and four raids on Britain dropping 5,683 kg of bombs. Destroyed by fire in its hanger along with L6, 16 September 1916.
6. Walter Goodin (1907–1992), the East Yorkshire artist, lived in Woodhouse Street and reminisced 'how he and others sought a dugout excavated in a nearby timber yard, and made a shelter there, during the Zeppelin raids'. See Wendy Loncaster and Malcolm Shields *Walter Goodin-Above all, the Sky* Ferens Art Gallery, Hull, 2008, p. 12.
7. L14 (LZ46), another navy Zeppelin 163.5 m (535 feet).Made 42 reconnaissance flights and no less than seventeen attacks on England dropping 22,045 kg of bombs. Destroyed by its crew after the Armistice. After a raid on London Böcker was brought down in L33, 24 September, 1916, at Little Wigborough, Essex, and he and his entire crew were captured.
8. L11 (LZ41) made 31 reconnaissance flights, and twelve raids on Britain, dropping 15,543 kg of bombs.
9. L24 (LZ69), naval airship; larger than previous examples 178.5 m (583 feet) with four, 240 hp Maybach engines. Made nineteen reconnaissance flights and four raids on England, dropping 8,510 kg of bombs. Destroyed by fire along with LZ53 while being drawn into its hanger, 28 December, 1916.
10. L23 (LZ66), naval airship; 178.5 m (583 feet). Made 51 reconnaissance flights and three attacks on England, dropping 5,254 kg of bombs. Shot down by Second Lieutenant Bernard A. Smart in a Sopwith 'Pup' launched from HMS *Yarmouth* 21 August 1917.
11. L41 (LZ80), naval airship 198 m (649 feet) long with six Maybach engines of 240 hp. Made fifteen reconnaissance flights and four attacks on England dropping 6,567 kg of bombs. Destroyed, like many others, by its crew after the Armistice, mirroring the scuttling of the surrendered German fleet at Scapa Flow.
12. L63 (LZ110), naval airship; 196.5 m (643 feet) with five Maybach engines of 240 hp. Made three attacks on England, including the last 5 August 1918. Dropped 8,915 kg of bombs and was destroyed by its crew after the Armistice.
13. L56 (LZ103), made seventeen reconnaissance missions and was destroyed by its crew after the Armistice.
14. L63 (LZ110).
15. *Hull Daily Mail* picture archive; reproduced 6 August 1958 and in *Flashback* 9 January 2004.
16. Actually the 118th Zeppelin to be constructed, others in the series remained on the drawing board or were not completed.
17. See Albert Sammt, *Mein leben für den Zeppelin* 1988; Sammt was the commander. The airship is also said to have encountered and photographed the Supermarine Spitfire, a number of which circled the intruder inside British airspace.

Appendix I: List of Zeppelin Raids across Britain

1. *Op. cit.*, Morris (1925); list of raids by airship pp. 265–8, by aeroplanes pp. 269–72, and German airships brought down by British forces.
2. Basil Thomson, *The Scene Changes* Doubleday, New York, pp. 263–4.
3. Lot 180, 'The David Kirch collection and other airship memorabilia' pt. 1, 21 March, 2012, Wallis and Wallis, Lewes, Sussex.
4. Captured, he remained in custody till the end of the war, and later wrote an account of his attack on London, 13 October 1915; 'How we bombed London' *Living Age*, January 1928.

5. Basil Thomson, *The Scene Changes* Doubleday, New York, p. 376.
6. Basil Thomson, *The Scene Changes* Doubleday, New York, p. 391.

Appendix IIa

1. Hydraulic power was used extensively in the dock system for opening and closing lock gates etc.
2. George Thorp, cuttings book, 'Cartoons etc', pp. 108–137, Box 2, L9. 7083, Hull History Centre.
3. A handful of photographs taken in the mortuary, probably by an official police photographer, are also preserved in the Hull Maritime Museum, each 9½ x 12 inches, showing women and children, killed in the first raid, 6–7 June 1915: Florence White (explosive bomb), Edward Jordan (explosive bomb), Elizabeth Slade (explosive bomb) and Maurice Richardson (incendiary). They are enclosed within a large envelope with MEDICAL OFFICER OF HEALTH HULL printed on the flap.

Appendix IIb

1. The implication was that he was signalling to the airship, but surely the most likely explanation is that the individual was trying to shine a light on it so as to see it better. With any normal sort of portable flash lamp a forlorn hope, but nowadays we constantly see individuals using flash and attempting to take photographs of something which is way out of range of a tiny portable camera.
2. There is absolutely no evidence of any such events taking place.
3. No; he shot down *LZ37*, not *L9* (= *LZ36*).
4. St Mary's Roman Catholic school, Wilton Street. Father Murphy extinguished the fire. A newspaper photograph appears in George Thorp, cuttings book, 'Cartoons etc', p. 135, Box 2, L. 9.7083 Hull History Centre.
5. *i.e.* chamber pots.
6. Presumably a reference to Sarah Bernhardt (1844–1923) famous for her strongly delivered dramatic and tragic roles.
7. In the 1939–45 war an unexpected effect of the concentrated fire-bombing was the 'firestorm', when intense heat would suck in air which fed the flames even more and resulted in devastation over a large area, as happened at Hamburg, Dresden and Tokyo. It is clear that during the Great War the German strategists had not appreciated the full destructive potential of aerial bombing, certainly in the early years when it was regarded more for its terror-inducing possibilities.
8. It is unclear whether he is referring to the normal commuter trains carrying workers between Hull and Withernsea, Hornsea, Bridlington etc. on the coast or whether numbers of people had decided to exit to the coast for the evening to avoid the bombing.
9. The east Yorkshire name for a sea mist or 'sea fret'; a description familiar in my childhood but now largely obsolete if not archaic.

Appendix III: Photographs of the Hull Raids

1. The sign of Laverack and Goddard, timber merchants, can be seen. Their headquarters were at Great Union Street, Drypool, with sawmills in Blenkin Street and yards in Coelus Street and Malton Street.

Appendix IV

Fryer's Maps

1. Hull History Centre TSH/2/5.

Appendix V

Memories of an Old Town Special

1. Sadly, there is no clue to his identity.
2. Concentration Point. Where the men received their orders; see note 16, *Warnings: the buzzers.*
3. This may be a reference to the shelter constructed in Regent House, premises of Turner and Drinkwaters, photographers.
4. Across the Humber between Hull and New Holland (Lincs.); passengers embarked and disembarked at the pier, Nelson Street.
5. Apparently referring to the buzzer.
6. But just such information we should dearly like to have!
7. See above.
8. Bristow and Co., grocers and provision merchants, 83–4 Queen Street.
9. This and the preceding somewhat oblique description of riotous behaviour suggests that someone had been the victim of assault.

Appendix VII: 'Buzzer nights'

1. *Hull and Lincolnshire Times* 25 January 1919, p. 7.

Appendix VIII

Artefacts in Hull museums

1. William Robert Simpson Ladell, born in Walsingham, Norfolk, is recorded in the 1891 census, aged 36 living in Islington with his wife Charlotte. He was an agricultural scientist by profession and spent most of his time overseas. He had been a private in the Malay States Volunteer Rifles, and in the Great War joined the Army Ordnance Department (later the Royal Army Ordnance Corps) rose to rank of Major. In 1919 he was living in Bangkok and was a member of the council of the Siam Society in 1928. My thanks to Michael J. Boyd for these details.
2. Admiralty War Staff, Intelligence Division, *German Rigid Airships* February 1917 p. 62 etc. Confidential document CB1265.
3. Basil Thomson, *The Scene Changes* Doubleday, New York, p. 263–4.
4. *Ibid.*
5. *Op. cit.*, Buttlar-Brandenfels 1919, pp. 24–5.
6. Gareth Jenkins, *Zeppelins over Bury; the Raids on Bury St Edmunds, 1915 and 1916* Moyses Hall Museum 1985. Unnumbered pages.
7. Peter J. C. Smith, *Zeppelins over Lancashire* Neil Richardson 1991, p. 11, illustrated.
8. This primitive method of dropping incendiaries was quickly superseded and they were

subsequently suspended from racks and released electrically like the HE bombs.
9. *Op. cit.*, Buttlar-Brandenfels, p. 53.
10. *Special Constables' Gazette* no. 3, 9 July 1915. Summarising the experience from raids across Britain a document came from the government: 'AIR RAID PRECAUTIONS Summary of official recommendations issued for the guidance of the public' *Special Constables' Gazette* no. 118, 5 October 1917, pp. 469-70.
11. Towards the end of 1914 the Admiralty and War Office purchased from Holland and Holland nine 12 bore, hammerless ejector Paradox shot and ball guns at £42 to 45 guineas each. This was followed by a series of orders for the Proprietary Pigeon Gun, a 12 bore box lock shot gun with two stage choke, totalling 125 weapons at £22 10s each; these became known as the Aero Gun and though retailed by Holland and Holland they were made by Webley and Scott, Birmingham. Supplied with chain-shot cartridges, each containing a large ball with six smaller balls strung on a single length of wire. Later an incendiary bullet filled with yellow phosphorus was also available. See David J. Baker and Roger E. Lake, *Paradox; the story of Col. G. V. Fosbery, Holland and Holland, and the Paradox* 2010, pp. 251-260.
12. The damaged remains were kept in a desk drawer in the same office until collected by the present writer.
13. Basil Thomson, *The Scene Changes* Doubleday, New York, p. 396.
14. Margery and James Fisher, *Shackleton* 1957, p. 430-1.